W9-AEP-613

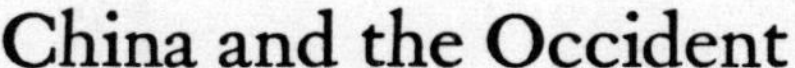

China and the Occident

China and the Occident

The Origin and Development of the Boxer Movement

By George Nye Steiger, Ph.D.

NEW YORK / RUSSELL & RUSSELL

1966

FIRST PUBLISHED IN 1927
REISSUED, 1966, BY RUSSELL & RUSSELL
A DIVISION OF ATHENEUM HOUSE, INC.
L. C. CATALOG CARD NO: 66—13256

REPRINTED FROM A COPY IN THE COLLECTIONS OF
THE BROOKLYN PUBLIC LIBRARY

PRINTED IN THE UNITED STATES OF AMERICA

Preface.

What was the Boxer Movement?—Unsatisfactory Answers—The Fundamental Conflict.

THE Boxer Movement was an episode—to many people an insignificant episode—in the relations between China and the West. It rose with a suddenness which astounded even the Diplomatic Body at Peking; for two months it occupied the place of honor in the newspapers of the world; it was suppressed by the action of the combined military forces of Japan and the Western powers; and a satisfactory punishment—all the traffic would bear—was imposed upon China for her guilt. When the incident was closed, in September, 1901, by the Protocol of Peking, the world proceeded to forget all about it; only to recall it dimly, a few years later, when the United States remitted a part of its share in the indemnity that had been imposed. Since that time, if the Boxer episode has been considered at all, it has usually been for the purpose of measuring the "progress" which has been made "even in China" since this agonizing attempt to oppose the irresistible "march of civilization."

Following the collapse of this midsummer madness which broke upon the world so unexpectedly, a multitude of books appeared dealing with the most spectacular aspects of the movement. The siege and relief of the legations of Peking, the adventures of the ill-fated Seymour Expedition, the massacres of Christian missionaries and their converts, the harrowing experiences of the missionaries who found their way to eventual safety; all these were described, and often well described, in the many narratives which poured from the presses of every Western country.

Other books dealt with prophecy concerning the probable future of the Chinese Empire, and indulged in optimistic speculation regarding the commercial and other benefits which reasonably might be expected, now that the power and pride of the reactionaries had been dragged in the dust. But the fundamental question in regard to the Boxer Movement was less satisfactorily treated.

The nature and origin of the movement, the seeds from which this evil weed had grown, were usually given but scant attention by the writers who hastened to place before a receptive public their accounts of those delirious months. For this neglect there were, at the time, several cogent reasons. In the first place, the reading public for which these books were intended wanted facts, not complicated explanations; a few strong generalizations, perhaps, to give the setting of the stage, and then the drama itself. Nor was it to be expected that the authors of these early accounts should concern themselves with the task of delving deeply into the labyrinth of historical evidence in search of hidden causes and ulterior motives. To the man or the woman who had lived through those eight weeks at Peking, to the missionary who had seen wife and children sicken and die under the hardships of a flight for life in the burning heat of a Chinese summer, the question—"how did it happen?"—seemed all too simple: The enemies of truth and progress had done this thing, and the chief among those enemies had been that monster of iniquity—the Empress Dowager.

Even the later writers, many of whom had not been called upon to endure the perils of the storm, have been equally unsatisfactory in their explanations of the causes which led to the Boxer outbreak. By the time these later books appeared, the assembled diplomats at Peking had put the seal of official approval upon a formula which satisfied the diplomatic necessities of the case. According to this formula, the movement was a rebellion; thus it was possible, while assessing China with an indemnity of 450,000,000 taels,[1] to hold the Empress Dowager innocent of all blame for what had taken place, and restore her to her position at the head of the Chinese Government.

For a quarter of a century, this interpretation of the upheaval which startled the world in the summer of 1900 has stood as official, and little effort has been made to go behind the diplomatic fiction so solemnly ratified by the eleven treaty powers which were represented at Peking. Few have raised the question as to why a "rebellion," aided and abetted by the most loyal supporters of the Empress Dowager, should have broken out in those particular provinces whose loyalty to the Manchu Dynasty was most enduring—the provinces which, during the revolution of 1911, supported the Manchus to the end—and yet should have found no adherents in the notoriously rebellious regions of mid-China and the south. As an alternative to this "official" interpretation of the outbreak, it has, at times, been characterized as an anti-Christian uprising, and as a gigantic conspiracy—organized by the Empress Dowager and her advisers—for the extermination of the foreigners; some writers have even described it as a combination of all three of these things. None of these explanations can, however, be regarded as satisfactory.

It is impossible to dismiss the Boxer outbreak as an insignificant episode in China's international relations, nor is it possible to rest satisfied with any explanation of the movement which fails to square with all the facts. No incident, indeed, in the course of the long contact between China and the West is more suitable for careful study than is the Boxer movement. The outbreak was not the climax

[1] Approximately equal to $330,000,000 in U. S. currency.

merely of the series of events precipitated by the German occupation of Kiaochow in November, 1897, or even of those consequent on China's defeat by Japan in 1894-1895; it was the culmination of the four centuries of relationship between the nations of the West and those of Asia, and had its origins in the essential differences between the civilization of the "Old East" and that newer civilization which was being brought to its doors by the merchants, the missionaries, and the men-of-war of Europe and America.

China, satisfied with the riches of her own ancient culture and resentful of the attempts which had been made by the "outside barbarians" to impose their innovations upon her, was stirred from her complacency by the events which followed the Japanese war and by the threat of annihilation which followed the seizure of Kiaochow. But any satisfactory study of the resultant furious outbreak against Western domination must go back of these liberating causes and must consider those characteristics of the Chinese state and of Chinese society which had made China so impervious to foreign innovations; which had prevented China from adopting, as Japan had adopted, enough of Western material civilization to be able to bid defiance to all threats of outside control.

The outcome of the Boxer movement was disastrous for China. Once more she saw herself compelled to undergo a humiliating settlement dictated by her conquerors. Yet the West, as well as China, learned some lessons from the event. The utter contempt in which the Empire had been held, since its defeat at the hands of the Japanese, gave way to a more healthy regard which almost amounted to respect. The plans for the partition of the country went into the waste-paper baskets of the several chancelleries of Europe; and the tradition that the Chinese people were utterly wanting in anything akin to the spirit of patriotism became one of the exploded myths of history. China, for her part, learned once more that her best hope for continued national existence lay, not in the appeal to arms, but in the cultural solidarity of her people.

Originally submitted to the Faculty of Harvard University in partial satisfaction of the requirements for the degree of Doctor of Philosophy, this study of the Boxer Movement has since been entirely rewritten with the addition of much new material. It is now offered to the reading public in the hope that it may contribute to a clearer appreciation of the modern problems of China and the West.

Among the many friends who have encouraged and assisted the completion of the work, especial acknowledgments are due to Professor A. C. Coolidge, of Harvard University, under whose guidance the original research was undertaken; to Professor F. W. Williams, of Yale University, who has kindly written a brief foreword for the book; and to Professor H. M. Varrell, my colleague in the History Department at Simmons College, for a critical reading of some parts of the manuscript.

Cambridge, Massachusetts,
February, 1927.

Contents.

Foreword.

THE literature upon the Boxer outbreak comprises more than a hundred volumes in European languages besides articles and reports of government bureaus. Evidently, as the third decade of our century approaches completion, there is occasion for a reasoned analysis of this movement and its causes. As an historical event the facts are sufficiently known and well attested, but the sources of the ferment behind the sudden uprising of millions of laborious peasants, as well as the motives prompting a desperate and insane hazard on the part of the imperial court, remain enigmas that demand solution. Professor Steiger's work, following the best traditions of modern historical scholarship, offers us an unbiased account of the incident itself—abounding in elemental passions fiercer and more delirious than any displayed in racial collisions since the Sepoy Mutiny—and resolves the seeming paradox of a dying nation quickened with the infinite possibilities of reincarnation in a world of new ideas.

At the risk of playing a repetend to the burden of his preface I must reaffirm the author's thesis that the Boxer movement is, perhaps, the most suitable for study of any in the course of the relations between East and West. He quite wisely abstains in his treatise from contrasts and comparisons with the turmoil in China today, for this is too inchoate as yet to be presented either as a catastrophe or a climax; but the reader will inevitably detect analogies in the news now coming from China and attempt some interpretations of his own. While this is a little dangerous it is very human. I may venture, however, to point to one or two factors in the present case that condition the problem of China's rehabilitation. The mental fiber of her people, their character and the influence of her institutions, are more intelligently appreciated under the existing unrest than ever before. If they are accounted mad by other nations there is method in their madness. They are finding leaders of a new sort, and we reckon ill who leave them out when we try to estimate the trend of a China which has already surrendered certain ancient ideals to adopt novel ideas from abroad.

With this in mind we can no longer interpret the agitation now rampant as the inevitable period of turbulence which has attended the downfall of every dynasty heretofore. Something unprecedented is happening. The nineteenth century with its industrial revolution made an end of the China of the past as effectually as the first century terminated the antique history of the Mediterranean basin. Owing to her geographical position, her race solidarity, and the discipline of her national experience China until the last century remained immune to foreign aggression, except for the barbarians on her northern frontiers. These, though not always successfully resisted, she could always absorb. The case was quite otherwise with the incessant impregnation of principles from beyond the sea. Hence came anomalous political and religious conceptions, economic preponderance, and unaccustomed methods of attack, before which other long-lived nations had crumbled ere the century closed. China's surrender to these imponderable forces has been slow but it is real. Her reluctant attitude is worthy of her ancient and great tradition of self-sufficiency. Her policy under the leadership of new men—for the moment intransigents inspired by Occidental extremists—shows a determination to renew the effort of 1900 without repeating its criminal follies and to regain a sovereignty nearly lost through the ignorance and ineptitude of her Manchu rulers. Whatever the outcome of the attempt the lesson of the Boxer misadventure is revealed in the entanglements of today.

F. W. Williams.

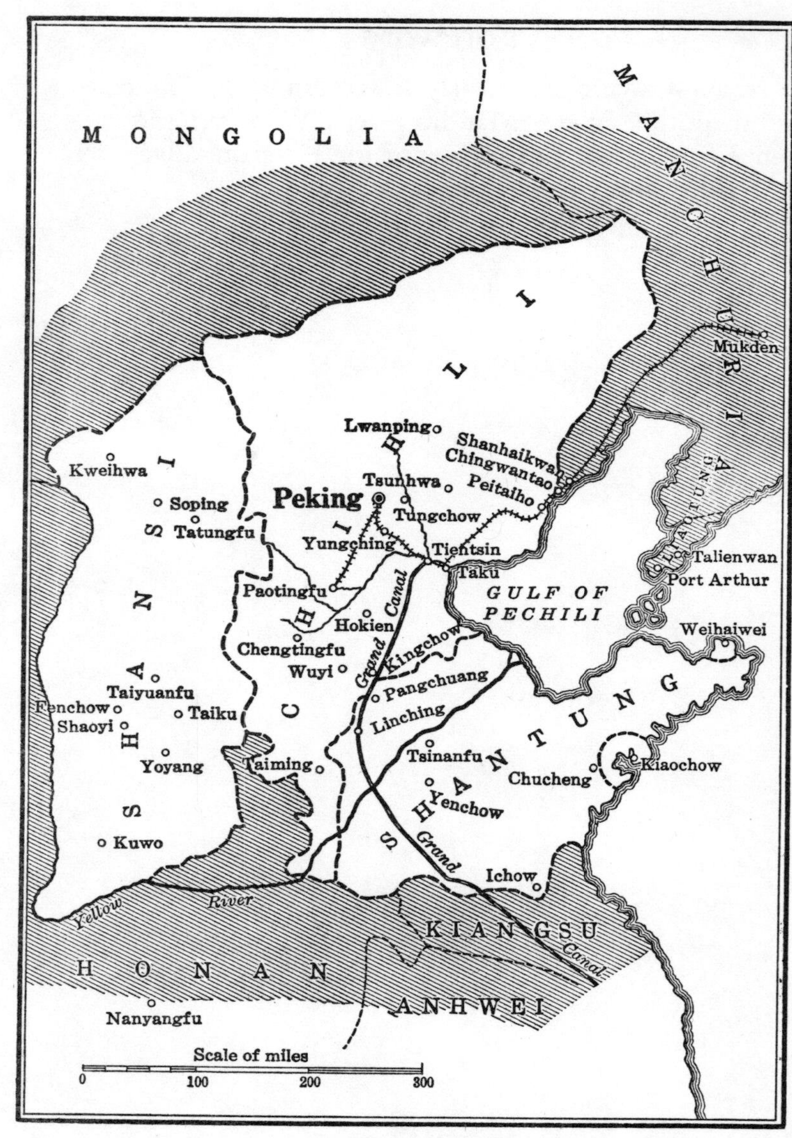

THEATER OF THE BOXER OUTBREAK.

The unshaded portion of the map shows the region in which the Boxer Movement developed and reached its greatest intensity.

China and the Occident

CHAPTER I.

The Chinese State and the Opening of Western Relations.

The Chinese State—Decentralization—Economic Theories—China and the Early Europeans—Toleration and Suppression of Christianity—Maritime Trade—Policy of the Ming Emperors—Changes under Kang Hi—Canton, the "Hoppo," and the "Co-hong"—The "Guild System" Applied to Foreigners—The Macartney and Amherst Embassies.

IN the year 1516, Rafael Perestrello, a Portuguese, reached the coast of China by a voyage from the recently acquired Portuguese possession of Malacca. The following year, Fernao Perez de Andrade, with a fleet of eight ships, arrived at San Chuan on the coast of Kwangtung province; and two of the ships, bearing an envoy from the Portuguese viceroy of Goa, were permitted to proceed to Canton. Perestrello, Fernao de Andrade, and the envoy, Thomé Pires, were all very circumspect in their behavior toward the Chinese; in 1520, therefore, Pires received permission to visit Peking for an audience with the Emperor. The favorable impression made by these earliest Portuguese was, however, soon nullified by the actions of later arrivals. Even before Pires reached Peking, the imperial government had received news of the high-handed proceedings of Simon de Andrade, the younger brother of Fernao. Simon had arrived at San Chuan with a fleet of four ships, had built a fort there, and was attempting to exercise jurisdiction over the inhabitants of the island. In consequence of this lawless behavior on the part of his fellow countryman, Pires met with a harsh reception at Peking; he was imprisoned and sent back in chains to Canton, where he died in 1523.

Such is the record of the earliest direct contact between China and the maritime nations of Western Europe; yet the four centuries of friction which have followed this inauspicious beginning cannot be attributed solely to the unfavorable impression made by the acts of Simon de Andrade. Other, and more worthy, representatives of European civilization followed this sixteenth-century buccaneer to the coasts of China, and many of these were honored and trusted by the Chinese government and people; but the friction continued, and China's hostility to the "outside barbarian" still remained.

The fundamental causes of conflict between China and the West are to be found in the character of the Chinese state. So different was this political organization from anything known to the Western world, so different were the political theories of China from those of Europe, that any understanding of the problems of China demands some examination into the nature and organization of the Chinese state.

Western visitors to China, prior to the overthrow of the Manchu Dynasty in 1912, have at all times been tremendously impressed with the outward appearances of autocracy. It is quite natural, therefore, that the great majority of writers on things Chinese should agree in characterizing the Empire as a typical oriental despotism. But this characterization is far from the truth. For a thousand years the government of China has been extremely democratic; it may, indeed, be safely asserted that, at the beginning of the nineteenth century, China was the only country in the world where essential democracy had been successfully worked out on a large scale. In no country which possessed a political organization worthy of the name were the lives and property of the people less at the mercy of officialdom; in no country were the officers of government, including the Emperor himself, more directly responsible to the people for the consequences of their acts, or more strictly circumscribed in their legitimate functions by the limitations of an unwritten constitution.

Within certain limits the absolutism of the Emperor was, indeed, complete; but those limits were well defined, and the Emperor who presumed to transgress them did so at his peril. The functions of the central government—the Emperor and his advisers—were simple and touched the mass of the people only in the appointment of provincial and district officials and in the punishment of crime; neither the right of legislation nor the power to impose taxes was reckoned among the prerogatives of the Throne. The provincial and local officials appointed by Peking were also strictly limited; their duties consisted in maintaining peace and order, in repeating to the people the Emperor's exhortations to right conduct, and in transmitting to Peking the taxes paid by the people. In the affairs of everyday life, the Chinese community enjoyed the highest degree of self-government. The taxes, which were ridiculously light, were collected by the officers of the community and could be increased only with the approval of the people. The administration of justice, except in criminal cases, was the affair of the community. In short, the Chinese Empire was a commonwealth of self-governing communities.

In this commonwealth, certain powers, of great importance in the cultural life of the people, but having little influence upon their economic life, were committed to the Emperor, who was assisted in his duties as head of the state by a central administration which had changed but little since it was originally organized at the time of the Chow Dynasty (1122-249 B.C.). Under the general supervision of the "Grand Council of State," closely akin to the "Privy Council" of a Western sovereign, the work of administration was divided among six "Boards" to which were referred, for consideration and advice, the various problems of government. The functions which the central government performed for the country are, therefore, outlined in the duties of these six boards.

The Board of Civil Appointments, which ranked first among them, was charged with the selection of men qualified for official position and with recommending to the Throne the appointments, promotions, and demotions which were necessary for keeping the administration of government at the highest pitch of efficiency. The Board of Revenue, second in rank, managed the imperial finances, but its powers did not include the right to impose new taxes or to increase the weight of old ones. The lightness with which the imperial taxation pressed upon the people, even after the influence of the West had added greatly to the functions and expenditures of the central government, may be deduced from an estimate made by Sir Robert Hart in 1901. According to this estimate, the total amount received by the imperial treasury in 1900, including the import and export duties collected by the foreign-managed Imperial Maritime Customs, was about 100,000,000 taels—approximately U. S. $74,000,000. Allowing 100% increase in this figure, to cover extortion, "squeeze," and the cost of transmission, Sir Robert calculated that the total taxation paid by the people amounted to 200,000,000 taels, of which less than 22,000,000 taels—about $16,000,000 U. S. gold—was spent for the Imperial Household, the Imperial Clan, and the upkeep of the

Manchu Garrisons.[1] The third board, the Board of Rites, had the oversight of ceremonial and etiquette in all their complex ramifications. The proper ordering of every function of the Imperial Court, the solution of every knotty question of propriety that arose throughout the Empire was referred to this board.

The three remaining boards were those of Punishments, War, and Public Works, of which the last two were far from having the importance which they would enjoy in any Western state. The Board of Works was chiefly concerned with the upkeep of the imperial mausolea and the care of the Yellow River embankments, and had annual expenditures of some six or eight million taels—$5,000,000 or $6,000,000; while the estimate of imperial finances in 1900, cited above, places the war budget of the Empire, even at that late date, at slightly under 32,000,000 taels—about $23,500,000. The Board of Punishments was the supreme court of review for all criminal cases. This and the Board of Civil Appointments, which served as a National Civil Service Commission, were, indeed, the only two branches of the central organization whose functions had any direct bearing upon the lives of the people; the other four were of importance to the body of officialdom, but affected the nation at large very incidentally, if at all.

One striking fact will be noted in this list of the boards of the central government: the absence of a Board of Foreign Affairs. There was no such board, for the sufficient reason that China had no foreign affairs. In 1860, when the Western powers obtained the right to have resident ministers at Peking, the "Tsungli Yamen"—which ranked only as a minor department—was created for the purpose of dealing with the foreign diplomats; but it was not until

[1] Report of the "Commission Chargée d'etudier la question des indemnités," Appendix, pp. 30-36.

the settlement of 1901 that China, at the demand of the powers, established a Board of Foreign Affairs—the "Waiwupu"—which henceforth ranked first among the boards of the central administration.

Quite as significant as the organization of the central administrative machinery was the absolute lack of legislative activity shown by the imperial government. In China, law was custom, hallowed by the test of time; legislation was an unknown art. From time to time, the Emperor, with the advice of the Grand Council, issued decrees in which he interpreted the existing laws in the light of new conditions; but he did not make new laws.[2] During the later part of the nineteenth century, the unwillingness, or inability, of the imperial government to adopt any sort of progressive legislative program was, to China's critics, convincing proof of national decadence; yet the experience of three thousand years had convinced the Chinese that the power to enact legislation touching the economic interests of the people—and no legislation can fail to touch those interests—was not a power which could safely be committed into the hands of any ruler. As a consequence of this reasonable suspicion, China never developed a body of civil—as distinct from criminal—law. In the Code of the Tsing Dynasty, which was largely taken over from that of the Mings, such laws as related to inheritance, mortgages, the transfer of property, and the like, are found scattered through the various sections of the criminal law. Civil law and the settlement of civil disputes were taken care of by the growth of trade customs which were enforced in the different guilds by the guild authorities, and by the almost universal recourse to arbitration in the case of disputes

[2] In general, the legislative power of the Chinese Emperor was not very different from that exercised by the Supreme Court of the United States.

between individuals who were not members of the same guild.

At the base of the Chinese social structure, permeating the administrative and legal systems, lay the principle of "responsibility," a principle to which, as it was worked out in actual practice, may be attributed both the stability and the flexibility which have made the Chinese Empire the most enduring state in the world's history. Every individual was responsible to the local official for the acts of the members of his family, as well as for those of his neighbors in any serious case; the local official was responsible to the district magistrate for the proper administration of justice and for the collection of the local taxes; the district magistrate was responsible to the provincial authorities; these, in turn, were responsible to the Emperor for peace and prosperity, and for the preservation of law and order in their respective areas. The circle of responsibility was completed by the Emperor's responsibility to Heaven for any misfortune which might afflict the Empire; for *vox populi vox dei* was no empty phrase in China, and found sanction not only in the ancient classics but also in the fall of successive dynasties, whose loss of the "Mandate of Heaven" had been demonstrated by popular uprisings which dismissed the unworthy rulers and confided the powers abused by them into more worthy hands.

While this chain of graduated responsibility—whose superficial resemblance to medieval feudalism misled many early European observers—established a certain necessary unity in the administration of the Empire, it also inevitably resulted in a high degree of local autonomy. Full responsibility could exist only if accompanied by an equally full reliance upon the individual initiative of the officer to whom authority had been delegated. Failure on the part of an official, in dealing with the problems of the area committed to his charge, was punished by demotion, dismissal, exile, or death; conspicuous success was attended by promotion to a higher sphere of activity; but the detailed measures by which any particular problem should be solved were seldom, if ever, dictated to an inferior officer by those above him. Hence the decrees, edicts, and rescripts of the Emperor, as well as the proclamations of the viceroys and governors, dwelt on glittering generalities and expounded the fundamental virtues of justice and propriety; the local official, being the man immediately responsible, must find for any given emergency a solution which, harmonizing with justice and propriety, did not offend the prejudices of his people and thus arouse fresh difficulties. "The Chinese idea," wrote Sir Robert Hart, in 1871, "is for the locality to *initiate*, and for the central authority to: (1) wink at, (2) tacitly permit, (3) openly allow, (4) officially recognise, (5) crystallize. It is useless to attempt—except where outside force does it—to get the central offices to *order* the adoption of *novelties*."[3]

The weakness of this political system, as it appeared to a Western critic, was well expressed by Sir George Staunton about the end of the eighteenth century: "That government is certainly the most firm in which a large portion of the subjects, as in Great Britain, are conscious of having an interest in its preservation. Such does not seem the general sentiment in China. . . . When personal attachment to the sovereign, to obtain which great pains have been taken in the present dynasty, ceases in consequence of any general evil pressing upon the people, which he is either supposed to have occasioned or not to have endeavoured to remedy, no sentiment of his having a claim of right to the throne he fills, which is elsewhere such a security to monarchs, ar-

[3] Quoted by Morse, *International Relations of the Chinese Empire*, vol. I, p. 6, note.

rests the disposition of endeavouring to make him yield it to another."[4]

In the abcence of any theory of "divine right" supported by the interest of a large part of the population, some other explanation must be sought for the permanence of the Chinese political structure; this is found, by the same author, in the cultural foundations of society: "The art of printing, practised probably at a very early period of the empire, has been the means of diffusing universally and establishing among all ranks of men, certain fixed principles of right and rules of moral rectitude which serve as so many dykes or barriers against the tumult of human passions and restrain the propensities of men in the plenitude of power. At every change in the government in the neighboring countries not so circumstanced, success, like a torrent, sweeps all before it and levels all former arrangements of society. But in China, institutions and opinions survive the wreck of revolutions. The sovereign may be removed, his whole family cut off; but the manners and condition of the people remain the same."[5] Thus, while the government lacked that strength which might have been derived from the existence of an important class whose economic interest dictated the support of the *status quo*, this lack was compensated by the fact that political revolution was not regarded, or utilized, as a means for readjusting the social and economic organization of society.

Inherent in the Chinese state there were, therefore, two noteworthy obstacles to the establishment of international trade relations such as had developed among the mercantile nations of the West, and such as these nations increasingly desired to form with China: first, the absence

[4] Staunton, *Authentic Account of an Embassy from the King of Great Britain to the Emperor of China*, vol. III, pp. 114-115.

[5] *Ibid.*, III, p. 116.

of a strongly centralized government, empowered to enter into treaty contracts which, even if they modified the existing law, would be regarded by the officials and people of the country as binding; second, the absence of any clearly defined body of civil or commercial law, on which the foreigner could rely as a guarantee for his property rights. The removal of these obstacles, the modification of Chinese political practice in such a way that these deficiencies would no longer exist, could be achieved only through a radical change of the Empire's political system, and of the political and social philosophy upon which this system was based.

The foundation upon which the Chinese state rested was the philosophy of Confucius (551-479 B.C.). Whether or not Confucianism should properly be regarded as a religion is a question which need not here be debated; it is the political philosophy of "China's Sage" which is of prime importance. This may fairly be reduced to the following principle: The ruler's first duty is to his people, not to property. Confucius looked upon the state as the guardian of morals and propriety; nothing in his teachings could be taken to justify a political system based upon the economic interests of a privileged class; and he expressly disapproved any grant, by the state, of monopoly rights which would enable the few to take advantage of the needs of the many.[6] Any attempt to weigh the comparative merits of the widely divergent social organizations of China and the West would involve endless speculation; it must, however, be borne in mind that the political and economic

[6] "As to natural monopoly," says a recent Chinese writer, "Confucius positively does not allow it. According to the principles of the 'Spring and Autumn,' the famous mountains and the great meres are not conferred to the feudal princes; 'Because they are the natural resourses of heaven and earth, which were not produced by human power, they ought to be shared in common with all the people.' . . . Since Confucius does not permit even the feudal princes to own the natural resourses, how can any private

theories of the West had, for the Chinese state, disruptive possibilities equal to those which the modern industrialized nations of Europe and America see in the doctrines of Bolshevism.

This incompatibility between the Chinese political system and the needs of the Western commercial countries will go far toward explaining the attitude of bitter anti-foreignism with which, from the close of the eighteenth century down to the present day, the Chinese people and officials have been so often charged. The hostility has been directed against the political institutions of the West—not against the westerners as individuals. The honorable treatment and official employment accorded to Marco Polo, at the end of the thirteenth century; to Ricci, at the close of the sixteenth century; to Schaal, Verbiest, and others, during the seventeenth and at the beginning of the eighteenth centuries give evidence that the Chinese government was, at these periods at least, remarkably free from race prejudice. The Mongol "Yuan" Emperors, the Chinese "Ming" Emperors, and the rulers of the Manchu "Tsing" Dynasty, all showed themselves willing to utilize the services of able men, irrespective of their alien origin. Nor do there appear to have been any evidences of popular antagonism, on racial grounds, toward the employment of these foreigners. When attacks were made upon the early Jesuits who were employed by the government, these attacks were attributable to three main causes: the personal jealousy of rivals in the official world, the suspicion evoked by the growth of a religious "secret society" under their leadership, and the

person have the right to own them? Subject to this principle is the modern development of franchise monopolies, such as railways, waterworks, etc."—H. C. Chen, *The Economic Principles of Confucius*, p. 540. This author is, however, of the opinion that Confucius would approve a limited legal monopoly, such as patents and copyrights; see *ibid.*, p. 537.

piratical activities of their fellow Europeans along the coast of the Empire.

Closely associated with the charge of anti-foreignism so often made against the Chinese is that of religious intolerance; on this point, the record of seventeenth-century China compared very favorably with that of contemporary Europe or even of America. During the last half century of the Ming Dynasty and the first seventy years of the Tsing, the propagation of the Gospel was openly carried on, both at Peking and in the provinces. Yet, within this period, we find the Thirty Years' War and the "dragonnades" of Louis XIV in continental Europe; the "Rule of the Saints" and the Clarendon Code in England; and the expulsion of Roger Williams and of Mrs. Anne Hutchinson from the colony of Massachusetts. Here and there in the Empire, the foreign faith was opposed by individual officials, to whose orthodox Confucianism the doctrines and rites of Christianity appeared in the light of degrading and superstitious practices which tended to undermine social morality; during the disturbances which accompanied the fall of the Ming Dynasty and the establishment of the Manchu rule, the missionaries and their adherents seem, at times, to have suffered rather more severely than other elements of society; but religious persecution, as such, was notably absent.

Because of his indifference to, or contempt for, the supernatural in religion, the Confucianist has never displayed enthusiasm in persecution for belief, or even for practice, where practice did not seem likely to result in scandal or in weakening the moral foundations of society.[7]

[7] Such is the almost unanimous testimony of Western writers, missionary and non-missionary. There is one outstanding exception: Prof. J. J. M. de Groot, in *Sectarianism and Religious Persecution in China*, undertakes to prove that the Chinese government is the most intolerant and the most

Thus there seemed, in the seventeenth century, to be no good reason why China should not be able to assimilate Christianity as she had already assimilated two other foreign religions—Buddhism and Mohammedanism. The possibility of this was, however, seriously compromised by the fact that Christianity retained a closer contact with its foreign source than had been the case with Buddhism; while the doctrine of the "Lord of Heaven" did not, like that of Islam, confine itself to a few outlying portions of the Empire. The difficulties in the way of absorbing the new doctrine became apparent in the reign of Kang Hi (1662-1723), who seems to have been convinced that the absorption was impossible by the outcome of the controversy which arose over the question of allowing the Chinese Christians to perform the customary rites of "ancestor worship." The Emperor had declared that these rites were not religious, and could properly be performed by the Christians; the declaration of the Pope contradicted this; the decision of the missionaries to accept the declaration of the Pope and to reject that of the Emperor resulted in the immediate loss of imperial favor. Rightly or wrongly, Kang Hi reached the conclusion that there was no place in China for a religious organization which rendered absolute obedience to a potentate residing outside his jurisdiction.

The immediate causes for the proscription of Christianity—first decreed in 1669 and subsequently reaffirmed in 1717—were, however, entirely political. The organization of Christianity had, in the eyes of the Chinese, all

bitterly persecuting government that the world has ever seen. I consider that Professor de Groot's thesis, in support of which he quotes copiously from Chinese sources, is totally disproved by the very material upon which he bases it.

the objectionable characteristics of a "secret society": a sworn membership, mysterious rites, an authoritative priestly leadership, and an ulterior motive which was not in harmony with the existing social status.[8] Moreover, the Chinese customarily identified the Christians with the members of the "Pa-lien-kiao"—White Lily, or White Lotus, Society—the most noted and most formidable of the indigenous secret organizations. The early Catholic missionaries had themselves been impressed by the resemblance between certain teachings and practices of the White Lotus and those of the Catholic Church,[9] and the Vicar-Apostolique of Szechuan, in the last quarter of the eighteenth century, gave, as the first of eight causes which brought persecution upon Christian converts, the fact that "Christians are often confounded with members of the Triad Society or of the White Lily Sect, both by their enemies and by persons belonging to those associations."[10] The growing strength of the new religion in various parts of the Empire, and especially among the officials and the members of the Imperial Clan at Peking, became a subject of concern to the central government, a concern which was considerably increased by the outcome of the dispute in regard to ancestor worship.

The final decision to renew the decree of 1669 against Christianity resulted from a memorial submitted to the Throne, in 1717, by a "military mandarin" in Kwang-tung named Tching-mao. The memorialist first advised the

[8] For a missionary corroboration of the Chinese tendency to class Christianity with the native secret societies, see Moule, *The Chinese People*, p. 191; "The numerous secret societies are probably the only thoroughly Chinese religious bodies with duly admitted and registered lay members."

[9] See Launay, *Histoire des Missions de Chine*, vol. I, p. 2.

[10] Quoted by Williams, *The Middle Kingdom*, vol. II, p. 320.

Emperor of the dangers which might result from the increasing number of European ships which were arriving at Canton. These ships were so powerfully armed that they could not be resisted, and he begged that orders be given for the authorities at Canton to take measures to guard against the danger. Turning to the subject of Christianity, Tching-mao related the earlier history of the European religion in Manila and Japan; in Manila the Christians had come as missionaries and had conquered the country; in Japan, also, they had attempted to conquer the country and the Japanese had been forced to expel all the Europeans. Now, he continued, they were building churches in all parts of China, spending great sums of money among the people, and attaching many of the people to their cause. Tching-mao knew nothing about the doctrines of the religion, but asked the Emperor to consider the political dangers which this growing organization might have for China, and decide what should be done about it.

Kang Hi submitted this memorial, in April, 1717, to the joint consideration of the heads of all the administrative boards; their report, on April 16, approved the reaffirmation of the anti-Christian decree of 1669 and the expulsion of all the missionaries. Referred back to the boards on May 11, and again on May 19, this decision was twice confirmed in spite of the efforts on the part of the missionaries and their friends to secure a reversal. The Imperial Rescript (answer to the memorial) ordered the mandarins to take all necessary precautions for the safety of the ports which were frequented by the foreign ships, and republished the proscription against Christianity. In order to remedy the abuses which had grown up during recent years, it was ordered that any European who desired to be allowed to remain in the country should apply for an imperial patent permitting him to do so.[11]

From this time until the treaty settlement of 1858, Christianity was outlawed in China. In some parts of the Empire the prohibition was strictly enforced; but, in general, the missionaries and their converts had little to fear so long as they behaved themselves with discretion. The real purpose of this, as of most Imperial Decrees, was to establish the strict accountability of the local officials for any disorders that might arise from the continuance of the prohibited practices. Local officials might be tolerant, if they so desired, and might even allow the foreign missionaries to reside quietly in their districts, but at their own risk if evil resulted.[12]

The reign of Kang Hi also saw the conclusion of a treaty with Russia, signed at Nertchinsk in 1689, the first treaty between China and a European power and the first which China had negotiated with any country on a basis of equality. Russia's eastward expansion across Siberia had begun about a century earlier, and, by 1658, had brought the Russians into conflict with the Chinese along the banks of the upper Amur River. The Treaty of Nertchinsk, which ended a long period of conflict, established the boundary between the two Empires, and provided that, in case any subject of one high contracting power should be guilty of crimes within the territories of the other, such offender should be seized and handed over to the authorities of his own country for punishment. In addition to these two points, the treaty also established a satisfactory

[11] The memorial of Tching-mao, the consequent deliberations, and the final decision are to be found in de Mailla, *Histoire Général de la Chine*, Tome XI, pp. 321 ff.

[12] It is interesting to compare this with the very similar policy in regard to Christianity adopted by Hideyoshi, in Japan, 130 years earlier; see Murdoch, *History of Japan*, vol. II, *passim*.

modus operandi for the frontier trade between the two countries.

Racial and religious intolerance were thus markedly absent at this early stage of China's intercourse with the West—a fact which might, perhaps, be attributed to a "superiority complex" on the part of the Chinese. The government at Peking had even shown itself willing and able to deal on terms of equality with an outside power, where such diplomatic dealings did not involve any necessary readjustment of internal policies. It was in her relations with the Western merchants who came by sea to trade at her ports, that China's incompatibility with the West was to become increasingly manifest. Her administrative and legal systems were, as has been shown, ill suited to the needs of modern international trade, and the complications arising out of this fact were to shake the fabric of the Chinese state to its very foundations.

During the sixteenth century, and down to the overthrow of the Ming Dynasty by the Manchus in 1644, European maritime trade with China was largely in the hands of the Portuguese, the successors of Perestrelo and the Andrades. The piratical activities of these rough-handed adventurers, at various points along the coast, quickly convinced government and people that the European, like all other foreigners, was an utter barbarian and must be subjected to strict control. The Ming emperors, therefore, prohibited European trade at any other port than Canton, and, in 1557, appointed the neighboring barren peninsula of Macao as a place where the Portuguese might reside under the watchful supervision of the Canton authorities.

The opening decades of the seventeenth century witnessed sporadic attempts, by the Dutch and English merchants, to establish a commercial foothold in China. Excluded from Canton by the jealous intrigues of the Portuguese, the newcomers were forced to confine their activities to the island of Formosa and the adjacent portions of the mainland. The English soon abandoned their efforts, but the Dutch succeeded in building up rather prosperous establishments in Formosa and at Amoy. The Manchu conquest, and the revolt of Koxinga—the pirate-patriot supporter of the Mings—wiped out the Dutch establishments; but, after the Manchus had consolidated their power, the Emperor Kang Hi, by the decree of 1685, threw open all the ports of the Empire to trade with the foreigners.

This liberal and progressive emperor soon discovered, however, what had been learned earlier by the Ming rulers: that the foreign traders were entirely too unruly to be allowed unrestricted access to all the ports of the country. The trade was, therefore, again restricted to Canton, and was there put under the management of a special officer who was known to the Europeans as the "Hoppo," or "Emperor's Merchant." In 1720, probably as the result of Tching-mao's memorial asking for more control over these dangerous outsiders, the Hoppo was reinforced in his task of overseeing the foreign merchants by the creation of the "Co-hong," a small group of merchants to whom was given the exclusive right of carrying on trade with the "outside barbarians," and who were to be securities for their lawful behavior.

The Co-hong was not a partnership and had corporate existence only in its collective responsibility for the maintenance of law and order among the Europeans, who could have no dealings at Canton except through one of the members of this guild. A buffer was thus set up between the outsider and the internal mechanism of the state. "Guild management" of the foreign trade rendered unnecessary any detailed legislation on this subject by the government, and supplied the lack of a code of commercial law. "Guild responsibility" for the behavior of the foreigner insured the satisfactory control of an element which was regarded with much the same suspicion as that which attached to the "landless man" in Norman England, or to the non-church member in the Massachusetts Bay Colony. The establishment of the Co-hong, an officially authorized monopoly, was the first attempt on the part of China to adapt herself to the impact of the West. Yet this contrivance, while it enabled the Chinese government to maintain its traditional policy of non-interference in purely commercial affairs, was in itself an important modification of traditional practice.[13]

The Co-hong was fairly effective as a method of maintaining the desired supervision over the foreigners, but it was never entirely satisfactory, even to the Chinese, whose dissatisfaction may be attributed to several undesirable aspects of the system. The existence of the monopoly opened the way for a great deal of official "graft," or "squeeze." The members of the Co-hong, in addition to paying heavily for their membership, were continually being forced to make large contributions to the officials. Although these contributions were probably no heavier burden than the legitimate taxation which would have been imposed in a Western country, the effect of this state of affairs was the growth of that very official interference in business which the Co-hong system had been designed to prevent. As "securities" for the foreigners, it was frequently necessary for the guild to resort to the threat—

[13] There was, of course, the already existing salt monopoly which, like the French *gabelle*, was a form of internal taxation; if we regard the Co-hong as essentially a revenue-producing scheme, it will appear in harmony with this precedent. I do not believe, however, that it can properly be so regarded; no similar monopoly was instituted for the purpose of deriving revenue from the Chinese-controlled trade with the Indies.

occasionally executed—of stopping the trade, in order to secure compliance with official commands. Some of the members admitted to the Co-hong were merchants whose assets were not sufficient for the trade which they attempted to transact, and the occasional bankruptcies among these weak brothers fell heavily upon the other members of the guild, whose corporate responsibility for the foreigners made them also jointly responsible to the foreigners in cases of this kind. Finally, there was much dissatisfaction among the "outside merchants"—the native merchants who were not in the Co-hong—due to their exclusion from the trade privileges enjoyed by the monopoly.

The keenest dissatisfaction in regard to the condition of trade at Canton was, however, on the foreign side, and was especially felt among the British merchants, who soon came to play the leading part in the maritime trade with China. The personal relations between the foreign merchants and the members of the Co-hong were usually most cordial, and the business relations were marked by the most punctilious commercial honor on the Chinese side; the dissatisfaction felt by the foreigners arose, partly, from the humiliating restrictions under which they lived, but was chiefly caused by the restriction of the trade to the single port of Canton, and the refusal of the Chinese to allow direct appeal to the officials. The first of these was attributed to the desire on the part of the Co-hong to retain its monopoly unimpaired, while the second was regarded as an obstacle raised by the monopoly merchants in order to prevent their shortcomings from being made known to the officials.

By the last decade of the eighteenth century, this discontent with the existing condition of the China trade led the British government to attempt relief by diplomatic means. The attempt took the form of the Embassy under

Lord Macartney, in 1793-1794, and was followed, after the close of the Napoleonic wars, by the Amherst Mission of 1816, which came to grief when Lord Amherst refused to perform the "kowtow"—the humble prostrations which court ceremony required of all who came into the presence of the Emperor.[14]

In spite of the dissatisfaction felt by the British at the Chinese restrictions, the trade at Canton was very profitable to the East India Company, which enjoyed a monopoly of British commerce in the Far East, and the Company exerted all its influence to maintain unimpaired the already existing commercial rights. Hence the representatives of the East India Company, who were attached to both of these Embassies as Junior Envoys, while interested in obtaining any possible amelioration of the existing conditions, were primarily concerned in preventing any step which might arouse the antagonism either of the central government or of the merchants and officials at Canton.

[14] Most English writers, and many Americans, accept without question the testimony of Staunton, in his *Authentic Account,* that Lord Macartney, at the time of the first Embassy, was received by the Emperor without complying with this custom; there still exists, however, a reasonable doubt on this point. The Chinese have always maintained that the kowtow was performed by the British Ambassador, and several of the French authorities accept the Chinese contention. The late W. W. Rockhill, in his *Diplomatic Audiences at the Court of China,* p. 31, presents some evidence in support of the Chinese statement. Especially significant is the fact that the younger Staunton, who accompanied the Macartney Embassy as a page and was a member of the Amherst Mission, evaded the question as to whether Lord Macartney had or had not performed the kowtow—when the Chinese officials appealed to him in the heat of the controversy in 1816—on the ground that he had been too young at that time to be a reliable witness as to what occurred. See Ellis, *Journal,* p. 108. Ellis also records the fact that Lord Amherst was, at one time, ready to perform the prostration, if he could be assured that the Chinese government would grant the British requests; and that the real reason for refusing was Staunton's argument that it would cause the East India Company to lose "face" if the ceremony was performed after the Envoy had declared that he would not do it.

Not until 1834, when the Company's monopoly of the China trade had been abolished, did the government of Great Britain embark upon a policy which, by bringing the two empires into direct conflict, was to usher in a new era in the relations between China and the West.

CHAPTER II.

The Opening of China.

The "Period of Conflict," 1834-1860—The Treaty Settlement—Treaty Ports and Tariff—Extraterritoriality—Diplomatic Intercourse—Christian Missions and Anti-foreignism—China and the "Balance of Power"—The Eastern Policies of Russia and Britain—France and the United States—Germany and Japan—The China-Japanese War.

THE first break in the long existing status of maritime trade at Canton came as a result of Great Britain's decision, in 1833, to abolish the monopoly of the China trade which had hitherto been enjoyed by the East India Company. On learning the intention of the British government, the Canton viceroy had informed the Select Committee of the Company, through the usual medium of the Co-hong, that it would be necessary for the British merchants to have a "headman" or "overseer"—in Chinese, "mok," *i.e.*, "eye"—who should perform for them the functions hitherto performed by the Select Committee. The duty of such a headman would be: to receive from the Co-hong the commands which that body issued in compliance with official instructions, to transmit these commands to his fellow nationals, to be generally responsible for the obedience of his fellow nationals to the commands so issued, and to compose any disputes which might arise among the British merchants so long as these disputes did not involve any question of Chinese law.

The person whose appointment was requested by the Chinese would thus correspond to the responsible head of a guild, through whom the activities of the guild and of its members are controlled. The Chinese did not contemplate any essential alteration in their own methods of controlling the situation at Canton, and their request was for the express purpose of making possible the continuance of those methods. Least of all did their request betoken any desire for the establishment of official intercourse between the authorities at Canton and a representative of the British Crown; such an eventuality would not merely involve a complete change in the method of controlling trade, it would constitute a violation of the imperial regulations which forbade dealings between provincial officials and the governments of foreign countries.[1]

In apparent conformity with the wish expressed by the Chinese authorities, the abolition of the East India Company's monopoly was accompanied by an act which provided for the appointment of a committee of three persons who should be known as His Majesty's superintendents of trade in China. On December 10, 1833, a royal commission was issued appointing Lord Napier, Mr. W. H. C. Plowden, and Mr. J. F. Davis to be first, second, and third superintendents of trade. The arrival of the superintendents at Canton in July, 1834, and Lord Napier's fruitless efforts to communicate directly with the viceroy—in accordance with the instructions which had been received from Lord Palmerston—marked the opening of a period of conflict which gradually ripened into war. After five years of friction, the conflict finally came to a head as a result of the steps taken by Commissioner Lin for the suppression of the opium trade, and the hostilities broke out which were terminated by the Treaty of Nanking, August 29, 1842.

This first war between Great Britain and China is usually

[1] Although the United States and France both had consuls at Canton, these officers confined their functions to limits harmonizing with the Chinese conception of the proper duties of a "headman."

called the "Opium War," a characterization against which many British writers protest as being grossly misleading. To the Chinese, the question of opium was the sole cause of the war, and this conception has been shared by many critics of the British government. The British apologists, on the other hand, have always maintained that the war was brought on by the corruption and barbarity of the Chinese officials, the arrogance with which they treated the representatives of the outside nations, and the unendurable restrictions which were imposed on trade of every sort. As the terms of the treaty which was imposed at Nanking contain no reference to opium, this settlement is held up as proof that opium was not the cause of the war. Yet it must be noted that the most aggressive element among the British traders at this period were those who dealt in the prohibited drug, and that opium constituted more than half of the British trade with China.[2]

The treaty imposed upon China in 1842, supplemented by the British, American, and French commercial treaties of 1843 and 1844, did no more than mark a truce in the struggle between China and the outside world. In the newly opened "Treaty Ports,"—Amoy, Foochow, Ningpo, and Shanghai,—commerce developed with comparatively little friction. The imperial government, regarding the opium question as the one cause of the late unpleasantness, attempted to avoid further difficulties by relaxing its efforts to stamp out the traffic, although the prohibition was not repealed. In Canton, however, the bitterness which had been aroused by the first war was intensified by the cession of Hongkong and by the bickering over the right of entry

[2] During the last six years of the East India Company's monopoly, despite the fact that the Company refused to take any part in *the Chinese end* of the illegal traffic, opium made up 54% of the total British imports amounting to $130,024,897. Mex.—Figures compiled from tables given in the Appendices of Gutzlaff, *History of China*, vol. II.

into the city of Canton, and it soon became obvious that a renewal of hostilities was almost inevitable. Nor was the arrogance, from which a renewal of war might come, all on the side of the Chinese. The foreign merchants and sailors, free at last from the humiliating restrictions which had been so long imposed by the Chinese, were not always careful to remain within the limits which they had fixed for themselves by treaty, and often exceeded their legal rights with an arrogance which did much to infuriate the already hostile Chinese.

The second war with China, 1856-1858—with an appendix in 1860—arose, like the first one, out of the British determination to establish their intercourse with China upon a satisfactory basis. The episode of the *lorcha* "Arrow," from which the war developed, was nothing more than a convenient pretext for hostilities. "I trust that you and I will see great changes in this great Empire before very long," wrote Mr. Parkes, at that time Her British Majesty's consul at Canton, and one of the principals in the "Arrow" controversy; "The issue of these troubles ought to be a resident Minister at Peking and liberty to go through the length and breadth of the land, and I trust it will be so. . . . It is the cause of the West against the East, of Paganism against Christianity, and what may we not look to as the result? The opening of China indeed I trust."[3]

French participation in the war in conjunction with the British was partly attributable to Napoleon III's policy of seeking the active alliance and friendship of Great Britain, and partly to his desire for the support of the clerical party in France. The excuse for French military action against China was found in the murder—or execution—of a French Roman Catholic missionary, August Chapdelaine,

[3] Lane-Poole and Dickins, *Life of Sir Harry Parkes*, vol. I, pp. 259-262.

in northwestern Kwangsi, earlier in the year 1856. Unsuccessful efforts were made by the allies to secure the active coöperation of Russia and also of the United States, whose increasing interest in Far Eastern affairs had recently been demonstrated by the dispatch of the Perry Expedition to Japan. These two powers refused, however, to take part in the coercion of China; although both availed themselves of the Anglo-French successes in order to obtain the long-desired revision of their own treaties.

The close of the twenty-six years of strife, 1834-1860, saw a complete reversal of the situation which had formerly existed. The control over relations between China and the West, previously in the hands of China, had now definitely passed into those of the foreigners. Henceforth China was not even to be the mistress of her own household. Aside from the indemnities of war, and the cession of Hongkong and the tip of the Kowloon Peninsula to the British, the rights obtained by the four "treaty powers" through the two settlements—1842-1844 and 1858-1860—may be briefly summarized under five points: Treaty Ports, Tariff, Extraterritoriality, Diplomatic Intercourse, and Christian Missions.

By the terms of the first of these treaty settlements, the foreigners acquired the right to trade at the five ports of Canton, Amoy, Foochow, Ningpo, and Shanghai, while ten additional ports were opened by the treaties of 1858. At these ports the merchants of the treaty powers were to be allowed to purchase or lease land, build or rent houses, employ servants, and trade freely with whomsoever they chose, without the intermediary of any specially commissioned group of native merchants. The abolition of the Co-hong monopoly at Canton was definitely provided by the British treaty of Nanking.

As a precaution against any attempt on the part of the

Chinese government, or the local officials, to crush the trade at any or all of these ports by the imposition of prohibitive import and export duties, China was compelled to agree to a negotiated tariff, which could not thereafter be altered except with the consent of the foreign powers. The foreign governments conceded China's right to demand a 5% tariff on all goods imported and exported, but insisted that the tariff be converted into a "specific tariff," based on the principle of 5% "ad valorem." Inasmuch as the prices of commodities, both imports and exports, have constantly appreciated in China since the imposition of these treaties, the Chinese government has been able to collect an effective 5% tariff only for short periods immediately after a revision of the tariff has been agreed to by the other parties to the treaties.

One point on which the Western powers were almost unanimous was their unwillingness to submit the lives and property of their nationals to the operation of Chinese law. Therefore their citizens and subjects were, by the terms of the treaties, withdrawn from the control of Chinese courts through the establishment of the right of extraterritoriality. Citizens, subjects, or protégés of these powers, resident in China, were amenable only to the laws of their own countries, as administered by their consular officers or other duly constituted authorities. In case of an offense committed by a foreigner in the interior of the country, the Chinese officials were empowered only to apprehend the offender and hand him over to the nearest consular officer of his country. It is a mistake to regard this immunity from the jurisdiction of the territorial sovereign as a mere extension of the arrangement adopted with Russia in 1689. By the Treaty of Nertchinsk, Chinese in Russian territory, and Russians in Chinese territory were subject to the control of the territorial authorities; but offenders against the peace were reciprocally handed across the frontier for punishment in their own countries. Under these new treaties, the foreign powers exercised jurisdiction over their nationals on Chinese soil, and, even in the case of offenses committed beyond the reach of consular authority, a Chinese official assumed considerable risk in laying violent hands upon a foreign offender.[4]

The treaties also extended partial immunity from native jurisdiction to Chinese in the employ of foreigners, to native crews of ships flying foreign flags, and, eventually, to the Chinese residents in the foreign settlements which grew up at the treaty ports. The Chinese authorities could apprehend offenders belonging in these categories only through the medium of the consular officials of the interested foreigner. On the other hand, the individual foreigner, having been completely withdrawn from the jurisdiction of the Chinese officials, had no right of direct access to the native magistrates; representations of any sort could be *legally* made to a Chinese authority only through his consular officers. In civil cases between Chinese and foreigners, and in all cases involving foreigners of different nationalities, the law of the defendant was applied and the case came before the defendant's court.

The refusal of the Peking government to treat with foreign powers on a basis of equality, and the laws forbidding the local officials to have any direct relations with the "outside barbarians" had long been grounds for Western dissatisfaction. One of the most important achievements of the treaty settlements was the alteration of this

[4] In connection with extraterritoriality, it is interesting to note that, according to Staunton, the "Tang-leu" or "Laws of the Tang Dynasty," edited in 654 A.D., direct that foreigners, in respect to disputes among themselves, should be governed by their own laws; but in respect to disputes with natives, or with other foreigners of a different nation, by the laws of China. See Staunton, *Miscellaneous Notes*, vol. I, p. 109.

state of affairs. In the treaties which followed the first war, detailed regulations were laid down for official correspondence between foreign representatives and the local and provincial officials of the Empire. The settlement of 1858, with the supplementary conventions signed at Peking in 1860, repeated and extended these regulations and also provided for resident diplomatic representatives at the imperial capital who should have the right to correspond with the high officers of the central administration. No longer were the local officials to be free to manage their affairs subject only to the approval of public opinion; if they refused to regard the claims put forward by the foreign consuls for the fulfilment of treaty stipulations, these claims were liable to be laid before the government at Peking in the form of demands—often supported by the threat to appeal to force if satisfaction was not forthcoming.

Finally, the government of China was compelled to alter its established policy in regard to the Christian religion. As we have already seen, Kang Hi, in 1717, had put the foreign religion under a ban; a decree which was so enforced—or non-enforced—as to allow the adherents of Christianity to live in comparative security, so long as they did nothing to arouse the hostility of other elements in their communities, or the suspicions of the local officials. In so doing, the Emperor had merely applied the policy which had usually been adopted in dealing with other heretical sects, such as Buddhism. After the negotiation of the French commercial treaty of 1844, M. de Legrené, the French plenipotentiary, urged upon Kiying, the Chinese negotiator, the desirability of establishing the liberty of the Catholic worship in China. As a result of these representations, transmitted to the Throne in a memorial from Kiying, Tao-kwang, by a rescript to Kiying's memorial, on December 28, 1844, and by a decree in February, 1846, granted toleration to all such followers of the "Lord of Heaven" as were guilty of no evil doing. In other words, the Emperor merely authorized the disregard of the ban imposed in 1717, without repealing the decree of that date; the prohibition against foreign missionaries going about through the country, which was being constantly violated, was reaffirmed.

This situation was completely changed by the treaties drawn up at Tientsin in 1858. The Chinese government bound itself to tolerate the Christian religion as professed by both Protestants and Roman Catholics, and also to protect the missionaries and their adherents from all persecution and interference, so long as they were guiltless of offending against the laws. The protection of foreign missionaries and native converts, even against popular hostility resulting from Christian disregard of community traditions, thus became a treaty obligation upon the government at Peking.

In breaking away from the humiliating conditions under which they had formerly been allowed to reside at Canton, the foreigners had gained not equality but supremacy in all points connected with their activities in China. Trade was carried on under regulations drafted by the foreign negotiators, and every advantage gained by the shrewdness of one foreign representative became, through the operation of "most favored nation" clauses, the privilege of all the other treaty powers. Living under the protection of their own foreign law-codes, the Westerners demanded for Chinese offenders punishments which were, at times, even in excess of those prescribed in the code of China. Their diplomatic negotiations with China had been carried on, and were to be carried on in the future, under the aegis of military and naval supremacy. "With the exception of the Alcock Convention," says Sir Robert Hart, "no negotiation, to the Chinese mind, has held the balance fairly. The non-ratification of that convention was damaging, for it had been negotiated leisurely and in a friendly spirit, and the Chinese officials regarded its rejection as equivalent to saying that their interests must always give way before what the foreigner thought to be his."[5]

The state of affairs created by these treaty obligations placed the imperial government "between the devil and the deep sea." It had been compelled to promise to the foreigners certain rights and privileges throughout the Empire, promises for which the beneficiaries of the treaties could be expected to hold Peking strictly accountable. Yet the fulfilment of these obligations imposed upon the central government the necessity of assuming, in regard to local affairs, an initiative which was wholly contrary to traditional practice. This assumption of initiative would, in many cases, be bitterly resented as an infringement upon cherished local rights, and might involve the dynasty in the popular hostility toward the foreigner who came violating customs and disturbing economic conditions. It has often been assumed, without sufficient ground, that anti-foreignism was fostered by the Manchus from a fear lest the introduction of Western progress would result in the overthrow of the dynasty. In addition to the early liberal policy of Kang Hi, who reversed the policy of the Chinese Mings in regard to foreign trade and opened, for a while, all the ports of the Empire, there is the testimony of Sir John F. Davis, Abbé Huc, and many others, to the effect that the Manchu officials were, almost without exception, more conciliatory than the Chinese in their dealings with the foreigners. While the Chinese officials shared the popular dislike for the foreign innovations, the Manchus were

[5] Hart, *These from the Land of Sinim*, p. 70.

chiefly interested in keeping peace with their formidable foes. It may also, perhaps, be conjectured that the Chinese officials had a clearer appreciation than had the Manchus of the essential incompatibility of these innovations and the Chinese social organization.

Until the closing years of the nineteenth century, anti-foreignism among the Chinese was almost entirely associated with the spread of Christian missions. This was largely due to the fact that the missionary was almost the only foreigner who came into close contact with the people outside the immediate environs of the treaty ports. Popular hostility to the missionaries and their work can be attributed partly to Chinese superstitions, partly to the exclusive—and, from the Chinese point of view, anti-social—character of the Christian religion, and partly to the privileges enjoyed by the missionary and his native adherents.

The grosser manifestations of Chinese superstition which appeared in connection with anti-missionary disturbances—the accusations in regard to various inhuman practices attributed to Christians—were the result rather than the cause of hostility. These charges were sometimes circulated by the officials, more often by the non-official "literati," to stir up opposition against new extensions of missionary work. Yet other aspects of superstition were real causes of hostility. Some of the superstitious fear and hatred toward the "foreign doctrine" must, indeed, be attributed to the teachings of the missionaries themselves. They were accustomed to preaching, often with little tact—and with only an elementary knowledge of the language which they were using—that the "True God" of the Christians was to triumph over the false gods of the heathen. There is little reason for wonder, then, that a Chinese should regard any local disaster, such as a flood or a drought, as the result of the conflict between his gods and those of the foreigner; or that he should, on such occasions, attempt to cast out the disturbing influence.

A more constant cause of popular opposition to Christianity was to be found in its social effects in those places where it succeeded in establishing itself. The convert to the religion was cut off from the community life as well as from the life of the family. Protestantism had followed the example of the Roman Catholics in forbidding its members to take part in the observance of ancestral rites—"ancestor worship." Thus the acceptance of Christianity by a single member of a family, especially by an eldest or only son, was bitterly resented as an unfilial act, and became the cause of hostility against the missionary. In much the same way, the Christian was cut off from the community in which he lived, and forbidden to participate in, or contribute toward, any of the community festivals or amusements in which there was a suggestion of honoring false gods. As almost all of the village festivals involved some recognition of the local deities, each additional convert to Christianity meant one less contributor to the expenses, and a corresponding additional burden to his fellow townsmen. The converts were, moreover, often accused by their neighbors of enjoying the performances to which their religious convictions would not allow them to contribute.

By far the greatest amount of friction between the Christians and non-Christians arose, however, out of the fact that the missionary was not amenable to the laws of the land, and out of the related fact that the treaties guaranteed to the native Christian freedom from religious persecution. Extraterritoriality for the foreigners resident in the treaty ports might, perhaps, have been a convenience for the Chinese authorities, in so far as it relieved them from the necessity of learning foreign ways and settling the commercial disputes that arose among these outsiders. Extraterritoriality carried about through the length and breadth of the land by the missionary was a constant source of internal trouble and a constant threat of external complications. Especially was this true when the missionary, espousing the cause of a convert who had become involved in legal difficulties, intervened on his behalf in the court of the local official. While the missionary had no right of direct approach to the native official, the official usually felt that, if the case was not settled in accordance with what the missionary considered to be justice, it would be taken up through diplomatic channels as a case of religious persecution and might lead to endless difficulties. In consequence of this feeling, cases between Christians and non-Christians were often decided in favor of the former, even when the facts and the law warranted a contrary decision.[6]

While the missionary question thus contained elements of popular friction and difficulties for the local officers, the treaty stipulations on this subject were also objectionable to the central government for reasons which had little to do with religious belief. In the first place, local difficulties in regard to missions soon proved to be a constantly recurring subject for diplomatic representations at Peking. The French legation particularly, in view of the insignificance of French commercial interests in China, was almost ex-

[6] Although the Catholic missionaries may have been more active in taking up cases directly with the local officials, the practice was also quite common among the Protestants. The most reliable evidence on this point is to be found in a paper by Dr. Bergen, later president of the Shantung Christian University, in the *Chinese Recorder* for June and July, 1899. In the same magazine, May, 1899, there appeared a communication from the United States consul at Canton, notifying American missionaries of the fact that they had no treaty right of direct access to the Chinese officials, and warning them that all complaints and demands must be taken up through their consular officers.

clusively concerned with questions arising out of the French protectorate over Catholic missions. The authorities at Peking were constantly receiving demands for the dismissal or reprimand of local officials, or for the payment of indemnities, as the result of anti-missionary disturbances here or there in the provinces.

There was a second, and equally important, reason for imperial dissatisfaction with the treaty-status of Christianity. In view of its secret and mysterious rites, the foreign religion was always regarded as a potential nucleus for revolutionary organizations—a danger accentuated by the treaty stipulations which debarred the government from exercising any effective oversight over such of its subjects as became converts. The Chinese always considered the Taiping Rebellion as a Christian movement, and held the missionaries responsible for the widespread desolation which this movement caused. Some justification for this belief is found in the proclamations issued by Hung Siu-tsuen, the Taiping emperor, who declared himself to be the representative and "younger brother" of Jesus. Even more justification lies in the fact that many of the Protestant missionaries during the early phases of the rebellion regarded Hung as a convert to the faith and hailed the movement as the beginning of the "conquest of China for Christ."[7]

The internal complications which have just been described were not, however, the only difficulties which China was to experience as a result of the changes brought about by her new treaty relationship with the West. From this time she was to find herself more and more deeply

[7] See *British Blue Books*, 1853, "Papers Respecting the Civil War in China," p. 41 ff., for Dr. Medhurst's summary of the *Taiping Tracts*. The later repudiation of the Taipings by the missionaries did not modify the Chinese opinion.

implicated in the international rivalries and jealousies of the European nations. The four powers whose representatives signed the treaties with China at Tientsin, in 1858, were, even at that time, not unaffected by mutual distrust; and the divergence of their aims and aspirations quickly developed after this date. On the subsequent resumption of hostilities by the Anglo-French allies, in 1860, the Russian representative took advantage of the situation to obtain from China, in return for his diplomatic assistance, a modification of the Russo-Chinese frontier. This gave Russia the valuable coastal province of Primorsk, including the excellent harbor which later became the site of the eastern stronghold, Vladivostok. At the same time, the British determination to demand the right of a resident minister at Peking was undoubtedly strengthened by suspicion in regard to Russian influence there.

From this period, Anglo-Russian rivalry was to play a prominent part in every phase of China's affairs. Both countries offered assistance to the imperial government for the suppression of the Taipings. The services of Gordon as leader of the "Ever Victorious Army," organized by the American, Ward, were accepted; but Russia's offer of an army of 30,000 men, and the British "Lay-Osborne Flotilla" were both rejected by the Chinese, who feared the complications which might result from the presence of a foreign-officered force independent of the local authorities. The Mohammedan uprisings of the '70's involved the Empire in difficulties with both countries. The revolt in Yunnan was the occasion of intrigue between the British officials in India and the rebels, which was resented by China; while the rise of Yakub Beg in Turkestan and the Dungan revolt in the Ili region led to the Kuldja dispute between China and Russia, and nearly brought on a war between the two countries before the territorial question was satisfactorily adjusted. The steady growth of Russian influence in Central Asia was a constant source of anxiety to the British government and, by 1890, this anxiety had become focussed upon Tibet, which became the center for diplomatic discussions and the subject of numerous agreements between China, Russia, and Great Britain.

Only a little less important than the Anglo-Russian rivalry was that which developed between the two countries whose combined military and naval power had forced upon China the final treaty settlement. Even before the withdrawal of the Allied forces from Peking, in the fall of 1860, the friendship between France and Britain had showed signs of cooling. France had taken advantage of the presence of her forces in the Far East to embark upon a policy of empire-building, and her acquisition of possessions in Indo-China led inevitably to a conflict between French and British aspirations in respect to the Chinese frontier provinces of Kwangsi and Yunnan. The growing rivalry between France and Great Britain in other parts of the world, and the *rapprochement* between France and Russia toward the close of the century, naturally served to intensify Anglo-French friction in the southern part of China.

Of the four original treaty powers, the policies of France and Russia were much alike and, as their interests lay in widely separated parts of the Empire, led to no difficulties between these two European states. The ambitions of each were primarily territorial. Russia, especially after British support of Turkey had barred the way to Constantinople, turned her attention more and more toward central and eastern Asia. The Russians had a considerable commercial interest in the northern parts of China, but their representative at Peking was chiefly concerned in preserving friendly relations along the common frontier and in establishing himself in the confidence of the Chinese as a dependable friend in case of any controversy between China and another foreign power.[8] France, after her humiliating defeat at the hands of Prussia, endeavored to reëstablish herself as a world power by building up an imposing colonial empire, and devoted a great deal of energy to extending and strengthening her position in Indo-China. The commercial activities of the French in China were negligible, and the diplomatic duties of their minister at Peking were limited almost entirely to questions arising out of the protection of Catholic missions. The protectorate over Catholic missions was, indeed, regarded by the French in the Far East as a valuable national asset, chiefly because it gave their minister an opportunity to play an important rôle at Peking and to maintain in the eyes of the Chinese the position of France as a first-rate power.

The policy of the British government in regard to China had two important objects: to maintain and—if possible—improve the facilities for trade, and to strengthen China so that she might become a bulwark against Russian expansion and thus serve as a protection to the Indian Empire. In pursuance of both of these aims the British necessarily became the chief advocates of reform and progress. The creation of the Imperial Maritime Customs, with an international personnel and a British inspector-general, insured the foreign importer against irregular exactions at the ports, and also secured to the central government a considerable increase of revenue from the foreign trade, revenue which could be utilized in strengthening the country against foreign aggression. It will be

[8] For an official exposition of this phase of Russian policy, see the memorandum submitted to Nicholas II, on June 4/17, 1900, by Count Mouravieff, *Krasny Arkhiv*, vol. XIV.

observed that the imperial government, for any further increase in the revenue derived from this source, was dependent not upon the consent of the Chinese people but on the good will of the treaty powers. In attempting to strengthen the central government, foreign influence was thus weakening the essential democracy of the Chinese state and, at the same time, putting a premium upon the government's subservience to the outside world.

The British government also encouraged China in the adoption of modern methods of warfare, especially by aiding her in the creation of a modern navy. For this purpose Chinese cadets were admitted to service in the schools and schoolships of the Royal Navy, and British naval officers were permitted to take service under the Chinese flag and to accept employment in the arsenals and navy-yards as construction engineers. While the British were moderately successful in developing China's navy and the customs service, and were able to obtain various minor concessions for the betterment of trade conditions, they met complete failure in their efforts to induce China to adopt a modern code of commercial law. Although this was repeatedly urged by the British commercial interests, China continued to reject it as an innovation which would strike at the very roots of her political system.

The policy of the United States—if that country can be said to have had a Chinese policy during this period—was entirely non-aggressive. During the thirty years which followed the close of the American Civil War, American commercial interest in China was insignificant. This fact was partly due to the decay of the American merchant marine; but it was also, to a considerable extent, due to America's absorption in the development of her own great natural resources in the West. Aside from the protection of American missionaries, almost the only issues that arose between the governments of China and the United States were those connected with Chinese immigration into America. The American minister was therefore generally able to assume the attitude of a disinterested friend, and if, like his British colleague, he often recommended the adoption of progressive Western institutions, there was no danger that the rejection of his proposals would lead to international complications.

During the decade which followed the settlement of 1858-1860, two new states, both destined to become first-rate powers, began to take part in the affairs of China. Of these two, Germany played a comparatively unimportant part for the next quarter of a century or more. Japan, however, soon became a source of new troubles for the Chinese government. Reopened to foreign influence by the American expedition under Commodore Perry, after more than two centuries of voluntary isolation, Japan had passed through a brief but turbulent period of readjustment which culminated, in 1868, in the abolition of the "Shogunate" and the establishment of a powerful centralized government under the "restored" Mikado. Following this reconstruction, Japan soon showed herself to be as quick as China had been slow in the assimilation of the material aspects of Western civilization, and, within a few years, discovered subjects for controversy with her less progressive neighbor on the continent.

The first clash between China and Japan arose over the Liu Chiu Islands, a group lying about midway between Formosa and the southernmost of the main Japanese Islands. Although the Liu Chius had been long regarded—and regarded themselves—as vassals of the Chinese Empire, Japan claimed them as an integral part of the Mikado's domains. Certain Liu Chiuan fishermen, shipwrecked on the shores of Formosa, having been murdered by the Formosans, Japan demanded of China an indemnity for the murdered men and the punishment of the authors of the outrage. China refused this demand on the grounds that the Liu Chiuans were vassals of China and that China assumed no responsibility, in any case, for the actions of the Formosans. Rejecting the first of these contentions, the Japanese accepted the second and, in 1874, dispatched a punitive expedition to Formosa. For a while war between the two empires seemed impending, but ultimately China agreed to pay compensation for the murdered men and an indemnity for the costs of the expedition, and to recognize Japan's claims to the Liu Chius.

Although the Liu Chiu affair had been a small matter, the results of the dispute encouraged the Japanese government to undertake the more ambitious project of dislodging China from her position as suzerain of Korea. In 1875 Japan negotiated with Korea a commercial treaty in which the latter country was officially represented as an independent sovereign state. China countered this move by encouraging Korea to enter into treaties with the various Western powers. In these later negotiations, the Korean government acknowledged the suzerainty of China, and the European countries avoided giving offense to China by the simple expedient of accrediting their diplomatic representatives at Peking to the court of Seoul as well. The United States refused to recognize the alleged relationship between China and Korea, and, like Japan, maintained a separate legation at the Korean capital. Having weakened, to some extent, the position of China as the suzerain of Korea, the Japanese proceeded to foster the growth of a pro-Japanese party in Korea, and conflicts began to arise between this new party and the conservatives, who were in favor of retaining the old relationship with China.

In 1885 Japan took advantage of an anti-Japanese uprising at Seoul, and of the fact that China was at this time engaged in war with France over Tong-king, to secure China's agreement to the famous Li-Ito Convention. This convention established a joint suzerainty over Korea and provided that either high contracting power should notify the other before sending troops into Korea for any purpose. Nine years later the outbreak of the "Tong-hak" disturbances in Korea led the Korean government to request military aid from China. In response to this request China dispatched a small force to Korea, and duly notified Japan of the move. At the same time Japan, although she had received no appeal for aid, sent a considerable force of her own troops into the peninsula. In the meantime the Korean authorities had succeeded in suppressing the disorders with their own resources. Japan now demanded the institution of sweeping reforms in Korea's internal affairs, and, when these demands were rejected by both China and Korea, declared that she would carry them out on her own authority. While the tension between China and Japan was at its height, the British steamer *Kowshing*, chartered by the Chinese as a transport and carrying reinforcements to Korea, was sunk by a Japanese warship—and war broke out.

That Japan deliberately forced the war with China is recognized by many of her own historians and by most neutrals. Her reasons for desiring war were mixed. One motive undoubtedly was the desire to resume the glorious but unsuccessful venture undertaken by Hideyoshi three centuries earlier. This was supplemented by resentment at the contemptuous treatment which she had always received from China, and by the necessity of utilizing abroad the pent-up energies of the people, which were threatening to create disturbances at home. But the dominating motives are to be found in the desire to test her newly organized military and naval machinery, and in the belief that only by showing herself to be a real military power could she hope to receive respectful treatment from the European nations.

Contrary to the expectations of most of the Europeans in the Far East—and contrary to the hopes of all, with the possible exception of the Protestant missionaries—the war was marked by an unbroken series of Japanese victories. Unable to stop the advance of the Mikado's armies, China was compelled to sue for peace and, on April 17, 1895, Li Hung-chang, as plenipotentiary for China, signed the humiliating Treaty of Shimonoseki. By this treaty, China recognized the independence of Korea; ceded Formosa, the Pescadores, and the Liao-tung peninsula to Japan; and agreed to pay a war indemnity of 200,000,000 taels. Severe as were the terms of the treaty, the indirect results of the war were destined to be even more serious. China lost at a single blow all the prestige which she had acquired by the suppression of the Dungan revolt, by her successful negotiations with Russia in regard to Kuldja, and by the respectable fight which she had made against France in the Tong-king War. Now she stood revealed to the world as a helpless giant, unable to raise a hand in defense of her vast possessions. The exaggerated esteem in which she had been held, by reason of her size and her apparent progress in the adoption of Western military equipment, now gave way to an equally exaggerated contempt. Nothing now remained to check the aggressions of the rapacious nations of the West save their own mutual jealousies and suspicions.

CHAPTER III.

Consequences of Shimonoseki.

Three-Power Intervention—Retrocession of Liaotung—Russian, French, and German Aspirations—British Policy—The "Denby Proposals"—Franco-Chinese Boundary Settlement—Anglo-Chinese Agreement of February 4, 1897—Russo-Chinese Treaty—Loans—Policy of China after the War—Military and Economic Reforms—Concessions.

THE outbreak of war between China and Japan in the summer of 1894 had aroused grave apprehension among the Western powers lest the conflict should destroy the *status quo* in the Far East. As a result of these apprehensions there were efforts to mediate between the belligerent empires, but the rivalries and the mutual suspicions which divided the neutrals prevented any effective coöperation for the restoration of peace. On October 7, 1894, the British government proposed that Britain, Germany, France, Russia, and the United States unite in "an intervention between Japan and China, which should have as its basis an indemnity to Japan for the expenses of the war and the independence of Corea, to be guaranteed by the Powers." As this proposal did not meet with a favorable reception in any quarter, the British government abandoned its plan as "premature." Toward the end of November the government of the United States made an isolated offer of friendly mediation, only to have its offer politely declined by the Japanese.

Following the failure of the American attempt at mediation, there were no further attempts to interfere in the progress of hostilities; but the opening of peace negotiations between China and Japan found the interested

Western powers busily engaged in exchanging views regarding the situation and the possible future developments in the Orient. On February 26, 1895, Mr. Denby, the American minister at Peking, reported that "for the last few days Li Hung-chang has been engaged in interviewing the heads of Legations here. . . . He puts to each Minister the question: 'Will your government intervene if China refuses to grant a cession of territory?' " Li's efforts soon produced tangible results: on March 8 the German minister at Tokyo, acting upon instructions from Berlin, recommended to the Japanese government the prompt conclusion of peace upon moderate terms. Baron Gutschmid informed the Japanese Foreign Office that some of the powers were inclined to respond to Chinese appeals for intervention, and his communication closed with the warning that "according to our present information, a Japanese demand for territorial acquisition on the mainland would be especially calculated to provoke intervention."

The Japanese demand for the cession of Liaotung, which became known to the European Foreign Offices on April 2, aroused three of the governments to definite action. On April 23, after much preliminary discussion and after an unsuccessful effort to secure British coöperation, the Russian, French, and German ministers at Tokyo called at the Ministry of Foreign Affairs to "advise" that Japan renounce her claim to the permanent possession of the Liaotung peninsula. Five days later this advice was reiterated, and, on the twenty-ninth, the three diplomats requested that the Japanese government honor them with an answer not later than May 8, the day fixed for the exchange of ratifications of the Shimonoseki treaty. On May 1 Japan attempted to compromise the matter by expressing her willingness, after the formal exchange of ratifications, to abandon all of Liaotung with the exception of Port Arthur. As the intervening powers insisted that the retention of Port Arthur was the one thing which was most objectionable, the compromise was not accepted and Japan ultimately gave way with regard to the entire area. On May 5 the Japanese ministers at Paris, Berlin, and St. Petersburg officially announced that the whole Liaotung peninsula, including Port Arthur, would be returned to China. The formal exchange of the treaty ratifications took place on May 8 at Chefoo, and, on the thirteenth of May, a proclamation by the Japanese Emperor announced the renunciation of the Liaotung territory. As compensation for the region thus abandoned, Japan obtained from China an additional indemnity of 30,000,000 taels.

The ringleader in this intervention had been Russia, whose action was dictated by very obvious motives. While it would be rash to assume that Russia, at this date, was already contemplating the absorption of Manchuria, including the Liaotung peninsula, into her own dominions, the government of the Czar had a very lively interest in the fate of this province. Russia could not fail to take offense at any territorial readjustment which would put an aggressive power, with a modern army and navy, on the flank of her recently commenced Trans-Siberian railway. Since Russia, of all the Western powers, had been the most successful in maintaining cordial diplomatic relations with the Court of Peking, it is improbable that she was any more anxious than Britain or the United States to see the partition of China. If, or when, the partition of the Empire should take place, however, the Liaotung peninsula was the one portion which Russia firmly intended should fall into no unfriendly hands.

France, in this affair, was merely supporting her Russian ally. With the exception of the Catholic missions in Manchuria, French interest in the region under discussion was practically "nil." In the light of subsequent developments, it may reasonably be presumed that the French government welcomed this opportunity to put China under obligations which would justify a demand for compensation in the form of new concessions in regions where French interests did exist; but the chief motives of the French action must be sought in Europe rather than in the Far East.

German participation in the move to prevent Japanese acquisition of a foothold upon the Chinese mainland may be partially explained by the Kaiser's exaggerated anticipation of the Japanese "Yellow Peril." In part, also, it was due to a legitimate fear that any essential modification of the *status quo* in the Far East would seriously threaten the growing German commerce in that part of the world. Indeed, if we avoid the temptation to explain Germany's actions at this time by reasoning back from her policy of two decades later, it will appear probable that the chief anxiety of the Berlin government was to prevent any radical change in the Far Eastern situation. To a certain extent, however, the German coöperation with Russia was dictated by European considerations. Since the accession of Nicholas II to the Russian throne, on November 1, 1894, the Berlin government had been endeavoring to foster more friendly relations with the Russian Court and weaken the Russo-French entente. German support of Russian policy in the Orient—where it was anticipated that France would prove a negligible factor—might achieve this end. It might also serve to turn Russia's attention from the Near East, thus eliminating the danger of a clash between Russia and Germany's Austrian ally.

Far more difficult to understand is the British attitude toward the partial dismemberment of China at the hands of Japan. British interests, commercial as well as imperial, had hitherto demanded the maintenance of China's sovereignty and territorial integrity. In October, as has been noted above, the British government had proposed an intervention on terms which would have precluded any cession of Chinese territory; and, as late as April 8, the German government counted upon British coöperation in the diplomatic intervention at Tokyo. Had it not been for the British proposal in October, the time relationship between the Anglo-Japanese treaty revision on July 16, 1894, and the outbreak of the China-Japanese War would suggest the possibility of a secret understanding, before the commencement of hostilities, whereby Japan should have a free hand in North China as compensation for future aid in checking the Russian advance.[1] The more probable explanation is that the British government, after witnessing the total collapse of China's military organization in the war with Japan, abandoned all hope that China could ever become an effective barrier against Russia, and therefore was willing to sacrifice British commercial interests in Manchuria for the sake of securing the friendship and future coöperation of China's conqueror.

Although it can only be conjectured that the British government regarded China's defeat as evidence that the Empire could no longer stand alone, much less resist the aggressions of any outside power, there is ample proof that this was the view of many Americans residing in China, including the American minister at Peking. The American missionaries, who had always considered the conservatism of the Manchus to be the chief obstacle to the Christianization of China, frankly welcomed the impending collapse of the existing régime and some of them even

[1] Professor Cordier, in his *Histoire des Relations de la Chine avec les Puissances Occidentales*, vol. III, p. 289, notes the possibility of this suspicion.

acclaimed the victorious armies of the Mikado as "the chosen instruments of Divine Providence." These missionary views may be taken at a considerable discount, since they expressed merely the private opinions of irresponsible parties. Real significance, however, must be attached to the views and recommendations of America's diplomatic representative, who, on May 8, submitted to Secretary Gresham a set of proposals which he regarded as a suitable basis for concerted action by the treaty powers for the readjustment of China's relations with the outside world.

Mr. Denby's nineteen proposals[2] were as follows:

Suggestions of Desired Reforms.

1st. During war Consuls of a friendly power acting for a belligerent to have all the jurisdiction that his Consul had during peace.

2nd. China to be open to foreign residence as Western countries are.

3rd. Whether article 2 be adopted or not, missionaries to go where they please, and to reside and buy land and be protected.

4th. Foreign goods to be subject to no taxation, except import duty, until they reach the consumer. They are not to be taxed as is now done as soon as they are landed.

5th. No internal revenue, or likin tax, to be levied on foreign goods which discriminates against them. No such tax to be prohibitory nor in any event to exceed 2%, and no internal revenue tax to be levied on foreign goods unless a similar tax is levied on native goods of the same character.

6th. Local authorities shall have no power to provide that

[2] These proposals are taken from Mr. Denby's dispatch No. 2192, which is to be found in the State Department Documents, "Dispatches from China," vol. 98. They are reproduced, with reasonable accuracy, in an editorial which appeared in the *North China Herald*, Shanghai, on July 12, 1895. The North China editorial asserts that they are reprinted from an American newspaper; but this intermediate publication has not been identified by the present writer.

freight shipped in native bottoms shall pay less duty than freight shipped in foreign bottoms. The export tax shall be uniform.

7th. Every port in China ordinarily used and frequented by seagoing ships shall be open to all the world.

8th. The coast-wise duty of 2½% on goods sent down the Yangtze and intended to be sent abroad shall not be paid in specie, but a bond shall be taken that if the goods are not exported in a certain time the coast-wise duty shall be paid.

9th. Drawbacks are abolished and bonds are substituted for the payment of coast-wise duties in order to relieve the commercial community from a useless expenditure.

10th. The Yangtze regulations to be amended or abolished. No bonds to be required that goods shipped from one point shall be delivered in toto at another. The existing regulation is entirely absurd.

11th. Private yachts, non-commercial ships, may ascend the Yangtze without taking out clearance at Chinkiang.

12th. The provincial authorities shall have no power to tax foreign goods for any purpose whatever. Such taxation shall be ordered by the Central Government only.

13th. Machinery may be imported.

14th. Foreigners may engage in manufacturing in China on the same terms as natives.

15th. Libellous and scandalous publications affecting foreigners shall be vigorously suppressed.

16th. Stringent measures shall be taken to prevent anti-foreign riots, and if any such occur the rioters shall be condignly punished, and besides damages shall be paid.

17th. All parts of China shall be open to foreign trade. This shall particularly apply to Peking or any other capital.

18th. The Viceroys, Governors, and the Provincial authorities generally, shall be prohibited to treat international matters, except to settle claims for injuries done to foreigners. All other questions affecting foreigners shall be cognizable at the capital and by the Central Government only.

19th. No Viceroy or Governor shall have the power to make

any contract with foreigners for the purchase or supply of any material. All such contracts shall be made or authorized by the Imperial or Central Government.

One apparent object of these proposals was to safeguard China against possible aggression on the part of isolated powers; this was to be achieved by making China the "ward" of all. The probable result of the reforms, if they had been adopted, would have been to put China absolutely under the management of the treaty powers; all important administrative functions would have been centralized in the hands of the government at Peking, where they would have been under effective control by the diplomatic body. As the policy suggested by Mr. Denby did not meet the approval of the Cleveland administration, it did not become the basis of any diplomatic action at that time; in the settlement of 1901, however, such of the proposals as dealt with the modification of existing customs regulations were essentially adopted by the powers.

While the general consensus of opinion among foreigners in the Orient anticipated the early dissolution of the Chinese state, it also was well understood that the three powers whose intervention had forced the modification of the Shimonoseki treaty had not been actuated by purely altruistic motives. Everyone felt confident that China would sooner or later be compelled to pay dearly for the services rendered.

France was the first kind friend to receive compensation for her assistance. M. Gerard and his government had long known exactly what they wanted; on June 20, 1895, therefore, a treaty was signed by the French minister and the representatives of the Chinese government providing for certain "rectifications" of the Annam-Chinese frontier. This treaty also provided that the French-Chinese Boundary Convention of June 26, 1887, should be immediately ratified by the Chinese Emperor. Since the rectification of the Annam-Chinese frontier was accomplished by surrendering to France certain territories which China held under the Anglo-Chinese Convention of March 1, 1894, the British minister at Peking, Sir Nicholas O'Conor, entered a vigorous protest against China's ratification of the new French treaty.

Whatever irritation Great Britain may have felt toward France for having taken these territories from China was cleared away by negotiations resulting in a declaration signed by representatives of the two countries on January 15, 1896, at London.[3] Although the British government was willing thus to compose its differences with France, China was not to be excused for her part in the objectionable treaty. In spite of the fact that China had merely submitted to French pressure and in spite of the fact that Britain had now secured a share in any of the benefits obtained by the French, the alienation of territory by China was taken as sufficient grounds for demanding compensatory concessions. On February 4, 1897, after considerable negotiation, a fresh agreement was signed by Li Hung-chang and the new British minister, Sir Claude MacDonald. The preamble of the agreement stated that it was made "in consideration of the Government of Great Britain consenting to withdraw its objections to the alienation by

[3] In addition to recognizing the new arrangement between France and China, the Anglo-French declaration provided—Article IV—"that all commercial and other privileges conceded in the two Chinese provinces of Yunnan and Szechuan either to Great Britain or France, in virtue of their respective conventions with China of the 1st March, 1894, and the 20th June, 1895, and all other privileges and advantages of any nature which may in the future be conceded in these two Chinese provinces, either to Great Britain or France, shall, so far as rests with them, be extended and rendered common to both powers."

China, by the Convention with France of the 20th June, 1895, of territory forming a portion of Kiang Hung, in derogation of the provisions of the Convention between Great Britain and China of the 1st March, 1894." As the price of this consent, Great Britain secured the cession of frontier territory amounting to something over 1000 square miles, the "perpetual lease" of a smaller area, a pledge of the non-alienation of any further territory along the Mekong, certain promises regarding the development of trade routes and railroads, and the opening of three new treaty ports and four "ports of call."

Great Britain's use of China's concessions to France as a "club" with which to secure compensations was in complete harmony with the traditions of European diplomacy; far more significant, however, was the provision for the transfer of territory under "perpetual lease."[4] Two earlier examples of leased territories are to be found in the history of China's relations with the West: the Portuguese settlement at Macao and the first Kowloon extension of the British colony of Hongkong. Both of these pieces of territory had been held originally on "lease"—and China had been compelled ultimately to cede outright both areas. But the principle of "leasing," although used only twice prior to February 4, 1897, was destined to become, after that date, a common and well-recognized expedient. In the course of little more than a year, China was to see pass from her control, by the operation of leases, most of those ports which had not already been opened to the world as treaty ports.

Except for the fact that Germany obtained "concessions"

[4] *Cf.* Cordier, *Histoire des Relations de la Chine avec les Puissances Occidentales*, vol. III, p. 183, "On voit ici reparaître ce fameux néologisme diplomatique de la 'cession à bail.' "

at Tientsin and Hankow similar to those already held, at these and other treaty ports, by a number of the powers, no territorial acquisitions were made, for more than two years, by the two governments which had been associated with France in protecting the integrity of China.

In the case of Germany, failure to claim prompt compensation for her valuable assistance was due partly to the difficulty experienced by the Berlin government in deciding upon the point which would prove most suitable as a base for subsequent activities in the Far East. The Kaiser and his ministers wished to secure on the coast of China a port —or ports—satisfactory, at the same time, as naval bases and as centers for commercial development. On April 17, 1895,[5] the German Foreign Office received from the Admiralty a confidential report discussing the comparative merits of six points along the coast: Montebello Island, off the southern point of Korea, Kiaochow Bay, the island of Chusan, Amoy, the Pescadores, and Mirs Bay, near Hongkong. Since the report showed that the Admiralty was unable to reach any definite decision between these six points, the Foreign Office marked time until a thorough survey could be made by naval and commercial experts. But this difficulty in making a proper choice of a suitable site was not the only cause for German delay. Much as the German government desired to secure a naval and commercial base on the coast of China, it was equally anxious to avoid any step which might endanger Germany's existing commercial interests, or which might compel Germany permanently to ally herself either with Great Britain or with Russia in Far Eastern affairs. Fearing that an aggressive policy might produce undesirable complications, the Berlin Foreign Office therefore spent two years in

[5] The day upon which the treaty of Shimonoseki was signed.

fruitless efforts to secure from China some voluntary concession in recognition of Germany's valuable services.[6]

Russia, the ringleader in the intervention on behalf of China, had even stronger reasons for not presenting an immediate bill for services rendered. Under the influence of Witte, Minister of Finance, Russia was endeavoring, at this time, to conciliate China and to strengthen the existing bonds of friendship between the two empires. This policy of leading the Chinese to feel that they had little to fear and much to hope from their neighbor on the north soon bore fruit: in May, 1896, a Russo-Chinese treaty was concluded at Moscow by Li Hung-chang and Prince Lobanov-Rostovski. Although the treaty granted to Russia the right of extending her Trans-Siberian railway across Manchuria, it also included the guarantee of Russian aid to China in case of any further aggression on the part of Japan. The treaty was therefore mutually advantageous, and it is easy to credit Count Witte's assurance that it was obtained without bribery of Li Hung-chang. A continuation of this moderate and far-sighted policy in dealing with China would have been extremely beneficial to Russia as well as to China; the reversal of policy two years later, when Russia forced the lease of Port Arthur, had disastrous consequences for both countries.[7]

[6] *Die Grosse Politik der Europäischen Kabinette, 1871-1914*, vols. IX and XIV, throws much new light upon Germany's Far Eastern policy during this period. Volume IX gives much valuable information concerning the "three-power intervention"; while volume XIV traces the story of the naval base, from the time of the Japanese war to the final acquisition of Kiaochow.

[7] Count Witte, in his *Memoirs*, chapter IV, gives a racy account of the negotiations with Li and an abstract of the treaty, as well as a valuable discussion of Russia's later change in policy. The treaty, in abbreviated form, was made public by the Chinese delegation at the Washington Conference and was sent out by the Associated Press under the date of January 24, 1922. The supposed treaty, as reported from Hongkong and printed

In the absence of any important moves against China's territorial integrity, the chief object of diplomatic rivalry at Peking, during the two years following the war with Japan, was the flotation of loans for the purpose of enabling China to meet the successive installments on the Japanese indemnity. The first of these loans, for 400,000,000 francs, was provided by Russia and France in an agreement concluded on July 1, 1895. This Russo-French diplomatic success was extremely distasteful both to Great Britain and to Germany. British dissatisfaction was due, partly, to the fact that British financiers had lost the opportunity of making this loan; but an even more serious ground for British objection to the loan agreement lay in the existence of a clause whereby the loan was to be guaranteed by the Russian government. Her British Majesty's Minister at Peking, Sir Nicholas O'Conor, expressed his disapproval of the loan with such vehemence—and with such disregard of diplomatic proprieties—that the "Tsungli Yamen"[8] requested and secured his recall. To Berlin the conclusion of the loan brought bitter disillusionment. The Kaiser's government had been striving to supplant France in Russia's affections, and the exclusion of Germany from a share in this important financial operation was regarded as an act of base ingratitude.[9] A consequence of this resentment was to drive Germany and Great Britain into closer coöperation, and the next loan to China was

in the London *Times* on October 25, 1895, may be considered as an "intelligent anticipation." For an excellent discussion of the entire question, see MacMurray, *Treaties and Agreements with and Concerning China*, vol. I. On the conclusion of the lease of Port Arthur, certain indiscreet remarks by the Russian representative at Peking, which were reported to the British Foreign Office, aroused suspicion and nearly betrayed the existence of the treaty; *cf. British Blue Books, China No. 1 (1899)*, document no. 24.

[8] Department of Foreign Affairs.

[9] For German resentment see *Grosse Politik*, vol. IX, documents no. 2280 (and footnote), 2283, 2290, 2296, 2297, and 2315.

arranged by the Anglo-German financial group—the Hongkong-Shanghai Bank and the Deutsche-Asiatische Bank—on March 23, 1896. This loan was for £16,000,000, at 5%, and was secured upon the revenues of the Imperial Maritime Customs.[10]

While the crushing defeat administered to China by the Japanese was generally regarded by foreign observers as evidence of China's approaching dissolution, the war had caused little popular excitement in the Empire except in the immediate field of military operations. At Canton a petition against the ratification of the Shimonoseki treaty was drawn up by a young scholar named Kang Yu-wei and was signed by 604 of the Cantonese literati; because of a confusion of dates, however, the petition reached Peking after ratifications had been exchanged and was never presented to the Throne.[11] An anti-foreign riot at Chengtu, the provincial capital of Szechuan, was partially caused by the popular feeling that the foreigners had been responsible for the Japanese attack on China; and a similar outbreak at Kiangyin, in Kiangsu province, may perhaps be attributed to the same belief that the foreigner was, in some way, responsible for Japanese aggression. On the other hand, reports from travellers in many parts of the country show the population to have been generally undisturbed and rather more friendly than usual.

In governmental circles, however, the outcome of the war led to considerable activity. This was first shown in the dismissal of a number of military officials who had been

[10] The third indemnity loan—for the same amount but at 4½%—was also financed by the Anglo-German group in March, 1898. As the negotiation of this last loan constituted an important feature in the "Battle of Concessions," it will be discussed in that connection in the next chapter.

[11] A translation of this petition, which marks the first appearance of Kang Yu-wei as an important factor in national affairs, was published in the *North China Herald* of December 6, 1895, vol. 55, p. 949.

guilty of incapacity or of cowardice during the war. The military house-cleaning was followed by the promulgation of a series of decrees calling for the general renovation of several branches of the civil service. Since Li Hung-chang had long been in control of the country's foreign policy and had negotiated the humiliating treaty with Japan, his enemies at Peking seized this opportunity to open a furious attack upon him as the man solely responsible for the disaster. Although Li's accusers failed in their efforts to have him brought to trial on capital charges, they did succeed in forcing his temporary retirement from official life, and, on August 30, Li was replaced as viceroy of Chihli by Wang Wen-shao, the former viceroy of Yun-Kwei.[12]

Even more noteworthy were the efforts put forth for the reorganization of national defenses. Steps were taken to centralize the general oversight of army and navy in the hands of a Grand Council of War Affairs, of which Yuan Shih-kai, recently Chinese resident in Korea, was appointed chief secretary. This council was commanded thoroughly to overhaul the military administrations in Manchuria, Chihli, Shantung, and the Liang-Kiang; to dismiss incompetent officers; and to reorganize the forces in accordance with the European system. Large quantities of arms and munitions were purchased, and a number of foreign officers were engaged to undertake the training and organization of the troops. A number of warships were ordered, some from England and some from Germany, to form the nucleus of a new Peiyang squadron; while several new ships, in addition to those ordered before the war but not yet delivered, were to be added to the Nanyang squadron. Captain W. M. Lang, R.N., who had rendered valuable service in the organization of China's first modern

[12] Yun-Kwei Viceroyalty includes the provinces of Yunnan and Kweichow.

navy, was requested to resume his old post; and the *North China Herald* reported on November 29, that Captain Lang had expressed his willingness to accept—subject to the approval of the British government—on condition that he should be guaranteed full control.[13]

The authorities at Peking showed also that they had begun to realize the necessity of making such changes in the economic system of the Empire as would enable China to avail herself of the superior Western methods in industry and transportation. On July 18 a member of the Board of Censors submitted a memorial to the Throne, recommending that the viceroys and governors of the various provinces be ordered to encourage the mercantile class to take over the government naval dockyards, arsenals, and ship-building yards in the provinces, and to work them on a commercial basis. The memorial was referred to the Board of Revenue for consideration, and on August 11, after a favorable report from the board, orders to this effect were issued to the provincial authorities. Other commands from the central government ordered the construction of three important railways: one from Shanghai to Soochow with a later extension to Chinkiang and Nanking; the second between Chinkiang and Tientsin; and the third from Tientsin to Lu-kou Chiao, some ten miles southwest of Peking. These railways were all to be constructed with Chinese capital, and the provincial authorities were instructed to arrange for organizing the necessary syndicates to handle the undertakings.

Although the innovations authorized by the imperial government appeared extremely moderate, even these cautious steps in the direction of Westernization entailed

[13] A satisfactory arrangement on this point was not reached at the time, and in 1898 China renewed her request for Lang's services; see *British Blue Books, China No. 1 (1898)*, document no. 145.

the possibility of unpleasant internal complications. In a land so densely populated as China, the introduction of factory production and of steam transportation could hardly fail to result in a serious dislocation of industrial conditions, producing problems of unemployment which were bound to require considerable readjustment. On the other hand, the government, in ordering the formation of syndicates to finance and manage these enterprises, was creating a situation which would involve the central authorities more and more deeply in the unfamiliar field of economic legislation.

Yet there were important considerations which made the Peking government anxious to see these innovations in industry and transportation adopted without loss of time. In the first place, China's rulers had at last come to appreciate the military importance of railways, of mines, and of modern factories, especially such as would be available for the manufacture of arms and munitions. If China was to regain the prestige which had been lost in the late war, she must follow the example of Japan and place herself in a position to arm and equip her military forces in modern fashion without having recourse to purchases from distant lands. A second, and even greater, reason for haste was the need of anticipating foreign demands for concessions, especially concessions relating to mines and railways. Only through immediate progressive action could these undertakings, so essential to national safety, be kept under Chinese control.

This hope—that immediate action would serve to keep in Chinese hands the control of mines and railways—was doomed to disappointment. The provincial officials, finding themselves unable to secure the necessary capital from exclusively native sources, were compelled—more or less surreptitiously—to admit foreign capital into the syndicates which they formed for carrying out the imperial commands. Hence the provincial and viceregal capitals were soon filled with the agents of the various European and American financial groups, all striving to find profitable investment for the superfluous capital of the West. Along with the duly accredited representatives of serious finance came also the adventurous "free-lance," who hoped, by intrigue or by good luck, to pick up some valuable concession which could later be sold at a handsome profit to a concern able to fulfil the contract. During a period of two years, this hunt for concessions was almost, if not entirely, free from the element of diplomatic pressure at Peking. The financial agents, like the agents for machinery, warships, cannon, and munitions, were usually recommended to the provincial authorities by fellow nationals in the service of China, or by prominent Chinese who had foreign connections. Foreign ministers at Peking occasionally urged upon the central government the favorable consideration of requests presented by their nationals; but diplomatic action was, for the most part, confined to protecting the concessionaire against the cancellation of his contract after it had been negotiated and duly signed.

Despite the fact that China, at the close of her war with Japan, appeared to be a hopeless wreck, more than two years elapsed before the opening of that phase of foreign activity which threatened the actual partition of the Empire. This lull before the storm was due in part to the intense jealousy between the various interested powers, in part to the fact that no one of them was quite sure that the results of a partition would not prove detrimental rather than beneficial to its own interests. All believed that the break-up of China was impending, yet each foreign government seemed to hope that the ultimate collapse might be deferred until such time as its own position in the Far East should have become sufficiently consolidated to enable it to obtain a lion's share of the spoils. Of the four European powers most vitally interested in the results of the contemplated partition—Britain, France, Russia, and Germany—only the last possessed no contiguous territory which might serve as the basis for substantial claims when the distribution should begin. Ever since the outbreak of the Japanese war, this handicap had been one of the chief anxieties of the Kaiser's government, and the thirty months which followed the conclusion of peace were spent in vain efforts to secure from China a concession which would put Germany upon a footing of equality with her rivals.

CHAPTER IV.

The "Battle of Concessions" and the "Hundred Days."

The Lease of Kiaochow—Port Arthur—Weihaiwei—Kwangchow-wan—The Third Indemnity Loan—China's Dilemma—The National Loan—Railroads—Kuang Hsu and Kang Yu-wei—The "Hundred Days of Reform"—Radicalism and Centralization—The Peking-Hankow Railway and British Demands—Collapse of the Reform Party.

ON November 1, 1897, two Roman Catholic priests of the German mission in Shantung, stopping for the night at the village of Yenchow, were murdered by a band of armed men who broke into the home of their host, the resident missionary. The nature of the band and the motives for the murder have never been conclusively established. It has been variously alleged that the murderers were armed robbers attacking the village; that they were a body of local ruffians, inspired by general hatred for the Christian religion; and that they were a group of men who had been roused to fury through the intermeddling of the local priest, who escaped by mere chance the vengeance which unintentionally fell upon his innocent guests. Writing a year later, Bishop Anzer, the German bishop of Shantung, identified the assassins as a band of the "Big Knife Society," but this identification is not entirely convincing.

On receiving news of the murder, Bishop Anzer—who was at that time in Germany—immediately telegraphed to the Kaiser asking protection for his mission.[1] William II

[1] See *Annales de l'Association de la propagation de la foi*, vol. 71, p. 208, for a letter of Mgr. Anzer: ". . . Mon premier mouvement fut une

needed no urging. For more than two years he had been advocating the forcible occupation of a desirable port on the Chinese coast—without awaiting any pretext—and, in November, 1896, was on the point of ordering the immediate seizure of Amoy as a preliminary to negotiations for a cession or lease. This step was prevented by the Chancellor, Hohenlohe, and the officials of the Foreign Office, who pointed out how, by such an act of naked force, Germany's policy in the Far East would be compromised to an extent that would not be compensated by the acquisition of a coaling station. At an interview on November 29, 1896, Hohenlohe recommended to his sovereign that "the Minister at Peking should be instructed to keep his eyes open for an event suitable as a cause for advance and, when such offers, to wire immediately."[2]

Nor does it appear that Bishop Anzer's telegram played any essential part in the events which followed, as may be seen from the Kaiser's note to the Foreign Office on November 6, 1897:

> I have just read in the press the news of the attack upon the German Catholic mission under my protection in Shantung. Plentiful atonement for this must be secured by energetic action of the fleet. The squadron must instantly proceed to Kiaochow, seize the port there, and threaten with severest repression unless the Chinese government instantly agree to a high compensation in gold as well as a really effective pursuit and punishment of the criminals. I am fully determined to abandon, henceforth, the

prière à Dieu; mon second fut un appel à l'Empereur d'Allemagne, le priant de soutenir efficacement mes collaborateurs et mon troupeau. Vous connaissez sa réponse et les conséquences de son intervention."

[2] See *Grosse Politik*, vol. XIV, documents nos. 3668, 3669, 3670 and footnote. Throughout the documents of this volume there is plentiful evidence that an aggressive policy in the Far East was a pet scheme of the Kaiser, but found little support among his ministers.

over-cautious policy which has been regarded throughout the East as weakness, and to show the Chinese, with full power and—if necessary—with brutal ruthlessness, that the German Emperor cannot be made sport of and that it is bad to have him as an enemy.

Please telegraph answer of agreement, so that I may immediately instruct the Admiral by telegraph.

Such energetic action is incumbent on me so that I may again show my Catholic supporters, including the Ultramontane group, that I have their welfare at heart, and that they can count upon my protection as well as my other subjects.

Wilhelm I. R.[3]

Having been furnished, at last, with a suitable pretext, Germany took prompt and decisive action. On November 14, eight days after the Kaiser learned of the murders, a German squadron steamed into Kiaochow Bay and landed a force of sailors and marines at the town of Tsingtau. Six days later the German minister at Peking, Baron von Heyking, informed the Tsungli Yamen that the German forces would not evacuate Kiaochow until the following demands had been granted: 1. The dismissal of Li Ping-heng, governor of Shantung; 2. The completion, at China's expense, of the cathedral started by Bishop Anzer, with the erection of an imperial "protection" tablet; 3. Severe punishment of all guilty parties, and an indemnity for injuries; 4. A satisfactory guarantee against any repetition of the late episode; 5. An indemnity to Germany for the costs of the operations; and 6. A priority for German interests with regard to a railway and related mining concessions in the province of Shantung.[4]

[3] *Grosse Politik*, vol. XIV, document no. 3686.

[4] See *Grosse Politik*, vol. XIV, document no. 3712 and note. A fairly accurate report of the German demands was reported to London by Sir Claude MacDonald on November 22; see *British Blue Books, China No. 1 (1898)*, document no. 5.

It soon became evident that these demands did not express the full extent of Germany's intentions. As early as November 15 a conference presided over by the Kaiser decided to keep in view the permanent possession of Kiaochow. On the twenty-third Baron von Heyking was instructed to inform the Yamen that, until the German demands were satisfied, Germany would hold the occupied place as a pledge and would set up a provisional government. A week later the British minister reported that an area had been defined around Kiaochow Bay, within which German law would be administered by the captain of S.M.S. *Arcona* as governor. On March 6, 1898, after negotiations lasting three and a half months, the German demands, with certain accretions, were conceded in full. Germany received Kiaochow as a coaling station and naval base on a ninety-nine year lease, while a separate agreement provided for German and Chinese coöperation in the building of railways and the working of mines.

Throughout these long negotiations China had sought in vain for foreign support against the German attack upon her territorial integrity. Russia, pledged to assist China in case of any renewed aggression on the part of Japan, put forth an embarrassing claim of a prior right to the port; but Russia had no intention of involving herself with Germany in behalf of China. Certain British objections to the sixth of the original German demands were withdrawn when Her Majesty's ministers learned that this demand did not infringe upon any existing concession previously granted to a British subject. In France, where traditional hostility to the German Empire had been accentuated by the fact that Germany's pretext for action was regarded as an infringement upon the French protectorate over Catholic missions, the "official" press contented itself with voicing its disapproval of this new development in the Far East. Japan and the United States made no move.[5]

Germany's procedure at Kiaochow was marked by a brutal disregard for Chinese susceptibilities which was to become characteristic of the ensuing period; yet these rough-handed methods, which were but a revival of the methods by which the West had gained its original foothold in the Far East, did not call forth any disapproval from the other foreigners resident in China. Even the Protestant missionaries in the Empire considered the Kaiser's actions to have been justifiable; Dr. H. D. Porter, of the American Board mission at Pang-chuang, Shantung, expressed, in a letter of May 30, 1898, his strong approval of Germany's procedure and his belief that the situation of all missionaries in Shantung would be much improved as a result. Germany's action, however, seriously affected the existing equilibrium in the Far East and precipitated the long-expected scramble for Chinese territory.

Russia, failing in her efforts to aid China against Germany's "mailed fist" diplomacy, determined to answer the occupation of Kiaochow by a similar acquisition in the Liaotung. Early in December, 1897, five Russian men-of-war were dispatched to Port Arthur, ostensibly for the purpose of wintering at a point which would enable them to protect China against any further acts of aggression. The friction which resulted from the appearance at this port of a British warship, actuated by the same high purpose,

[5] In addition to volume XIV of the *Grosse Politik*, much valuable source material is to be found in the *British Blue Books, China No. 1 (1898)*; documents 1-131, with a few exceptions, relate to the Kiaochow lease. Although not entirely approving German methods, the British government rather favored the establishment of a German naval station in North China, since this might serve as an additional check to Russian aspirations. The oft-repeated statement that Great Britain took Weihaiwei as a counterpoise to Kiaochow is an anachronism.

soon showed the existence of an ulterior motive in Russia's fleet movement; and Great Britain's suspicions regarding Russia's real intentions were demonstrated by her attempt, in the pending loan negotiations, to secure the opening of Talienwan[6] as a treaty port. The secret of the Russian negotiations was well kept, and it was not until March 7, 1898, that Sir Claude MacDonald was able definitely to report Russia's demand for a lease and for the right to build a railroad connecting Port Arthur with the Trans-Siberian line.[7] Three weeks later—as the result of bribes, an ultimatum, and the presence at Port Arthur of the Russian squadron in battle array—the Chinese representatives signed the agreement leasing to Russia for twenty-five years the most valuable portion of the territory which, less than three years earlier, had been rescued from Japan.

The details of the bribery in connection with Port Arthur have recently become available. From the following documents published in the *Krasny Arkhiv*,[8] it is apparent that bribery was attempted first in negotiations for a loan to pay off the final installment of China's indemnity to Japan.[9] The authors of the telegrams were Pavloff, the Russian chargé d'affaires at Peking, and Pokotiloff, the Peking representative of Minister of Finances Witte.

Telegram, in cypher, from Pokotiloff to Witte.

Peking, January 8/20, 1898.

The procrastination in the matter of the loan must be attributed to the intrigues of the Chinese against Li Hung-chang and to the unwillingness on the part of the other ministers to leave the settlement of this affair to him. On the other hand, there is some information indicating that the British have promised the minis-

[6] Later known as Dalny and Dairen.

[7] Baron von Heyking made a similar report one day earlier.

[8] See *Krasny Arkhiv*, vol. II, pp. 287-293.

[9] See below, p. 74.

ters a large bribe for the arrangement of a loan. Rumors to the effect that we have no intention of evacuating Port Arthur and Talienwan are being circulated among the members of the Tsungli Yamen.

Telegram, in cypher, Pokotiloff to Witte.

Peking, January 12/24, 1898.

Last night Li Hung-chang visited our chargé d'affaires, at the latter's invitation, to confer with him in my presence. We called his attention to the seriousness of the consequences that can result for China in case the loan is placed in England and promised 500,000 Taels to him if the loan is placed with us. Li Hung-chang pointed out that the main difficulty is that the British offer advantageous terms, namely: to issue the loan at 100 and allow China to pay off, for 50 years, 4% on the amount of the loan per annum. Li Hung-chang said that it might be possible to arrange the matter; he also said that China is afraid of England's revenge in case her offers are declined. A conference between Pavloff and Prince Tung is set for today at the Tsungli Yamen.

Telegram, in cypher, Pavloff to Foreign Office.

Peking, January 15/27, 1898.

Yesterday Pokotiloff and I had a secret interview with Chang Yin-huan and promised him 200,000 Taels under the same conditions as to Li Hung-chang. Chang Yin-huan assured us that we can absolutely rely on him in this and any subsequent affair. The minister of finance Weng Tung-ho declined to attend a secret meeting, fearing to arouse suspicion as he never has any relations with foreigners; but I am aware of the fact that he has come to an agreement with Li Hung-chang, who will let him have his share.

After the failure of the loan negotiations, the Russians increased the amount of their offers, now as an inducement for signing the Port Arthur lease.

Telegram, in cypher, Pokotiloff to Witte.

Peking, March 9/21, 1898.

In company with the chargé d'affaires I had today a confidential conversation with Li Hung-chang and Chang Yin-huan and promised each 500,000 Taels if the business in Port Arthur and Talienwan is consummated on the date fixed by us and without extreme measures on our part. Both ministers complained about the extreme difficulty of their position and the great excitement prevailing among the bureaucratic classes. The Emperor receives innumerable requests not to yield to our demands. Tomorrow both ministers will report to the Emperor. The Chinese minister at London telegraphed to the Tsungli Yamen of Britain's opposition to our conditions.

Telegram, in cypher, Pokotiloff to Witte.

Peking, March 16/28, 1898.

I paid today to Li Hung-chang 500,000 Taels. Li Hung-chang is greatly pleased and requested me to convey his deep gratitude to you. At the same time I am wiring about it to Rothstein. I had no occasion to remit money to Chang Yin-huan, who behaves with much caution.

The British government, which had seen no cause for alarm in Germany's acquisition of Kiaochow, was stirred to immediate and vigorous action by the lease of Port Arthur. The counter-move to this latest Russian advance took the form of the acquisition of Weihaiwei as a naval station which would enable the British fleet to share with the Russians the control over the Gulf of Pechili. Britain's negotiations for the lease of Weihaiwei were brief and sharp.

On February 25, 1898, Sir Claude MacDonald had telegraphed to Lord Salisbury as follows: "I have heard from a Chinese Minister, who is probably well informed, that Chinese Government would offer lease of Weihaiwei to British Government if they thought their request would meet with a favorable response." The nature of the Chinese government's "request," to which the telegram referred, was not disclosed. On the same day, Lord Salisbury wired in reply that "the discussion of any proposal for the lease of Weihaiwei would . . . be premature, provided the existing position is not materially altered by the action of other Powers." Ten days later the British Premier wired his representative at Peking in a different tone. "The influence of Russia over the Government of Peking will be so increased to the detriment of that of Her Majesty's Government, if, as the *Times* reports, the Russians are to have a lease of Port Arthur and Talienwan on the same terms as Germany of Kiaochow, that it seems desirable for us to make some counter-move. The best plan would perhaps be, on the cession of Weihaiwei by the Japanese, to insist on the refusal of a lease of that port on terms similar to those granted to Germany." Later on the same day the Foreign Office received from MacDonald a telegram confirming the *Times* report, and, on March 15, instructions were sent to Sir E. Satow, Minister to Japan, to sound the Japanese government as to its attitude toward a British lease of Weihaiwei.

On March 25, two days before the lease of Port Arthur was actually signed, Lord Salisbury sent to Sir Claude MacDonald his definite instructions concerning Weihaiwei. "Balance of power in Gulf of Pechili is materially altered by surrender of Port Arthur by Yamen to Russia. It is therefore necessary to obtain, in the manner you think most efficacious and speedy, the refusal of Weihaiwei on the departure of the Japanese. The terms should be similar to those granted to Russia for Port Arthur. British fleet is on its way from Hongkong to Gulf of Pechili." On the following day the British minister at Berlin was authorized to assure the German government that Great Britain intended no interference with German interests in the province of Shantung. At Peking two stormy interviews took place between Sir Claude MacDonald and the Tsungli Yamen; one on March 28, the other on the thirty-first. At the second of these interviews, a two-day ultimatum was presented by the British minister, and, on the morning of April 3, he was able to telegraph to his government that his demands had been granted on the preceding day. Since Weihaiwei was still occupied by the Japanese, pending the full payment of the war-indemnity, the formal lease of the port to Great Britain was not definitely signed until July 1.[10]

France joined the ranks of the lease-holders a week after the conclusion of the preliminary agreement concerning Weihaiwei. Anti-missionary disturbances in the province of Kwangtung furnished a suitable pretext for the landing of a French force at the Bay of Kwang-chow-wan, and, on the ninth and tenth of April, an exchange of notes provided for the lease of the bay to France as a coaling station. This new French position constituted a possible threat to Hongkong; so the British government now had satisfactory grounds for demanding such an extension of her holdings on the adjacent peninsula of Kowloon as would insure the safety of the colony. The area to be demanded for this new extension had been agreed upon by the military authorities of Hongkong as early as November, 1894, and Sir Claude had recently been furnished with a map

[10] The above citations are from *British Blue Books, China No. 1 (1898)*, documents nos. 90, 91, 95, 96, 129, 144; and *China No. 1 (1899)*, documents nos. 35, in which Sir E. Satow acknowledges Lord Salisbury's instructions of March 15, and 154, in which Sir Claude MacDonald gives a detailed report of his negotiations with the Tsungli Yamen. The generally accepted tradition that China willingly granted the lease of Weihaiwei cannot stand in the light of this last bit of evidence.

illustrating these desiderata. As the British fleet was still at Chefoo, and as the British minister ostentatiously departed on a visit to the Admiral the day after he had laid his draft agreement before the members of the Yamen, it was a comparatively easy matter to convince the Chinese government of the "reasonableness" of the British desires; on June 9, the lease of the Kowloon extension was signed.

Shortly after the German landing at Kiaochow, and while Russia was preparing to demand the lease of Port Arthur and the Liaotung Peninsula, a three-cornered diplomatic struggle developed, between Great Britain, Russia, and China, over a loan to China for paying off the last installment of the Japanese indemnity. A loan for this purpose had been offered to China in June, 1897, by the British minister on behalf of the Anglo-German Syndicate,[11] but the terms proposed had not seemed acceptable to the Chinese government. In December, Russia offered China a 4% guaranteed loan, at 93, in exchange for which Russia was to have the financing, construction, and control of all railways in Manchuria and North China; China was also to promise that a Russian would be appointed Inspector-General of the Imperial Maritime Customs when that post should become vacant. China considered these conditions unacceptable—or feared the wrath of Great Britain if she should dare to accept them—and attempted to revive the earlier offer of the Anglo-German Syndicate, only to be presented with an imposing list of concessions which the British would demand in return for their services in arranging a direct or a guaranteed loan.

The British proposals, especially the demand that Talienwan be opened as a treaty port, were immediately

[11] Composed of the Hongkong-Shanghai Bank and the Deutsche-Asiatische Bank.

protested by Russia; while France objected to an isolated guarantee of the loan by the British government, to the railway clause, and to the demand that Nanningfu be opened as a treaty port. The Tsungli Yamen, in its conversations with the British minister, advanced the Russian and French objections as arguments for the modification of the list of concessions. In answer to this, Sir Claude pointed out that China had asked Great Britain to guarantee a loan, which the British government had consented to do; if, after all that had passed, China now rejected the proposed loan, she must be prepared for the consequences. On January 28 it was reported that China would attempt to compromise the matter by proposing that the loan be divided between Great Britain and Russia. Three days later the Yamen told the British minister that they saw no way out of the difficulty except by coming to some arrangement with Japan, and borrowing neither from Great Britain nor Russia; a definite decision not to borrow at all was communicated to MacDonald on February 3.

In a series of interviews between the Tsungli Yamen and MacDonald, beginning on February 5, the Yamen discovered that China's abandonment of her intention to borrow the money would not mean an end to the British demands. The British government had, at China's request, "reluctantly agreed to do her a very exceptional favor, and had a right to feel deeply affronted by what had occurred." Sir Claude would not be answerable for the consequences if the Yamen now declined to make to Great Britain such concessions as even they had frequently admitted to be in China's own interests. Finding that they would have to pay the same price in concessions whether or not they accepted the loan, the Yamen again resumed negotiations for the loan.

That the concessions to Great Britain might not be taken

by Russia as grounds for demanding counter-concessions for the rejection of her own offer the British minister consented that these should appear as steps spontaneously taken by China. On February 14 he reported that he had received from the Yamen definite assurances on three important points:

(1) A declaration, on February 11, in regard to the non-alienation of territory in the Yangtze Valley.

(2) A declaration, on February 13, to the effect that the office of Inspector-General of Customs should be held by a British subject so long as the British trade with China exceeded that of any other nation.

(3) An assurance in regard to the loan.

Five days later the formal preliminary agreement for the loan was signed by the Yamen and the representative of the Hongkong-Shanghai Bank.

The decision of the Chinese government, announced on February 3, to break off all loan negotiations and borrow from neither of her importunate friends, had been only partly due to the desire to extricate itself from the Anglo-Russian dilemma. To a considerable extent this decision had been due to the disapproval of the proposed loan expressed by various officials, notably by Chang Chih-tung, the viceroy of the Hukwang. From Wuchang this able official telegraphed repeatedly to the Tsungli Yamen, pointing out in detail the dangers which the proposed concessions contained for China, and remonstrating against the conclusion of the agreement. The British demands, he argued, would, if conceded, place the whole commercial situation in the twelve southern provinces in the grasp of England during times of peace, and would give her a strong military position when peace was threatened. Rather than thus to put the English in absolute control of so great a part of the Empire, China should leave Weihaiwei temporarily in the hands of Japan until the indemnity could be paid off in such annual installments as China could raise without having recourse to a foreign loan.[12]

In response to these and similar remonstrances, and in the effort to find some way out of its diplomatic and financial difficulties, the imperial government, on February 4, issued the following decree:

We have received the report of the Board of Revenue, made in obedience to our commands, with reference to a memorial by Huang Sze-jung, a member of the Supervisorate of Instruction of the Heir-Apparent, in which is recommended the issuance of Government Bonds for the purpose of raising funds for the Imperial Exchequer. The said Board, having gone carefully and minutely over the memorial in question, agree with the views contained therein, recommending that "the said Board of Revenue shall print one million Bond certificates (of Tls. 100 each), to be styled 'Sincerity Bonds' and distributed for sale at Peking and in the various provinces of the Empire; the said Bonds to bear interest at the rate of 5% per annum, the same to be all redeemed by the Imperial Government within the period of twenty years, interest to be paid up to date of redemption. The said Bonds are also to be saleable and transferable at all times within the above period and their actual value shall be guaranteed by the Imperial Government. At the several periods set for the redemption of the said Bonds, the holders thereof shall have liberty to use the said Bonds in payment of land taxes and salt duties. The said Bonds shall be distributed and sold to all classes of the country, beginning from the Princes, Dukes, and Nobles downwards in Peking, and from the Tartar-Generals, Viceroys, and Governors in the provinces down to their civil and military subordinates of

[12] The arguments of Chang Chih-tung, which have been summarized above, are given more fully in an article in the Tientsin *Kuo Wen Pao*, February 3, 1898. A translation of this article was inclosed in Sir Claude MacDonald's dispatch to Lord Salisbury of February 15, 1898; see *British Blue Books, China No. 1 (1898)*, document no. 18.

every rank, grade and class, whether substantive or expectant. These shall buy up and pay cash for the said Bonds so as to set an example to the business men of the country. Those of the business classes and others amongst the people of the Empire having shown a desire also to buy the said Bonds shall have perfect liberty to do so, in which case it shall be the duty of the Governor of the Imperial Prefecture of Shuntien, at Peking, and the various Tartar-Generals, Viceroys, and Governors, in the provinces, to proclaim at once to the people at large the regulations settled upon by the said Board of Revenue governing the issuance and sale of said Bonds. The said High Authorities shall also appoint Deputies to explain to the people the true nature of the said Bonds, and any attempts by the said Deputies to take advantage of the occasion to extort and force the sale of the said Bonds upon the masses must be strictly prohibited. The Deputies charged with the sale of the said Bonds to the people who shall succeed in obtaining large sums therefrom will be rewarded with extraordinary promotion in recognition of their energy and ability."

The said Board having agreed to the above quoted proposition, we hereby command that the same be forthwith regarded as Law.

In a crisis like the present when the Imperial Exchequer is depleted, we feel sure that our Princes, Dukes, Nobles, and Ministers in the capital and the high authorities in the provinces who have been the recipients of our special Bounty will surely show their gratitude to the Throne by heartily responding to the needs of the Government. Nay, even the gentry, notables, and business men down to the common people must surely know their duty and loyalty to the Imperial Dynasty and hasten to the succor of the Throne at this time of emergency. Finally, as it is decided by the said Board of Revenue, the present movement is entirely different from the former methods of calling upon the people of the Empire to render help to the Imperial Government, nor will any force be permitted to compel the masses to buy the said Bonds, the present scheme being on the basis of a commercial transaction where a regular interest shall be paid at stated intervals, we trust that there will be no delay in encompassing the object of this Loan and that our people will not simply look on and remain indifferent (to the needs of the Empire).

Let the above be promulgated to all the people of the Empire.[13]

Although this decree antedates, by more than four months, the opening of the so-called "Hundred Days of Reform," it is to be associated with the policy adopted by the government at Peking at this later period. This association is necessary by reason of the fact that such a method of national financing involved a radical departure from time-honored practices, and also because this, like the later decrees, represented a desperate attempt to find relief from the pressure of foreign demands.

Any hope that the Emperor and the Grand Council may have entertained, as to the benefits which would result from this move, proved illusory. As we have already seen, China was so deeply involved in her negotiations with the British government that it was no longer possible for her to refuse the loan and its attendant list of concessions. On the other hand, this financial innovation, while it produced but a small fraction of the desired 100,000,000 taels, soon gave rise to internal difficulties. There were repeated complaints that local and provincial officials were bringing pressure upon the people under their jurisdiction to compel them to subscribe to the loan, and the Throne was forced to issue edicts, on May 18 and July 5, denouncing this practice and explaining that the loan was to be purely voluntary.[14]

The Russian and British proposals for the final indemnity loan had both contained provisions whereby China was to grant valuable railway concessions to the capitalists

[13] The above translation is taken from the *North China Herald* of February 14, 1898, vol. 60, p. 241.

[14] These two edicts can be found in the *North China Herald* of August 22, 1898, and September 19, 1898, vol. 61, pp. 346 and 535.

of the lending countries. Similar concessions were demanded, and obtained, in connection with each of the five territorial leases, with the exception of that of Weihaiwei. Germany obtained a prior claim to the construction of any railroad which should, in the future, be undertaken in the province of Shantung. Russia obtained, in connection with the Port Arthur lease, the right to connect Port Arthur with the Trans-Siberian Railway and the monopoly of all subsequent railway construction in Manchuria. The French lease of Kwang-chow-wan carried with it, among other concessions, the right to construct a railroad from Yunnan-fu to connect with the French line in Tongking at some point on the frontier. So, also, the British demand for the Kowloon extension had included a demand for railway concessions, particularly the right to build a line from Burma into Yunnan.

When the rush for territorial concessions had abated, the several diplomatic agents at Peking continued to press upon the Tsungli Yamen the requests of their respective nationals for additional concessions for railroads and for the mining rights which usually accompanied these. On June 23, 1898, Lord Salisbury telegraphed to Sir Claude MacDonald: "It is desirable, now that Kowloon and Weihaiwei are arranged, that we should settle the order in which the other projects should be pressed on the Yamen. I should put first Messrs. Jardines' railway from Nanking; then the Peking Syndicate's lines; then the right of the Hongkong Bank to finance the Newchwang line; and then the opening of Nanningfu. It is urgent at the same time to extend the opening of the rivers to non-treaty provinces. Telegraph whether you agree in this list, and if there are others." Three days later Sir Claude wired in reply: "All the projects mentioned in your Lordship's telegram of the 23rd June are being pressed on the Yamen, as well as the scheme proposed by Mr. Pritchard-Morgan for a central Mining Administration; the relative urgency of each of these must be decided by circumstances. I will press the lines of the Peking Syndicate as soon as the latter have decided what they want, but as complicated commercial details are impossible for me to arrange, and seeing that the value of a concession in general terms is almost nil, the negotiations should be carried on by their agent."[15]

In the meantime, however, the continued pressure of foreign demands had stirred the Chinese government to action. Although the national loan, decreed on February 5, had proved an inauspicious venture into the field of foreign innovations, desperate measures were necessary if the Empire was to have any hope of resisting the apparently endless series of encroachments by the Western powers. Two weeks before the above telegrams were exchanged between the British Foreign Office and the legation at Peking, the Emperor Kuang Hsu, under the guidance of Kang Yu-wei, Liang Chih-chao, and others, had inaugurated an ambitious program of radical reform. The plan of Kuang Hsu and his young advisers was to make China strong by a rapid introduction of Western ideas and by a reorganization of the government along the lines of greater centralization of power. At the same time they hoped that this voluntary adoption of Western methods by China would disarm her critics and lead to a cessation of the flood of foreign demands.

On June 11 the opening of what later became known as the "Hundred Days" of reform was marked by the appearance of two long imperial decrees in the *Peking Gazette*. The first of these emphasized the importance, in the present crisis, of having able men to represent the

[15] These two telegrams are to be found in *British Blue Books, China No. 1 (1898)*, documents nos. 202 and 205.

Empire in foreign lands, and commanded the viceroys and governors to recommend to the Throne any men of high ability who were suitable for such appointment. The second decree, after rehearsing the efforts which had already been made to introduce much-needed reforms, announced that a great national university was to be established at Peking for the purpose of giving instruction in all branches of modern learning, and that this institution was to serve as a model and be copied in all the provincial capitals.

From this moderate beginning, the pace of reform steadily quickened. On June 23, a somewhat more radical decree ordered that, henceforth, in all literary examinations, the "wen-chang," or literary essay, should be abolished. In the place of this time-honored requirement, the candidates for degrees would, in the future, be required to produce a number of short essays on subjects drawn from the *Analects*.[16] An even more striking departure from tradition was indicated by a decree which appeared on July 7. It was herein commanded that subjects of the Empire who wrote useful books on new topics, or who invented any new machine, should henceforth be rewarded by granting them copyrights or patents. The significance of this step lay in the fact that it marked the introduction of the principle of private monopoly rights guaranteed by law, a principle which would necessarily involve the government in a program of economic legislation.

These first reforms, although they did considerable violence to tradition, had enough practical value to commend themselves to the conservative judgment of the body of officialdom. Now, however, the Emperor and his iconoclastic mentors began to modify the administrative system

[16] The *Lun Yu*, or *Analects*, records the conversations of Confucius with his disciples, and covers practically the entire range of human relationships.

of the Empire. A number of minor boards at Peking were abolished, on the ground that they served no useful purpose. The governorships of Kwangtung, Hupeh, and Yunnan were abolished, as unnecessary, and the viceroys of Liangkwang, Hukwang, and Yun-Kwei were instructed to take over the duties which had hitherto been performed by the incumbents of the discontinued offices. The right of submitting memorials directly to the Throne was extended to officials of all grades, and, when the Board of Rites attempted to sift out memorials which they considered ill-advised, the entire Board was summarily dismissed.

It has been customary—in discussing the wholesale abolition of posts which the reformers judged superfluous—to emphasize the "economy motive" on the part of the Emperor, and the consequent discontent and hostility among the officials who were thus removed from positions of honor and profit. These considerations did unquestionably exist; but it seems equally certain that other, and more important, factors were also involved. Many of the discontinued offices were superfluous only if it was the intention of the Emperor to bring under the direct control of the central government many of the functions hitherto performed by the provincial officials, and to reduce these latter to the status of mere administrative officers carrying out the detailed instructions of the central government. The conjecture that this was the Emperor's purpose finds confirmation in his action in extending to all ranks of officials the right of directly memorializing the Throne, a right which had formerly been enjoyed only by the viceroys, tartar-generals, and governors in the provinces, and by the higher officers at Peking. This fundamental change in the direction of greater centralization constitutes the keynote of the program into which the Emperor had been led by the "young reformers."

Whatever eventual benefits China might have derived from this change—assuming that such a change could have been imposed on the Chinese state—the immediate fruits of the reform policy were insignificant. Despite the lavish praise that has been bestowed upon the efforts of the reformers of the "Hundred Days," a careful consideration of the many decrees and edicts which followed the inaugural decrees of June 11 leads to the conviction that there was only one which could be regarded as having any practical value to China in the existing crisis: on September 5, the Emperor approved a plan for raising and drilling a national army along Western lines. If the reform party had remained in power, and if this preparedness plan had been carried out, some effective opposition might have been raised to the threatened partition of the Empire.[17]

The professed purpose of the reform party was to save the Empire from foreign aggression; success in this would have been the one possible justification, in Chinese eyes, for the radical changes which were made in governmental affairs. But in this important respect the Emperor's program failed completely. Not only did the "Battle of Concessions" continue throughout the "Hundred Days"; it actually increased in intensity, and the Tsungli Yamen was deluged with the demands and counter-demands which poured in from the rival diplomatic representatives.

The struggle for concessions reached its climax in connection with the contract which was signed on June 27, between China and the Belgian Syndicate, for the construction of the Peking-Hankow Railway. The British

[17] A valuable summary of the more important of the decrees which appeared between June 11 and September 21 can be found in Morse, *International Relations of the Chinese Empire*, vol. III, pp. 137-139. The decrees can be found in full in the *North China Herald* for 1898 and 1899, vols. 61, 62, and 63, *passim.*

minister, believing or knowing that the Belgian Syndicate was merely a dummy representing French and Russian influence, demanded that he be allowed to see the contract before it was ratified, in order that he might have an opportunity for objecting to any possible infringement on British interests. A promise to this effect was given by the Yamen; but on August 12 the contract was ratified without Sir Claude having had an opportunity to inspect it.

The British government regarded this as a breach of faith on China's part which could not safely be overlooked. MacDonald was accordingly instructed, on August 17, to demand that the Tientsin-Chinkiang line, the Shanghai-Nanking line, and lines in Honan and Shansi be immediately granted to the British syndicates which were negotiating for the same, on terms identical with those in the Peking-Hankow contract. The minister was authorized to present these demands in the form of an ultimatum if he considered such a step necessary. A week later he was further authorized "to inform the Yamen that, unless the very moderate terms already demanded are immediately complied with, we shall, in addition, require the concession of another line on the same conditions . . ., and that additional demands will be preferred as the result of further delay."

On September 7 Li Hung-chang was relieved of his duties as a member of the Tsungli Yamen. Li was commonly regarded by the British in the Far East as hostile to British interests, and his removal from office was hailed by the treaty port newspapers as a concession forced from the Chinese government by the British minister; although no evidence that this was the case can be found in official documents. On September 14 the British demands were fully satisfied. Sir Claude had not found it necessary to put the demands in the form of an ultimatum, but, as he expressed it in a telegram ten days earlier, "the fact that the fleet is concentrating is, of course, known to them."[18]

This episode marked, if it did not actually cause, the close of the reform era. One week later the power was taken out of the hands of the Emperor by the Empress Dowager; Kang Yu-wei and some of his fellow reformers found safety in flight; six of the party were arrested, tried, and executed; and a new régime was established. The policy of the new administration, like that of the one which it superseded, was to be directed toward the preservation of national independence and integrity; but its methods were to be based on the ancient traditions of the Empire.[19]

[18] An interesting time relationship exists between this telegram and the Emperor's decree of September 5, recommending the formation of a "National Army."

[19] The traditional, and extremely dramatic, story of the "Hundred Days" and the *coup d'état*—which is told with especial effectiveness by Bland and Backhouse in *China under the Empress Dowager*—represents the period as merely one of party struggle and completely ignores the influence of foreign complications. Sergeant, in *The Great Empress Dowager,* is one of the few English writers to note the fact that the pressure for concessions ran through the entire "Hundred Days." The strongest argument against the "party struggle" explanation of the period is to be found in the small number of important changes among the high officials at Peking or in the provinces, either at the beginning of the reform period or at the time of the *coup d'état;* Kang Yi, Jung Lu, Yu Lu, Yu Hsien, Wang Wen-shao, Li Hung-chang, Chang Chih-tung, Liu Kun-yih—to mention only a few of the most important—held office before, during and after the "Hundred Days." Although there was great opposition, a few months later, to the reported plan of the Empress Dowager to dethrone the Emperor, public opinion throughout the country seems generally to have approved her assumption of power in September. Pinon, in *La Chine qui s'ouvre*, p. 68, note, regards the *coup d'état* as a victory for Russia over British and Japanese influence at Peking.

CHAPTER V.

The Empress Dowager and Conservative Reform.

China at the Close of the "Hundred Days"—Perils and Problems—Check to Concession Hunting—Restoration of Provincial Autonomy—Diplomatic Decentralization—Decree of March 15, 1899—Official Status for Missionaries—Purpose of Decree—Final Attempt to Absorb Christianity—Military Reorganization—Revival of the Local Militia.

"THE control of the Government as held by the Emperor has been rendered, by Imperial Edict, subject to the advice of the Empress Dowager. This step may lead to important results. It shows that the measures recently taken by the Emperor are not approved." So ran the telegram of Sir Claude MacDonald to Lord Salisbury on September 22, 1898, as the hastily erected structure of Western reform fell in ruins and the architects of the edifice fled to the safe refuge of foreign lands.

The Empress Dowager Tzu Hsi, who was at that time sixty-three years of age, had been living in semi-retirement since Kuang Hsu attained his majority some nine years earlier. Although she had never completely abandoned her advisory relationship to the government, especially in regard to the appointment of high officials, she had little direct responsibility for the disasters which had befallen the Empire during the last four years. During the brief period of reform, she had maintained an attitude of silent watchfulness. Whether her forceful resumption of the reins of government at this time was due to anxiety for the fate of

China or, as has been held by unsympathetic writers, to the desire to save herself from extinction and a horde of clamoring officials from the necessity of earning an honest living, she now found herself faced with a number of serious problems which demanded almost instant action as well as a high degree of constructive statesmanship.

The situation in which China found herself at the close of the "Hundred Days" was one which could not be relieved by mere negative action; the fate of the dynasty, the very existence of the Empire seemed to be trembling in the balance. Unless the Manchu rulers could evolve some means by which to put an end to the continued aggressions of the powerful Western nations, the dynasty's "mandate from Heaven" would be regarded as having become exhausted. In this event, an anti-dynastic movement, which might easily originate in any one of a dozen parts of the Empire, would sweep out the old régime and bring in a new one to take its place. The chief internal danger for the dynasty did not lie in the small but vociferous groups of "reformers," with their theories and programs, who were gathered in the safe sanctuaries of Shanghai, Hongkong, and Singapore; it lay rather in the great mass of conservative people, the uneducated as well as the "literati," who saw traditional government falling into decay and giving place to anarchy and chaos.

In addition to the danger of an avowedly anti-dynastic movement, there were even graver dangers in the possibility of a popular uprising against the foreigners. Such an uprising might occur at almost any point in the South, the West, along the Yangtze River, or in the vicinity of the recently surrendered leased territories in the North. Should an uprising of this sort take place, it would furnish the powers with ample pretext for embarking upon their contemplated partition of the Empire. Finally, there was the danger that the foreign powers, considering the "sick man of the Far East" to be beyond all hope of recovery, would begin the work of final dismemberment without awaiting any pretext in the form of new internal disorders.

For the avoidance of all these manifold dangers, it was primarily necessary that the prestige of the imperial government be restored, at home as well as abroad. The mass of the Chinese people had to be assured that the dynasty was still capable of performing its duties; that the time-honored relationship between government and people was not to be discarded in favor of untried innovations from abroad; that there was no reason to fear any further extension of foreign control, and hence no cause for anti-foreign sentiment. It was equally necessary, moreover, to convince the foreign diplomats that China must still be regarded with respect, and that the imperial government was fully determined to maintain China's national sovereignty and independence.

Evidence as to the Empress Dowager's intention to terminate the "Battle of Concessions" was not slow to appear. One immediate result of the *coup d'état* had been a cessation of the flood of demands, which, during the "Hundred Days," had poured in upon the Tsungli Yamen. This temporary pause was probably due, in part, to the popular excitement which had attended the overthrow of the reformers, and to the general tension at Peking—which had been accentuated by the summoning of foreign marines to guard the legations. In part, also, it may have been due to the fact that, so far as British demands were concerned, most of the outstanding desires had been obtained in the sweeping diplomatic victory which had so closely coincided with, and had contributed to, the collapse of the reform party. That the cessation was to be something more than temporary was shown by an imperial decree which the

Tsungli Yamen, on December 15, communicated to the members of the diplomatic body. The government announced that it would, for the present, undertake the construction of no more railroads, therefore it would be unnecessary for the foreign representatives to submit any new proposals. Nor would the Yamen receive at this time any tentative proposals which might, in the future, become the basis for claims of priority.

A more striking display of the new temper of the Chinese government was afforded, a few months later, in connection with the Italian demand for the "lease" of Sanmen Bay, in Chekiang province, as a coaling station. This demand[1] had the open diplomatic support of the British government as well as the approval of Germany, and Italy appeared, for a while, to be preparing to use any necessary force in support of her claims. Yet China absolutely refused to make any further grants of territory, and backed up her refusal by preparing to resist the anticipated attack.

The government's prestige in the eyes of the Chinese people could not, however, be completely restored by merely putting a stop to concession-grabbing and compulsory leases. It was equally necessary to bring to an end the practice of foreign interference between the central government and the provincial officials, a practice which was demoralizing the administrative system of the Empire. This method of securing the fulfilment of treaty obligations—at first employed only as a last resort and usually in connection with officials of minor rank—had, since the Japanese war, been rapidly extended both in its frequency of application and in the rank of the officials whose dismissal was demanded.

From the foreign point of view there was much that could be said in justification of the practice. The fulfilment

[1] To which further reference will be made in the succeeding chapter.

of the treaties was a matter which depended upon the local administration, and the difficulties met by the foreigners in obtaining complete enjoyment of their treaty rights were usually attributed to the inefficiency, or the open hostility, of the local officials. The Chinese principle of responsibility, moreover, seemed fully to justify a demand for the dismissal of any official within whose jurisdiction treaty rights had been denied or anti-foreign outrages had taken place. Yet, even for the foreigners, the policy was of doubtful advantage. Every dismissal which resulted from diplomatic pressure created at least one more bitter enemy for the foreigners in the ranks of officialdom; while the fact that an anti-foreign riot could always be counted on as a means of getting rid of an unpopular official occasionally led to anti-foreign disturbances where no actual hostility to foreigners existed.[2]

To the imperial authorities, the practice was an unqualified evil. Through its operation they had lost the services of some of their most capable officers, sometimes on frivolous or unsubstantiated charges.[3] The officials and the people soon came to understand that every post in the country, whose jurisdiction in any way affected foreigners, was at the mercy of the diplomatic body. This knowledge induced popular contempt for the officials and for the central government, and furnished a potent reason for official obstruction to the spread of foreign activities into any hitherto unaffected region. Finally, since most of the "scape-goats" in these cases were Chinese and not Man-

[2] The riots in Changsha, in 1909,—where a considerable amount of missionary property was destroyed after the missionaries had been warned and given ample time to escape,—were for the deliberate purpose of securing the dismissal of certain local officials.

[3] *E.g.*, Li Ping-heng, former governor of Shantung, who, in 1897, was dismissed, "never to be employed again," at the demand of the German minister.

chus, the dynasty was in danger of being regarded as "the foreign slave of foreign masters," which willingly gave way to the demands of the diplomats and welcomed the opportunity to lessen, in favor of the Manchu officers, the proportion of native Chinese in the high provincial offices.

In the twenty months which followed the Empress Dowager's *coup d'état* of September, 1898, we find no case where a viceroy or governor was dismissed from office in compliance with demands put forward by members of the diplomatic body; although there were at least three cases in which such demands were made. On June 9, 1899, the British chargé, after a month's warning, demanded that the governor of Kweichow be dismissed because of his failure to discover and apprehend the chief culprit in the murder of a missionary, Mr. Fleming. The Tsungli Yamen refused to submit a memorial to the Throne asking for the governor's dismissal, and persisted in this refusal for nearly four months. The ultimate arrest of the guilty man, on October 2, resulted in the British chargé withdrawing the demand, to which the Chinese government's resistance was especially remarkable since it coincided with the period when war with Italy seemed imminent. Later in the year 1899, the foreign ministers whose nationals were engaged in missionary work in the province of Shantung centered their attack upon Governor Yu Hsien, whom they regarded as mainly responsible for the anti-foreign disturbances in that province, and Minister Conger suggested the desirability of his dismissal. On this occasion the imperial government avoided a trial of strength, and compromised the matter by calling Yu Hsien to Peking and sending Yuan Shih-kai to Shantung as *acting* governor, an appointment which was made "substantive" only after Yu Hsien was transferred to the governorship of the neighboring province of Shansi. The third high official to become the object of attack during this period was Tan Chung-lin, viceroy of the Liang Kwang, whose removal was demanded by the French on the ground that he was responsible for the anti-French and anti-Catholic outbreaks in Kwangtung and Kwangsi. Here again the Empress Dowager compromised by summoning the officer to Peking "for a consultation" and sending the aged Li Hung-chang to Canton as *acting* viceroy.

This rehabilitation of the governors and viceroys in their respective provinces and viceroyalties was a fundamental part of the policy determined upon by the Empress Dowager. As the program of the Emperor and Kang Yu-wei had been "reorganization along western lines," so that of the new régime may be described as "restoration and reform." The state was to be reconstructed in accordance with tradition, with only such modifications as might be absolutely necessary to enable it to adjust itself to its new environment. Not only were the recent steps toward centralization to be retraced, but the provincial authorities were to be restored, as far as possible, to the position of practical autonomy which they had held prior to the establishment of treaty relations with the West.

An important step in this direction was proclaimed in a decree which appeared in the *Peking Gazette* on January 3, 1899:

> The Tartar-Generals, Viceroys, and Governors of the maritime and riverine provinces of the Empire, having under their jurisdiction the treaty ports, naturally have considerable additional work in relation to international intercourse, while those of the inland provinces are constantly appealed to in cases regarding disputes between missionaries and their converts against the masses. In this connection the high provincial authorities often seem to be inclined to shirk responsibility and trouble by sending all such cases to the Tsungli Yamen to be dealt with, thereby frequently

causing much delay before any arrangement can be arrived at. To obviate this, I, the Empress Dowager, have now decided to increase the powers of all Tartar-Generals, Viceroys, and Governors of provinces and make them ex-officio members of the Tsungli Yamen so that they may decide matters without loss of time, while at the same time they are also expected to communicate with the Princes and Ministers of the Tsungli Yamen thereanent.

As this step met with some objection, a supplementary decree, in the *Peking Gazette* of January 8, explained more fully the purpose of the Empress:

Chun Liang, a sub-Chancellor of the Grand Secretariat, thinks that a recent innovation of mine will lead easily to misunderstandings between my Ministers in Peking and the high provincial authorities, and therefore prophesies that there will be trouble in the future instead of simplifying matters as I intended. Under these circumstances the memorialist prays that I recall my decree and allow things to go on in the old way, etc. The other day, in consideration of the numerous delays made by the Tsungli Yamen in settling international trade litigations and disputes between missionaries and the masses, I decided that, to remedy matters, power should be given to Tartar-Generals, Viceroys, and Governors of provinces, as ex-officio members of the Tsungli Yamen, to settle all such disputes off-hand, apprising the Tsungli Yamen, pari passu, by telegraph of what was being done, so that this department may have proper information of what is going on throughout the Empire. I decided this way because I felt that the high provincial authorities, being on the spot, could have every information at first hand and so could decide in a much quicker manner than if, according to old custom, the Tsungli Yamen many miles away had to be first communicated with; while the time taken to investigate and settle matters would be interminable, giving the litigants much proper cause for complaint. I see nothing undesirable in my decision and if only the high Ministers and officials do their respective duties properly and be of mutual help to each other, the saving of time aimed at could easily be accomplished. Indeed the successful accomplishment of my object does not depend upon the innovation commanded by me, but really upon the calibre and conscientiousness of the officials entrusted with these duties. There is, therefore, no reason why there should be any further discussion of the said sub-Chancellor's memorial which is hereby refused.[4]

The apparent intention of Tzu Hsi, in so modifying the machinery of China's international relations, was to re-establish local autonomy, even in questions arising out of treaty commitments, thereby reducing to a minimum the occasions for diplomatic pressure at Peking. For a proper appreciation of these two decrees, however, they must be considered in connection with a third which appeared about two months later: the much quoted, and much misunderstood, decree of March 15, 1899:

Churches of the Catholic religion, the propagation of which has been long since authorised by the Imperial Government, having been built at this time in all the provinces of China, we long to see the Christians and the people live in peace, and in order to make their protection more easy, it has been agreed that local Authorities shall exchange visits with missionaries under the conditions indicated in the following articles:

1. In the different degrees of the ecclesiastical hierarchy, Bishops being in rank and dignity the equals of Viceroys and Governors, it is agreed to authorise them to demand to see Viceroys and Governors.

In the case of a Bishop being called home on business, or of his death, the priest charged to replace the Bishop will be authorised to demand to see the Viceroy and Governor.

Vicars-General and Archdeacons will be authorised to demand to see Provincial Treasurers and Judges, and Taotais.

Other priests will be authorised to demand to see prefects of

[4] These two decrees are taken from the *North China Herald* of November 20, 1899, vol. 63, p. 1021.

the 1st and 2nd class, independent prefects, sub-prefects, and other functionaries.

Viceroys, Governors, Provincial Treasurers and Judges, Taotais, prefects of the 1st and 2nd class, independent prefects, subprefects and other functionaries will naturally respond, according to their rank, with the same courtesies.

Articles 2, 3, and 4 merely give the detailed regulations which shall govern the intercourse between the officials and the missionaries, but the final article is important.

5. The local authorities shall give timely warning to the people of the place and exhort them earnestly to live on good terms with the Christians; they must not cherish hatred and cause trouble. Bishops and priests shall in the same way exhort the Christians to devote themselves to well-doing so as to maintain the good name of the Catholic religion, and act so that the people will be contented and grateful.

Wherever a suit takes place between the people and the Christians, the local Authorities shall hear and decide it equitably; the missionaries must not mix themselves up in it and show partiality in giving their protection; so that the people and the Christians may live in peace.[5]

It has been customary to regard this remarkable decree as an innovation extorted from the Chinese by the machiavellian diplomacy of the Catholic authorities at Peking,

[5] This translation of the Decree is taken from the *North China Herald* of May 22, 1899. The official French translation can be found in Boell, *La Protectorat des missions catholiques en Chine . . .*, p. 2; in Cordier, *Histoire des relations de la Chine avec les puissances occidentales*, vol. III, p. 469; in Pinon, *La Chine qui s'ouvre*, p. 296; also in *Les Missions Catholiques* and in *Annales de l'Association de la propagation de la foi*. The most illuminating discussion of the decree—one with which, however, I cannot fully agree—is given in M. Boell's monograph. The views which I have set forth briefly in this chapter are more fully elaborated in my article, "China's Attempt to Absorb Christianity," in the second issue of *T'oung Pao* for 1925-1926.

who, in turn, were the dupes of German intrigue directed against the French protectorate of Catholicism.[6] Although internal evidence points unmistakably to the fact that the promulgation of the decree was preceded by discussions between the Tsungli Yamen and the representatives of the Catholic missions, there are valid reasons for accepting the statement of Bishop Favier that the step was taken by the Chinese government on its own initiative.

In the first place, this new arrangement coincides so nicely with the policy already indicated in the decrees of January 3 and 8 as to make it almost certain that this was but the logical development of that policy. In spite of recent economic and territorial developments, missionary questions still furnished, as they had for the last three decades, the chief subject matter of diplomatic representations at Peking. If, therefore, any considerable portion of these difficulties could be settled locally, without finding their way into consular and diplomatic channels, the necessity for intervention by the central government in the administration of provincial affairs would be correspondingly diminished. This interpretation of the Empress Dowager's purpose finds confirmation in the fact that similar privileges were offered to the various Protestant missionary bodies; an offer which was ultimately rejected in spite of the sound arguments in favor of acceptance advanced by some of the ablest of their members.

It must also be noted that the "right" conferred upon the members of the Catholic hierarchy by this decree—namely, that of making formal visits to the Yamens of local and provincial officials—had hitherto been commonly exercised *illegally,* as has already been pointed out, by a

[6] Pinon, in particular, dwells at length upon the efforts made by Wilhelm II to ingratiate himself with the Pope and to oust the French from their place as the protectors of the church in heathen lands.

considerable portion of the missionaries, Protestant as well as Catholic. The real effect of the innovation was, therefore, merely to legalize a practice which had grown up and which could probably not be checked either by the Chinese government or by the national authorities of the missionaries. On the other hand, the very legalization of the practice would presumably result in making it less likely to become a source of local friction and misunderstanding. Thus the imperial government was but following the policy, mentioned by Sir Robert Hart, of ultimately accepting and regularizing local practices which had at first developed surreptitiously.

Finally—if it be argued that the decree of March 15 conferred not merely official "status," but also official powers, upon the missionaries—we may regard the move as a renewed attempt to assimilate the foreign religion into the Chinese state. Instead of being a step toward the creation of an *imperium in imperio*, as most of the Protestants have contended, it was actually designed to prevent that development. As has been seen in an earlier chapter, imperial opposition to Christianity arose, not out of the fact that it was foreign, but out of the conviction that it would always remain foreign; that it would always render allegiance first to its foreign head. This conviction had, in the early years of the eighteenth century, led to the outlawing of the religion, a solution of the problem which, by reason of the religious toleration clauses in the various treaties signed by China, was no longer possible at the close of the nineteenth century. Since the exclusion of Christianity was impossible, it is not surprising that the government should attempt to regain control over its Christian subjects by incorporating their spiritual leaders into the official system of the Empire, a policy which had been successfully adopted with Buddhism throughout the country, and with Mohammedanism in Yunnan, Shensi, Kansu, and Chinese Turkestan.

The Empress Dowager's policy of administrative and diplomatic decentralization was also extended to economic affairs. As early as December 2, 1898, Sir Claude MacDonald reported to his government the appointment of a board of Sub-Commissioners of Mines for the province of Szechuan, which was to have control over all mines in that province except those already in operation. All proposals for new concessions would, in the future, have to be taken up with this board. The removal of questions relating to mining concessions in Szechuan from the hands of the General Board of Mines and Railways, if followed by similar action with regard to the other provinces, would still further reduce the reasons for diplomatic pressure upon the Tsungli Yamen, and at the same time increase the direct control of viceroys and governors over provincial affairs.

A firm resistance to all further humiliation at the hands of the foreign powers, and the restoration of the traditional relations between central and provincial governments thus constituted two essential features of the new imperial policy. The first of these two points could be maintained, in the face of an almost certain continuance of foreign demands, only by increasing China's ability to oppose threats of force with some military preparedness of her own. Yet the development of national defenses must be accomplished in a way which did not violate the other essential feature of the conservative-reform policy, namely, the restoration of provincial and viceregal autonomy.

The low rate of taxation in China, and the certainty that any appreciable increase in that rate would result in violent popular disapproval, rendered impossible any addition to the imperial revenues by means of new or increased imposts. If it was out of the question for the government to finance its schemes of preparedness by increased taxation, so, also, was it impracticable for it to utilize other methods which would have appeared obvious to the financiers of any Western state. The flotation of a foreign loan would have been only too easy, but this would have involved opening the door to fresh demands by the lending powers and the imposition of increasing foreign control over the financial affairs of the country. On the other hand, the "Patriotic Loan" which had been authorized in February, 1898, had not proved successful; it was too much of an innovation to command popular support, and had already resulted in scandals arising out of the methods by which certain officials were attempting to secure contributions. For financial reasons, therefore, as well as for reasons connected with administrative policy, it was necessary that the utmost use be made of provincial and local agencies in the development of a system of national defense.

The first step taken by the Empress Dowager toward military reorganization was the unification of the command over all defensive forces in the vicinity of Peking. By an imperial decree which was issued six days after the *coup d'état*, Jung Lu, Viceroy of Chihli, was transferred to Peking and made a member of the Grand Council, his cousin Yu Lu succeeding him as Viceroy of Chihli and Superintendent of Trade for the Northern Ports. The command of the military and naval forces attached to the Peiyang Administration was, however, retained by Jung Lu instead of being handed over to the new viceroy. On October 11, the Empress Dowager issued another decree appointing Jung Lu Imperial High Commissioner, and giving him "supreme command, with powers of life and death" over the four army corps which constituted the defense forces of the metropolitan district, and which were severally commanded by General Sung Ching, General Tung Fu-hsiang, General Nieh Sze-ching, and General Yuan Shih-kai. The decree exhorted the new high commissioner "to use every effort in personally attending to the welfare and discipline of the troops under his supreme command, so that they may form a rock of defense around the capital of the Empire."

Two additional decrees relating to the reorganization and arming of the "Grand Army of the North" appeared on December 7. The first of these decrees sanctioned the formation of a Headquarters Corps, to be under Jung Lu's special command, in addition to the four existing army corps, and provided that the sum of 400,000 taels necessary for the equipment of this new force should be drawn from funds contributed by the various viceroys and governors for the reorganization of the Foochow arsenal and dockyard. The second decree, which, like the first, was in response to a memorial from Jung Lu, ordered the viceroys and governors who had arsenals and small-arms factories within their jurisdictions to pay especial attention to turning out "quick-firing, small-bore rifles of the Mauser pattern as fast and as many as each establishment can." This decree also commanded that military maps of the Peiyang district, including the coast, be prepared, and copies be sent to the officers of the entire army.

The forces in Chihli, the metropolitan province, were thus taken out of the control of the viceroy and placed under the command of Jung Lu; Shantung, while not actually attached to any viceroyalty, was, to a certain extent, under the influence of the Chihli viceroy, and was now included in the metropolitan defense area; the forces in the rest of the Empire remained under the command of the various viceroys and governors. Apart from Chihli and

Shantung, the portions of the Empire which were liable to attack lay within the jurisdictions of four great viceroyalties: the "Hukwang"—consisting of Hupeh and Hunan—under Chang Chih-tung, residing at Wuchang; the "Liangkiang"—Kiangsi, Anhwei, and Kiangsu—under Liu Kun-yih, at Nanking; the "Min-Che"—Fukien and Chekiang—under Hsu Ying-kuei, at Foochow; and the "Liangkwang"—Kwangtung and Kwangsi—under Tan Chung-lin, at Canton. The first two of these, comprising the entire Yangtze Valley except for Szechuan, were considered the most important, and defensive preparations here received the most careful attention; although, during the trouble with Italy in the summer of 1899, considerable activity was displayed in connection with the defenses of the Min-Che. The military preparations in the two Yangtze viceroyalties were second only to those of the metropolitan district in respect to the energy with which they were carried on. Chang Chih-tung and Liu Kun-yih were two of the most capable officials in the Empire, and Chang was especially progressive in his adoption of Western armaments.

On January 29 a decree was published ordering all Tartar-generals, viceroys, and governors to exercise energy and vigilance in the inspection and drilling of their provincial armies so as to keep them ever ready for possible emergencies. Recruits for the provincial armies, as well as for the forces under the command of Jung Lu, were to be sought among the idle, the desperate, and the lawless. "Good iron," says an old Chinese proverb, "is not used for nails, nor good men for soldiers." As early as October 24, 1898, a decree appeared in the *Peking Gazette* calling upon desperate men, who had become robbers and bandits, to reform themselves and enlist for the defense of their country in the various regiments which were being formed, and the viceroys and governors were commanded to supplement this appeal by proclamations to the same effect.

The provincial armies, however, like those under the direct control of the imperial government, were necessarily limited by the amount that could be spent upon their maintenance. The dangers to be apprehended from any increase in the burden of taxation were alike in both cases. It was, therefore, chiefly with the idea of providing a force which might be an auxiliary to these regular organizations, without entailing any additional expense, that the following decree, the importance of which can hardly be overestimated, was issued on November 5, 1898—a decree which will hereafter be repeatedly referred to as "the Decree of November 5":

> I, the Empress Dowager, having at heart the welfare of my people and the permanence of the dynasty, am of the opinion that every effort should be made to establish reserve granaries and volunteer military organization throughout the country, as these are actually the basis of a strong Empire. With full reserve granaries on hand in every district of the Empire, whenever an emergency arises, or famine, the people will have plenty to sustain themselves with and there will be no great sufferings by which the starved people will have to be driven to become robbers for sustenance. *With trained volunteers in all the cities, towns, and villages, and the people accustomed to the use of arms and the drills and discipline of the regular army, the whole country can be turned into a great armed camp to fight for their homes should the exigencies of the moment call our people forth.*[7] We can then depend upon ourselves for the safety of our homes and families. *I hereby command that the Viceroys and Governors of Chihli, Fengtien, Shantung, and Shansi be the first to inaugurate the systems advocated above*[7] and then let the Viceroys, Governors, and Tartar-Generals of other provinces follow in the footsteps

[7] The author's italics.

of the Northern authorities; and above all let there be diligence, energy, and care exercised in the manipulation of the grand work in hand. The sovereign on the Throne considers the whole Empire as one great family with Peking, and all must, therefore, depend upon one another. Let there be no timidity or loss of courage at the magnitude of the task before us, but let us, one and all, aim for the perfection of our duty and there will be no labor lost.

The commands uttered in this decree were repeated at greater length in a second decree on the subject which was issued on the last day of December:

The principle of true government lies in the determination to seek for the substance of all things. Of late, owing to the difficulties of the times, the Throne has in all things sought to effect the welfare of the people, and whenever our Ministers and lower officials memorialized on subjects having reference to the strengthening of the country we have never failed to approve of them with the command to bring such measures into force at once, while the number of decrees issued on these subjects has, indeed, not been few. If, therefore, the high officials, both in Peking and in the provinces, set earnestly to work in obeying our commands there would never have been any difficulty in obtaining substantial results therefrom. Unfortunately old practices have been so deeply rooted in the hearts of all these officials that it seems impossible to make them break through such barriers. For whenever they receive an Imperial edict they think that all that is needed of them is to transmit our commands to their subordinates; they never make any attempt to see that our edicts are put into force. And when chided for dilatoriness, excuses and false attestations are put forward to cover their faults. It follows, therefore, that our decrees are looked upon only as so much waste paper and never have we heard of any substantial results arising from them. Why is it then, that having received such gracious bounties from the Throne, our Viceroys and Governors never seek to help us bear our burdens, which cause us anxious days and sleepless nights? *We, therefore, now call upon these high officials to set to work at once upon all matters of immediate importance, such as the disciplining and organizing of the territorial armies; the Pao-chia or Military Police organizations;*[8] the creation of reserve granaries; and the encouragement of agriculture, mechanical arts, and commerce. Let there be no further delay and let every one tremblingly obey our commands. Those among the high officials who have already reported to us on such matters are hereby commanded to begin at once to put them into execution, while to those who have not we grant one month to report to us what they can do in this direction. Moreover, having begun on such reform measures the said high officials are to report to us at various intervals upon the progress of their work so that we may send special commissioners to examine them. In conclusion, all our high officials are expected, after receiving this edict, to rouse themselves up into active and earnest effort and they are warned from attending to the advice of crafty secretaries and slippery subordinates, accustomed to a life of fraud and falsehood; for, if it be hereafter discovered that empty show instead of solid substance has been attempted, we will consider it to be a wish to deceive the Throne and the delinquent guilty of such conduct will be punished according to the law provided for such crimes. Let it not be said that warning has not been given in time.[9]

"Conservative Reform" adequately characterizes the policy of the Empress Dowager during the months which immediately followed the *coup d'état*. Such of the Em-

[8] Author's italics.

[9] The first of these decrees did not appear in the *North China Herald* until October 30, 1899, but the second is to be found in the issue of January 9, 1899. Bland and Backhouse, in *China under the Empress Dowager*, p. 241, give a decree, somewhat similar to these two, which they say was "promulgated towards the close of the year." I have been unable to find any other decree on the subject appearing at this period, and am forced to regard the version given by Bland and Backhouse as an abstract of these two; particularly as they fail to give a precise date for the decree which they quote.

peror's reform edicts as constituted a violent departure from the political or economic traditions of the Empire were repealed; those few which seemed harmless and likely to aid in developing the national strength were retained. At the same time positive steps were taken to raise the prestige of the government in the eyes of its own people and in the estimation of the outside world; to reestablish the traditionally Chinese system of administrative decentralization; and to reduce, in every possible way, the danger of missionary difficulties which might furnish the foreign powers with pretexts for fresh aggressive steps. Finally, in the shrewd belief that foreign aggression could not be forestalled merely by the maintenance of internal peace, every effort was made so to strengthen the military resources of the Empire that China would be able to meet any new humiliating demands with a flat refusal, and to support such refusal, if necessary, by opposing force with force.

CHAPTER VI.

Foreign Relations after the *Coup d' Etat.*

Peace with Dignity—Difficulties—Marine Guards for Peking—Tung Fu-hsiang's Troops—Italy and Sanmen Bay—China's Readiness to Fight—Edict of Empress Dowager—General Forebodings—The "Open Door" Negotiations—Preparedness—Kang Yi, the "Imperial High Extortioner"—Rise of Militant Patriotism.

AS has been pointed out in the preceding chapter, the basic principle in the foreign policy of China after the *coup d'état* was a resistance to all foreign demands which would constitute new infringements upon China's sovereignty, or which might involve the humiliation of the government in the eyes of the people. This aspect of the government's policy was, however, tempered by the desire, apparently sincere, to maintain peaceable and friendly relations with the powers, so far as this was possible. In her anxiety to convince everyone that the recent change in government did not mean that China had any intention of adopting an aggressive anti-foreign and anti-Christian policy, the Empress Dowager issued, on October 6,[1] an "edict of toleration." The gentry and literati of all the provinces were warned that they must maintain peace and harmony between the Christians and non-Christians, and must treat cordially all missionaries who came among them; while the high provincial officials were ordered to do justice promptly in all cases of dispute between the converts and the people, and to furnish adequate protection to all places of Christian worship within their jurisdiction.

[1] *I.e.*, fifteen days after her assumption of power.

The maintenance of peace with dignity was to prove no easy task. The spirit of anti-foreignism, which had been steadily growing since the close of the war with Japan, was a source of constant danger. At the same time, there was no good reason to expect that the foreign powers had any intention of modifying their policies toward China. Regarding the *coup d'état* as a mere episode in palace intrigue, or as the final convulsive struggle of the decadent Manchu Dynasty, they were not apt to treat the new régime with any more consideration than they had shown to the one which had preceded. Indeed, as the conviction grew that the final dissolution of the Empire was at hand, it was but natural for the Western governments to prepare to maintain by force the rights and concessions which had been obtained by threats of force.

Evidence of the difficulties which were to be encountered in keeping on good terms with the outside world was not long in appearing. On September 30 several foreigners, one a member of the British legation, were attacked by a mob, while on their way from the railway station to the legation quarter, and were severely pelted with mud and stones. Although Sir Claude MacDonald, in reporting the incident, stated that "a member of the United States legation had one of his ribs broken," Mr. Conger informed the State Department that no one had been seriously injured.[2]

There is a considerable amount of reason in the contention that this and similar anti-foreign demonstrations which followed were the direct result of the overthrow of the Reform Party, an event which the people naturally interpreted as foreshadowing a bitterly anti-foreign reaction. But another very probable cause of the outbreak—

[2] See *British Blue Books, China No. 1 (1899)*, document no. 344; and *Foreign Relations of the United States, 1898*, p. 225.

certainly a contributing cause—is to be found in the concentration of the British fleet in the Gulf of Pechili, which had taken place in the early part of the month as support for the latest block of railway demands. On September 4 Sir Claude MacDonald had reported to his government that he had not presented his demands to the Tsungli Yamen in the form of an ultimatum, but added: "The fact that the fleet is concentrating is, of course, known to them." Nor was this fact known only to the government. On September 20 Mr. H. T. Pitkin, an American missionary, wrote from Peitaiho that the Chinese in the vicinity were much alarmed over the appearance of warships off the coast, and that one of his own servants had asked if it was true that some power was at war with China. In view of the leases which had recently been forced from China by "gunboat diplomacy," it was not unreasonable that the common knowledge of this naval concentration should produce popular apprehension and suppressed anti-foreignism; nor was it strange that these feelings should find open expression as soon as the "pro-foreign" government had been overthrown.[3]

As a result of this anti-foreign disturbance at Peking, "strong representations" were made to the Tsungli Yamen. The diplomats whose governments had naval forces in Eastern waters immediately requested that ships be dispatched to Taku, and, on October 6, guards of marines were brought up for the British, German, and Russian legations; a similar guard was brought up for the American legation a month later. The Tsungli Yamen protested vehemently against this step, and vainly attempted to convince the foreign ministers that it would inevitably

[3] While it is not entirely correct to describe the government during the "Hundred Days" as "pro-foreign," such was the popular estimate which resulted from the program that it had adopted.

lead to increased anti-foreign sentiment; their arguments were regarded as idle efforts to save the government from a well-deserved "loss of face." A precedent for summoning guards for the legations had been established in February, 1895, during the tension which marked the closing period of the Japanese war, and no arguments against the proceeding would now be admitted as valid. It is well to note, however, that Secretary Gresham, in a dispatch to Minister Denby, in 1895, had discussed at length the alleged treaty right of the foreign representatives to summon armed guards for their legations and had denied the existence of such a right. On this later occasion, also, Secretary Hay, when informing Mr. Conger that a ship with marines had been ordered to Taku, advised him to summon guards to Peking "only in case of necessity."

The need of the guards at Peking was denied by at least one competent foreign observer, the Rev. W. S. Ament of the American Board mission. Mr. Ament was, at the time, very sympathetic toward the program of the Reform Party, and decidedly hostile to the Empress Dowager, yet it was his opinion that the step taken by the foreign diplomats had forced upon the foreign community at Peking protection which was not required. While it is quite probable that the foreign representatives were acting in good faith when they summoned guards for the legations, it is equally probable that mutual suspicion among the foreign powers was an important factor in keeping the marines at Peking through the winter. Lord Salisbury, in response to the requests of the Chinese minister at the Court of St. James for the removal of the guards, replied that the British guards could not be withdrawn from Peking so long as the Russian guards remained.

Whether because of the presence of the guards, or because of the Empress Dowager's bona fide desire to protect foreigners throughout the Empire, there were no further popular anti-foreign demonstrations. Friction of another sort, however, almost immediately appeared. In connection with the reorganization of the "Grand Army of the North," as outlined in the decree on October 11 (to which reference was made in the preceding chapter), the troops of Tung Fu-hsiang were moved to Peking and quartered at the Hunting Park, about two miles south of the city. On October 22 a party of these soldiers met four Europeans, one of them a member of the British legation, at Lu-kou-chiao on the Peking-Tientsin railway, and a conflict arose which, according to the British report, appears to have been precipitated when the Europeans ordered the soldiers away from the railway embankment.

This body of troops was entirely composed of Kansu men, and had served with distinction in the suppression of a Mohammedan uprising in that province during the years 1895 and 1896. Their presence in Chihli was, however, regarded by the foreigners as a grave threat to the peace, and complaints had already been made to the effect that these Kansu men were undisciplined and beyond all control. Immediately after the trouble on October 11, therefore, the foreign ministers protested against keeping this force at Peking, and finally demanded, on November 6, that the Kansu Army Corps be removed from the province of Chihli within nine days.

As Tung Fu-hsiang's soldiers were the most efficient part of the imperial forces—the only portion, in fact, which had given evidence of military efficiency in actual warfare—the Chinese government had no intention of yielding to this demand. It is, indeed, highly improbable that the Tsungli Yamen would have dared to submit a memorial to the Throne asking that these troops be removed from the province. Therefore the complaining diplomats were ultimately compelled to recede from their demand and to content themselves with the transfer of the objectionable troops to Chichou, a post about fifty miles east of Peking, on the road to Shanhaikwan. Since the Chinese government had already shown considerable anxiety to guard against the possibility of an attack on Peking from the direction of the coast, this disposition of General Tung's forces did not in any way interfere with its plans for the defense of the metropolitan district.

Aside from the fact that the diplomatic body had been forced to compromise on this matter, the demand for the removal of the Kansu Army Corps to a point "outside the province of Chihli," where they would not have been readily available for the defense of Peking, had certain unfortunate consequences. It served to convince many of the officials at Peking that the powers were contemplating some further move against the peace and dignity of the Empire. The ranks of the extreme anti-foreign party were considerably augmented, and it became increasingly difficult for any official to advocate a conciliatory attitude toward the Westerners without exposing himself to the suspicion of being a traitor to his country.

For the next month or two, no new difficulty arose with the outside world, but, during the early months of the year 1899, friction developed between China and the recipients of practically all the concessions which had been granted during the scramble of the preceding year. In the Liao-tung peninsula, Russia denied the right of the Chinese authorities to collect the customary taxes, and, in February, as a result of attempts by the Russian officials to collect the land tax, disturbances broke out which cost the lives of a large number of Chinese. At about the same time it was rumored that Great Britain had demanded assurance of the non-alienation of any part of Honan province, on the ground that Honan was a part of the Yangtze Valley and should, therefore, be brought under the declaration that China had already made concerning the Yangtze.

In March the British authorities at Weihaiwei followed the example which had been set by the Russians in the Liao-tung, and issued a proclamation forbidding anyone within their newly leased territory to pay taxes of any kind to the Chinese officials. Toward the end of the same month, troubles arose in Shantung as the result of attacks upon German engineers in the neighborhood of Jihchow. These troubles led to the occupation of Jihchow by a German force, and to the dispatch of a punitive expedition to the spot where the attacks had occurred. In April there were disturbances at Kowloon in connection with the delimitation of the new extension and its surrender to the British.

During the same general period, there were riots at Shanghai, arising out of demands for the extension of the French concession there; it was vaguely rumored that either Russia or Japan had demanded a lease of the island of Yang-mao, near Shanhaikwan; Japan was pressing for a concession at Amoy; and even the United States, through its consul at Amoy, was negotiating for some sort of a concession at that port which would serve as a base of communications with Manila.[4]

The minor conflicts which have here been briefly catalogued, were overshadowed by the clash between China and Italy in March, 1899. The Italian demands, to which Sir Claude MacDonald had, on February 25, been instructed to give diplomatic support,[5] were presented to

[4] The American minister at Peking, Mr. Conger, had no knowledge of the nature or extent of these negotiations until after the Tsungli Yamen had raised the question whether these were in conflict with the demands of Japan. For his correspondence with the State Department on the subject, see *Foreign Relations of the United States, 1899*, pp. 150-152.

[5] See *Parliamentary Debates*, vol. 68 (4th Series), p. 1321.

the Tsungli Yamen on February 28. Italy requested the lease of Sanmen Bay, in Chekiang province, to serve as a coaling station, and also a "sphere of interest" covering the southern two-thirds of Chekiang: that portion of the province which Great Britain was willing to consider as not a part of the Yangtze Valley, and therefore not included in the Chinese pledge of non-alienation.

At Peking, as well as at the various European capitals, it was generally expected that the Chinese government would offer a certain amount of resistance, but would eventually give way to these demands as it had, in the preceding twelve months, given way to so many others of the same nature.[6] With the possible exception of Russia, China could hope for no support against Italy. The United States maintained its customary attitude of neutrality, an attitude in which it was joined by Japan. Germany and Austria, the allies of Italy, professed absolute disinterest, but would probably aid Italy against any outside power which might take the side of China. France, although it was reported that her minister at Peking had warned the Tsungli Yamen of the impending demands several days before they were presented, denied, semi-officially, that she was in any way opposed to Italy's aspirations. On the other hand, Italy had the avowed diplomatic support of Great Britain, the power most vitally interested in this part of the China coast.

On March 4 China refused the demands, and the refusal took a rather unusual form: the Italian minister's dispatch was returned with an accompanying note which stated, in curt language, that the government of China was unable to consider the subject. This action by the

[6] But Japanese correspondents at Peking reported, on March 2, that China, on the advice of another power, would refuse the demands. See *Japan Chronicle*, Kobe, vol. IV, p. 186.

Tsungli Yamen was regarded by Signor Martino and his government as a deliberate insult to Italy, and there were ominous suggestions that, although Italy would prefer to obtain her objects by peaceful means if possible, the attitude of China might compel the use of force. To a note from Sir Claude MacDonald, supporting the Italian requests, the Tsungli Yamen returned an answer couched in the same uncompromising terms: the Chinese government regarded the matter as impossible of negotiation, and refused to discuss it.

The Italian minister sent a second dispatch to the Yamen on March 10. He now demanded that the Yamen should, within four days, request the return of his earlier dispatch, which had been so unceremoniously rejected; that it approve, in principle, the request for a coaling station and a sphere of interest; and that it resume friendly negotiations for the arrangement of details. Three days later this second dispatch was disavowed by the Italian government; in an official note published at Rome, it was announced that Signor Martino had therein exceeded his instructions, which had not authorized the presentation of an ultimatum. The discredited minister was immediately recalled, and the British minister was asked to take charge of the interests of Italy pending the arrival of Signor Martino's successor.

In spite of this retreat, Italy persisted in her resolve to obtain Sanmen Bay, at the same time declaring that she would do her utmost to avoid the necessity of using force, and the summer was spent in vain attempts to bring the Yamen to a more conciliatory attitude on the subject. Early in August, an "inspired" article in the *Milan Corrier* announced that Italy had abandoned her claim to Sanmen Bay, and did not intend to demand a new coaling station. A fresh set of demands was now presented, which included certain mining rights in Chekiang and Kiangsi, a railway concession in Chekiang, a railroad between Peking and the western hills with the right of working the coal mines there, and the establishment of a chair of Italian literature in Peking University. Yet even these moderate requests failed to obtain favorable consideration from the Chinese government, which saw no good reason for departing from its recently adopted policy of opposing all further grants of concessions. Despite the Italian threat that China's persistent refusal might lead to unfortunate complications, Italy's venture into the field of Far Eastern concession hunting remained fruitless, or resulted only in an increase of hostility toward Italy and all the other European powers.

In China, as in Europe, the Italian demands were regarded as the final test of the Empire's ability to resist total dismemberment. If the imperial government submitted to this fresh incroachment, the rush for the last remaining morsels—which had been checked by the change of administration in September—would be resumed with redoubled energy.

The Empress Dowager and her government showed their appreciation of the desperate nature of the emergency which was facing China by immediately speeding up the defense program along all lines. As soon as the first Italian demand was presented, telegrams were sent to generals commanding forces in Shansi, Shensi, Honan, and even as far away as Kansu, ordering them to concentrate their best troops as quickly as possible in the vicinity of Peking. As the result of a meeting of the Grand Council which was held two days after Signor Martino had been repudiated by his government, an edict was sent to Governor Liu, of Chekiang, ordering him to report upon the number of disciplined and modern armed troops available for the defense of his province, and authorizing him to call upon the viceroys at Nanking and Foochow for additional soldiers, if he considered them necessary. A week later, secret instructions were sent to the viceroys and governors of the maritime and Yangtze provinces, authorizing them to resist by force the landing of foreign troops anywhere along the coast, and ordering them to rearm and redrill all their forces according to modern requirements with all possible haste.

Toward the end of May these instructions were repeated to Liu Kun-yih, viceroy of the Liang-Kiang and imperial high commissioner for the Nanyang Administration, in the following terms:

> In the event of the landing of armed forces of European Powers within the jurisdiction of the Imperial Commissionership of the Nanyang, you are hereby granted perfect liberty to employ armed resistance thereto. There will be no necessity of waiting for further instructions from the Throne, as in critical times it is not unusual that telegraphic communications may be stopped between the Capital and other points in the Empire. You will be held responsible should there be any failure in obeying these instructions, and it shall be your duty to notify our commands to the various Viceroys, Governors, and Provincial Commanders-in-Chief of the maritime and riverine provinces comprised in your jurisdiction, and to see to it that effective opposition be given to the foreign aggressors. Liberty is also given to you to keep back taxes destined for the Imperial Exchequer in the event of lack of funds to prosecute the war.
>
> Obey this in fear and trembling![7]

[7] Taken from the *North China Herald* of June 12, 1899, vol. 62, p. 1049. Although this edict has not the full authenticity which attaches to the translations from the *Peking Gazette* which appear in the columns of the same paper, it is printed by the *North China* as having been received from its Nanking native correspondent, and may be accepted as substantially accurate.

Anxiety as to the possibility of war with Italy was, it is true, considerably abated by the modification of the Italian demands at the beginning of August. Yet the Chinese continued, through the late summer and fall, to regard with suspicion the reported activities of Italian naval forces in Chinese waters. This suspicion was further complicated, in November, by the development of new conflicts with the French in the province of Kwangsi. The attitude of the Empress Dowager, in the face of these growing complications, is admirably illustrated by the following secret edict which was sent, on November 21, to the viceroys, governors, Tartar-generals, and provincial commanders-in-chief throughout the Empire:

Our Empire is now laboring under great difficulties which are becoming daily more serious. The various Powers cast upon us looks of tiger-like voracity, hustling each other in their endeavors to be the first to seize upon our innermost territories. *They think that China, having neither money nor troops, would never venture to go to war with them. They fail to understand, however, that there are certain things which this Empire can never consent to, and that, if hardly pressed upon, we have no alternative but to rely upon the justice of our cause, the knowledge of which in our breasts strengthens our resolves and steels us to present a united front against our aggressors.*[8] No one can guarantee under such circumstances who will be the victor and who the conquered in the end. But there is an evil habit which has become almost a custom amongst our Viceroys and Governors which, however, must be eradicated at all costs. For instance, whenever these high officials have had on their hands a case of international dispute, all their actions seem to be guided by the belief in their breasts that such cases would eventually be "amicably arranged." These words seem never to be out of their thoughts; hence, when matters do come to a crisis, they, of course, find themselves utterly unprepared to resist any hostile aggressions on the part of the for-

[8] Author's italics.

eigner. We, indeed, consider this the most serious failure in the duty which the high provincial officials owe to the Throne and we now find it incumbent upon ourselves to censure such conduct in the most severe terms.

It is our special command, therefore, that should any high official find himself so hard pressed by circumstances that nothing short of a war would settle matters, he is expected to set himself resolutely to work out his duty to this end. Or perhaps, it would be that war has already actually been declared; under such circumstances there is no possible chance of the Imperial Government consenting to an immediate conference for the restoration of peace. It behooves, therefore, that our Viceroys, Governors, and Commanders-in-Chief throughout the whole Empire unite forces and act together without distinction or particularising of jurisdictions so as to present a combined front to the enemy, exhorting and encouraging their officers and soldiers in person to fight for the preservation of their homes and native soil from the encroaching footsteps of the foreign aggressor. Never should the word "Peace" fall from the mouths of our high officials, nor should they even allow it to rest for a moment within their breasts. With such a country as ours, with her vast area, stretching out for several tens of thousands of li, her immense natural resources, and her hundreds of millions of inhabitants, if only each of you would prove his loyalty to his Emperor and love of country, what, indeed, is there to fear from any invader? Let no one think of making peace, but let each strive to preserve from destruction and spoliation his ancestral home and graves from the ruthless hands of the invader. Let these our words be made known to each and all within our dominions.

This secret edict was supplemented, early in December, by the following circular dispatch from the Tsungli Yamen, which was addressed to the provincial authorities of the maritime and Yangtze provinces:

As the Italians have not had their ambitions gratified with respect to the cession of Sanmen Bay to them, it is apprehended that they may try to seek opportunity for seizing other portions of our coast. Moreover the arbitrary and aggressive actions of the French at Kwangchowwan, where they are stirring up disturbances in order to obtain further pretexts for demanding concessions from the Imperial Government, may lead to actual hostilities between China and France. It behooves us, therefore, to exercise the utmost vigilance and watchfulness to guard against sudden aggression, and to be always prepared to resist an enemy. Your Excellency is, therefore, urged to enjoin all this upon the Generals and Commanders of troops garrisoning important points within your jurisdiction, and not only this, but to be prepared also to give aid to your brother Viceroys and Governors, whose territories adjoin your own. It has been an evil practice among the high provincial authorities to consider that the duty of any one of them lies only in guarding safely the region lying within his own jurisdiction, ignoring the crisis that may be taking place in the next adjoining provinces, forgetting that his neighbors being overcome his turn for overthrow becomes a near possibility. This lack of union is lamentable, but it must not continue from this date. *This Yamen has received the special commands of Her Imperial Majesty, the Empress Dowager, and His Imperial Majesty, the Emperor, to grant you full power and liberty to resist by force of arms all aggressions upon your several jurisdictions, proclaiming a state of war, if necessary, without first asking for instructions from Peking;*[9] for this loss of time may be fatal to your security and enable the enemy to make good his footing against your forces. Finally, Your Excellency will be held responsible for any repetition of indecision or too great trustfulness in the declaration of an encroaching enemy, such as happened, for instance, to General Chang Kao-yuan in Shantung. [Chang Kao-yuan was in command at Tsingtao when the Germans landed.][10]

[9] Author's italics.

[10] These two documents were printed in the *North China Herald* of December 27, 1899, vol. 63, p. 1289; and are also to be found in the *Foreign Relations of the United States, 1900*, p. 85. The secret instructions given in May to Liu Kun-yih (printed above) have been ignored by—are not known to—other historians of this period, hence these two expres-

Foreign Relations after the *Coup d'Etat*

It is difficult to deny the accuracy with which the Empress Dowager described, in her secret edict of November 21, the intentions of the Western powers; nor can the instructions which were issued to the provincial authorities be regarded as unduly belligerent, or as lacking in justification. The forebodings so graphically expressed by Tzu Hsi were, indeed, shared by the government of the United States. In September, 1899, Secretary Hay had instructed the ambassadors of the United States at London, Paris, Berlin, and St. Petersburg to request from the governments to which they were accredited formal assurances "that each within its respective spheres of whatever interest:

"First: Will in no way interfere with any treaty port or any vested interest within any so-called 'sphere of interest' or leased territory it may have in China.

"Second: That the Chinese treaty tariff of the time being shall apply to all merchandise landed or shipped to all such ports as are within said 'sphere of interest' (unless they be 'free ports'), no matter to what nationality it may belong, and that duties so leviable shall be collected by the Chinese government.

"Third: That it will levy no higher harbor dues on vessels of another nationality frequenting any port in such 'sphere' than shall be levied on vessels of its own nationality, and no higher railroad charges over lines built, controlled, or operated within its 'sphere' on merchandise belonging to citizens or subjects of other nationalities transported through such 'sphere' than shall be levied on similar merchandise belonging to its own nationals transported over equal distances."

In November similar requests were addressed to the

sions of the imperial will have been generally regarded as marking a sudden change in policy at Peking in November and December of 1899.

governments of Italy and Japan, and, by February 19, satisfactory written replies to these efforts to maintain the "Open Door and Equal Opportunity" were received from each of the six governments.

Although the second of the three points upon which the government of the United States desired to receive assurances included the provision "that the duties . . . shall be collected by the Chinese government," the notes of the American Department of State recognized "spheres of influence or interest" as established facts. Indeed, the official documents, as well as the private letters of Secretary Hay, indicate that the authorities at Washington anticipated the extinction of Chinese sovereignty, and were primarily concerned with safeguarding existing American rights in the event of such a development. If not the purpose, at least the effect, of the assurances received by the government of the United States, was to secure for American treaty rights, in case of the partition of China, the status of "international servitudes," which would continue effective regardless of any transfer of sovereignty which might take place.

The immediate responsibility for resisting any possible attack, on the part of Italy or other powers, was delegated to the several provincial governments, and especial emphasis was laid upon the development of modern armed forces; yet the imperial government neglected no possible means of supplementing these arrangements for defense. On March 14 the day after the unauthorized ultimatum of Signor Martino was repudiated by the government at Rome, Yu Hsien—who subsequently became notorious for his bitter anti-foreign spirit—was appointed governor of Shantung to replace the inefficient Chang Ju-mei, the apparent purpose of this appointment being to put a capable and energetic official in this important post at a moment when war seemed impending. The rise of this Manchu officer had been exceedingly rapid during the preceding few months. In the spring of 1898 Yu Hsien was a simple "Taotai" (magistrate of a circuit) in the province of Shantung; during the summer of that year, *i.e.*, during the period of "reform government," he was raised to the post of provincial judge. In October he was appointed provincial treasurer for the neighboring province of Honan, but, before he had time to proceed to his new post, the Tartar-general at Nanking died, and Yu Hsien was appointed acting Tartar-general. He took over the seals of this office on December 31 and remained here until March 14, when he was made governor of the province in which, less than a year before, he had been only a "Taotai."[11]

Three days after this appointment, an imperial decree commanded the viceroys and governors to hasten the work of organizing the reserve granaries, military police, and volunteer militia within their respective jurisdictions, in accordance with the decrees issued on November 5 and December 31, since this work was of vital importance to the safety of the Empire. Two months later the imperial government still further demonstrated the important part which the militia system played in its military calculations. On May 21 Kang Yi, president of the Board of War, was appointed to act as imperial high commissioner on a tour of inspection in Kiangsu Province. The appointment of Kang Yi was partly for the purpose of searching out and

[11] In this connection it must be noted that Professor Cordier, in his *Histoire des relations de la Chine avec les puissances occidentales*, vol. III, p. 456, errs in making Yu Hsien the immediate successor of Li Pingheng as governor of Shantung. This error, of a sort which is exceedingly rare in any work by Cordier, has been followed by a number of lesser writers, with the consequence that Yu Hsien is generally held responsible for the anti-foreign disturbances in Shantung during the winter of 1898-1899, a period when he was absent from the province.

punishing corruption in official circles. But the chief objects of his mission were to inspect the defenses; to investigate the system of public granaries; to consider possible measures for the thorough reorganization of the volunteer, or train-band, system; and to devise some means for increasing the amount of imperial revenue which could be derived from the province.

The visit of Kang Yi to Kiangsu did not result in any very important development of the volunteer system in that province. A movement was set on foot for the organization of a volunteer company at Shanghai, armed and drilled along Western lines, and a few bodies of local militia were formed at other points; otherwise no considerable activity in this respect can be noted. The high commissioner's financial efforts were, however, more fruitful. Besides recommending a number of possible sources for new revenue, which were approved by imperial decrees, he was able to effect considerable economies by weeding out a number of corrupt and incapable officials, and by abolishing a number of superfluous offices. In addition to these accomplishments, Kang Yi succeeded in obtaining, by pressure upon various other local officers, a sum amounting to more than a million taels which the provincial authorities were ordered to devote to the extraordinary military expenses of the province. So successful was Kang Yi in this form of activity that he was always referred to, thereafter, in the foreign press, as the "Imperial High Extortioner." He was ordered to continue his tour to Kwangtung, where his efforts resulted in "increasing the revenue of the Imperial Exchequer by over 1,600,000 taels."

While the imperial, provincial, and local officials were thus putting forth unprecedented efforts to strengthen the military resources of the country, often to the neglect of other governmental duties, there was developing among the people of the Empire a feeling of national consciousness such as had, on earlier occasions of conflict between China and the outside world, been conspicuous by its absence. Apprehension of foreign aggression and resentment toward the powers for their aggressions in the past were no longer confined to the population of the areas directly affected.

In May, 1899, the students in one of the mission colleges at Shanghai debated the question "Whether the European powers are justified in partitioning China." At Peking, during the month of August, the air was filled with rumors, and the people seemed to have a dull apprehension that, in some way or other, the foreigners were going to injure them or their country. The talk on the streets was that China was to be terrorized by the foreigners. At Canton, in the latter part of October, the most influential daily paper in the city published a series of articles which were intended to rouse the people from their indifference by showing how the foreigners were planning to divide up China "like a water-melon."

This growing fear and hatred with regard to the foreigners tended to focus upon the Christian missionaries throughout the Empire, and upon their native adherents. "Why the educated classes of this land should be so inveterately hostile to the foreigners is a difficult question to answer," wrote the British consul at Foochow, in August, 1899. "It has been suggested that the Chinese of this type have an ineradicable conviction that every European is at heart a 'land-grabber'; that missionaries are the advance agents of their governments; that the Bible is the certain fore-runner of the gunboat; and that where the missionary comes as a sojourner he means to stay as a proprietor; consequently, that the only hope of integrity for China is that her loyal sons should on every occasion destroy the baneful germs."[12] If, as Mr. Playfair here suggests, the missionary was regarded in the light of a spy or an advance agent for a land-grabbing government, the native convert was looked upon as a traitor, who was contributing—perhaps unwittingly—to the dismemberment of his native land. It was, therefore, not without reason that the fear of foreign aggression often found expression in attacks upon the mission stations, both Protestant and Catholic.

The year which followed the *coup d'état* was a year of gathering storm clouds. The apparent desire of the Empress Dowager to avoid conflict with the Western powers and to quiet the growing anti-foreign bitterness—which might precipitate a struggle that would be fatal alike to the Dynasty and the Empire—was set at naught by the continued and increasing aggression of the West. The demands of Italy had, indeed, been successfully repulsed; but these new demands, and the efforts which had been made to prepare for effective resistance, had filled the country with military activity. The Empress Dowager's program of economic and administrative reform, along lines which would harmonize with Chinese traditions and political theory, had been subordinated to the pressing need of immediately reorganizing and financing the nation's armed forces. In official circles, both at Peking and in the provinces, an increasing hostility toward the outside nations became manifest, not as a result of any change of personnel in government offices but because every capable official in the Empire believed those nations to be contemplating the dismemberment of the country. Finally this

[12] *British Blue Books, China No. 1 (1900)*, inclosure in document no. 384.

fear of the foreign powers was spreading among the people in all parts of the land, and was beginning to produce among the mass of the Chinese people a spirit of militant national patriotism.

CHAPTER VII.

The Boxers: "I-ho Chuan" or "I-ho Tuan."

The Traditional Explanation of the Boxers—Weakness of this Explanation—Earliest Use of "I-ho Chuan"—"Ihonokinen"—Prior Use of "Boxer"—"Tuan," not "Chuan"—The "Ta Tao Hui" or "Big Sword Society"—Amalgamation of the "Big Sword" by the "Boxers"—Origins of the Boxer Spiritism—A Boxer Placard—Not "Rebels," but Lawful Militia.

THE explanation of the "Boxer Movement" which has been accepted as authoritative by a majority of writers first made its appearance some time during the winter of 1899-1900 in a brochure written by Lao Nai-hsuan, sub-prefect of Wuchiao. According to this explanation, the "I-ho Chuan"—"Righteous Harmony Fist"—existed in the early part of the nineteenth century as a secret society associated with the "White Lotus Society," the "Eight Dragons Sect," the "Red Fist Society," and similar heretical and revolutionary organizations. All of these societies were suppressed, in 1808, by a decree issued by the Emperor Chia Ching. At the time of this earlier existence, the I-ho Chuan had no anti-Christian tendencies but was purely revolutionary in its aims. For ninety years after its suppression by Chia Ching, the society maintained an obscure existence in many districts of Chihli and Shantung, and ultimately reappeared, in 1898, as an active and anti-Christian organization.[1]

[1] The most complete abstract of this work by Lao Nai-hsuan—French romanization, Liao-ngai-siuen—is to be found in the little Jesuit magazine, *Chine et Ceylan* for August, 1900, pp. 11-12. It is quoted by Cordier in his *Histoire des relations de la Chine avec les puissances occidentales,*

At the time this work appeared, Yuan Shih-kai, as acting governor of Shantung, was endeavoring to check the spread of the I-ho Chuan in his jurisdiction, and this explanation of the nature and origin of the movement received his official sanction; Lao Nai-hsuan's booklet was officially printed and distributed in large numbers throughout the province as a warning to the people not to support or join the organization.

Yet this explanation of the movement is in such complete disaccord with a number of important facts that it must be rejected as absolutely untenable. In the first place, it is impossible to believe that a secret society, holding heretical doctrines and known to have revolutionary aims, would deliberately go out of its way to institute a campaign of bitter hostility against Christian missions, and thus stir up against itself the activities of the officials and the complaints of the foreign diplomats. Such procedure would have been contrary to all that is known of the history of secret societies in China, and is without precedence in the history of the country.

There is but one recorded and authentic instance of a deliberate attack upon Christianity by a *religious* secret society, and, even in this case, the motive for the attack was non-religious. In the summer of 1895, the "Chi-tsai-ti," or "Vegetarians," massacred a number of Protestant missionaries at Kucheng, in the province of Fukien. In the trial of the murderers, it was proved that the Vegetarians had attacked the missionaries because they considered them responsible for having had the governor of

vol. III, p. 451, and by de Groot in *Sectarianism and Religious Persecution in China*, p. 430. References to the brochure also occur in the "Outport Correspondence" of the *North China Herald* during the early months of 1900, and in the contemporary letters of the missionaries of the American Board in North China.

the province move troops into the districts where the Vegetarians were practically in control. It is true that the "Ko Lao Hui," "Elder Brother Society," was often implicated in anti-foreign outbreaks; but the Ko Lao Hui was a purely revolutionary organization, with no religious significance, and its avowed purpose in attacking foreigners was to involve the Manchu Dynasty in difficulties with the foreign powers.

Some writers have attempted to avoid this weak point in the account given by Lao Nai-hsuan by assuming that the I-ho Chuan was originally heretical and revolutionary, but that it was later "captured" by the Empress Dowager and her lieutenants, and turned against the hated foreigners. In support of this theory—which is obviously a rejection of the original account—it has been asserted that the organization was first called the "I-ho Chuan Hui" ("Hui" being the generic term for secret societies) and that the term "Hui" was later abandoned in return for imperial sanction. Although the I-ho Chuan did, as will be seen, practically absorb a society known as the "Ta Tao Hui," "Big Knife Society," there is no contemporary evidence that the I-ho Chuan was ever called a "Hui."

Aside from this essay by the sub-prefect of Wuchiao, the only substantiation for the claim that the I-ho Chuan was originally a secret society is found in an imperial decree which was published on June 6, 1900, and in the proclamations which were issued by the "neutral" viceroys and governors after June 17. The decree of June 6 was, as will be seen later, issued under conditions which were hardly conducive to disingenuousness; hence the reference to the suppression of secret societies in the reign of Chia Ching, and the statement that these present organizations had been tolerated because they were merely training themselves in the arts of self-defense, cannot be regarded as conclusive proof on any point. After June 17 the viceroys and governors of central and southern China, in order to keep the movement from spreading into their own portions of the Empire, denounced it as a rebellion, and attributed its origin to a secret society. As these proclamations were dictated by considerations which were entirely dissociated with any desire for historical accuracy, they are entitled to little consideration as evidence of the origin and nature of the movement.

More positive evidence for rejecting the assumption that the I-ho Chuan was a branch of the White Lotus—or White Lily—Society is furnished by Dr. Arthur H. Smith. "There has long been in Shantung," he writes, "a society called the 'Six Times Sect,' which was regarded as a branch of the White Lily Society and was frequently broken up by the magistrates. Yet in the villages where this society flourished it had no connection whatever with the I-ho Chuan, either upon its first appearance or at any later period."[2]

So far as it has been possible to discover, the earliest use of the name "I-ho Chuan," by any foreigner in China, was in a letter written on October 14, 1899, by Dr. H. D. Porter, of the American Board mission at Pang-chuang, in Shantung. "It is just a month this morning since we first secured a few soldiers from the District city to defend us against a possible, but seemingly imminent, attack upon us by turbulent members of the Yi Ho Chuan Society. The last character in the combination of three in the name of the society is 'Fist,' or 'Boxers,' and the Society has been named for the past year 'Spirit Boxers,' a company of young fellows who have gathered together for wrestling and general gymnastics, with the underlying purpose of combining against all foreigners within range. Under the

[2] *China in Convulsion*, vol. I, p. 171.

pretence of a patriotic purpose 'Exalting the Dynasty and Destroying the Foreigners,' these companies have increased in great numbers until the whole region about us was wholly infiltrated with them. . . ." It will be observed that Dr. Porter makes no reference to any revolutionary or "secret society" aspects in his description of these bands; that he does not give "Hui" as part of the name of the organization; and that he puts the first appearance of the bands at about a year prior to the date of his letter—*i.e.*, at about the date when the Empress Dowager began to emphasize the reorganization of the local volunteer bands. Dr. Porter had been a missionary in Shantung for twenty years, yet he found it necessary to give a translation of the name "Yi Ho Chuan," evidence that this was the first time he had used the name in a letter to his correspondent —the secretary of his Mission Board.

While Dr. Porter's report is the earliest which uses the name I-ho Chuan in approximately its accepted form, an earlier report of what must certainly have been the same organization came from the Jesuit mission in southeastern Chihli. In the journal of P. Remy Isoré, S. J., who was located at Tchao-kia-tchoang, the following entry appears under the date of October 25, 1898: "At six o'clock in the morning, I was informed of the uprising of the 'Ihono-kinen' (a hostile sect). These rebels have as their insignia a sort of turban and boots; their weapons are muskets or lances; their ensign, a yellow flag with a black border, carrying the motto, 'Obedience to the Tsing, Death to the Europeans'; their object, to provoke a general revolution at the beginning of the year; in the meantime, to recruit, to drill, and to conciliate the officials by attacking only the Christians."[3] Father Isoré was, like Dr. Porter, an old

[3] *Chine et Ceylan,* vol. I, p. 106.

resident in China, having arrived in the country in 1882, and his description of this hostile sect differs from that of his Protestant contemporary only in the ulterior motive which he ascribes to the organization. The form of the name, as it appears in the journal of the Jesuit Father, would suggest that it was unfamiliar to the writer and had been transcribed from the oral report of a badly frightened native adherent; although "kinen" is quite probably a typographical error, in the French magazine, for "kiuen" which is the accepted French romanization of the character meaning "Fist."

The term "Boxer," either alone or in various picturesque combinations, was used by the English-speaking missionaries in Shantung several months before they became acquainted with the name I-ho Chuan. It first appeared in the *North China Herald*, whose "outport news" was largely drawn from its missionary correspondents, on October 2, 1899, in an item dated "Tientsin, September 21st," and appeared again, the following week, in a letter from Linching, Shantung, which bore the same date as the Tientsin letter. The term was used much earlier, however, by the missionaries in their mission correspondence; Dr. Porter, in a letter to the secretary of the American Board, on January 13, 1899, identified the "Boxers" with the "Big Sword Society," "Ta Tao Hui," and proceeded to give the following description of the organization:

> The "Boxers" were the people so stirred up over the Roman Catholic troubles west of Linching. They broke out again in August, but were put to flight by the prefect of Feng Chang and a few soldiers. . . . This Society, something like the German Turners, add a kind of spiritism to their gymnastics. They suppose that their trainer is a medium. The fellows, mostly young men, practice under him and fancy themselves under the influence of a spirit. In this condition they pretend that nothing

can harm or injure them. They assume great bravado, and boast of great strength and skill. . . .

Subsequent correspondence of Dr. Porter and other members of the American Board mission contains frequent references to the "Boxers," the "Spirit Boxers," and the "Plum Boxing Society."

The name "Boxer" was thus in common use for some months before any reference was made to the term "I-ho Chuan," and seems originally to have been adopted as one which satisfactorily described the gymnastic activities of the organization. When, therefore, the Chinese name was later reported to the missionaries, they readily accepted "Chuan," or "Fist," as the third character in the name, and translated the whole as "Society of Harmonious Fists," the title by which the society has, from that time, been almost universally known.

"I-ho Chuan" was the name by which the society was designated in all the diplomatic correspondence at Peking, and even in the translations of the decrees which were eventually issued by the imperial government, but this is not the name which the organization had adopted. The "official," or correct, name for the organization was "I-ho Tuan," "Righteous and Harmonious Band," or "Militia"; the substitution of "Chuan" for "Tuan," as the third character in the name of the organization, was simply a pun which was perpetrated by its opponents.[4]

[4] The original name and its corruption are ably discussed in Couling's *Encyclopedia Sinica*, in an article by Evan Morgan. Dr. A. H. Smith, in the first volume of his *China in Convulsion*, also demonstrates that the organization was a "Tuan." In *The Diary of His Excellency Ching Shan*, see Duyvendak's reproduction of the text, "Tuan" is always used; the diarist speaks of "I Ho Tuan," "Shen Tuan," and "Tuan min." On the other hand, the Chinese history of the Boxer movement, the *Ch'uan fei chi lueh*, published in 1903, appears always to have used "Ch'uan"—so far as can be judged from Duyvendak's citations. The councillor of the Chi-

"I-ho Chuan" or "I-ho Tuan"

The "Tuan," or local militia, had long been a recognized feature in Chinese local administration. Dr. J. C. Ferguson, in an article on Wang An-shih—a radical premier during the Sung Dynasty, about the last quarter of the eleventh century—attributes the origin of the system to the militia organizations which were instituted as a feature of Wang's reforms. "The Boxer movement three years ago was founded upon the idea of a defensive militia, and in its organization used many of the terms which have been handed down from the time of Wang An-shih. This feature of his reform schemes has had more permanence than any other, and is to be praised for its low estimate of militarism."[5] These "Tuan," which were primarily for defense against bandits and armed robbers, were entirely voluntary but were recognized by the government as lawful bodies.[6]

On September 5, 1898, shortly before the close of the Reform Period, the Emperor Kwang Hsu issued a decree which, if it had been put into execution, would have re-

nese Legation at Washington informs me that "Ch'uan" was always used in the communications from the Tsungli Yamen. The British minister at Peking used "Chuan" in all his earlier dispatches to his government, although "Tuan" is used in translating the Imperial Proclamations of June 28, 1900—see *British Blue Books, China No. 6 (1901)*, inclosure in no. 16. The original of Yuan Shih-kai's "Ode"—see Appendix A—has not been available, but the translation would indicate that Yuan used "Ch'uan." In general, it would seem that "Tuan" was always used by those who sympathized with the movement, and "Ch'uan" by those who opposed it.

[5] *Journal of the Royal Asiatic Society, China Branch*, vol. XXXV (1903-1904), p. 73.

[6] A current events article in the *Prussische Jahrbücher* for July, 1900, vol. 101, p. 187, describes them as "Leute deren Geschäfte es bisher war, den Reisenden als Sicherheitswache zu dienen, und die nun durch die Eisenbahnen brotlos geworden sind." This unique explanation of the disturbances at that time going on evinces considerable understanding of the nature of the Tuan, but is open to the objection that railroads were not yet in operation in the regions where the I-ho Tuan first began to cause disturbance.

placed these militia bands by a National Army. It was the Emperor's intention that this army should eventually include, as active or reserve members, every able-bodied male subject of the Empire, drilled and trained along Western lines. The provincial authorities of Kwangtung and Kwangsi were ordered to take immediate steps for carrying out the scheme within their jurisdictions, to be followed in time by the other provinces. This ambitious project, which would probably have proved utterly unworkable, was abandoned after the *coup d'état*.

The Empress Dowager—who was more of a "realist" than Kwang Hsu and his youthful advisers, and who was anxious to adhere as closely as possible to tradition in working out her reforms—turned her attention to the utilization of the existing Tuan system. In her decrees of November 5 and December 31, 1898 (given in chapter VI), and of March 17, 1899 (to which reference has been made in chapter VII), she ordered that the local militia be strengthened and improved, and that they be instructed in the use of modern arms and in the drill and discipline of the regular army.

The Emperor had commanded the authorities of the Liang Kwang to make the first experiments in the application of his plan, but the Empress Dowager ordered that her decrees be first carried out in the provinces of Chihli, Shantung, Shansi, and Fengtien (Manchuria), to be followed by the other provinces if it proved successful in these four. The reason for this difference is quite easy to understand: the Reform Party, upon which the Emperor relied, was strongest in Kwangtung and Kwangsi, while Tzu Hsi distrusted the revolutionary temper of the south but had full confidence in the loyalty of the north. The immediate purpose of the Empress Dowager was probably to provide local forces for the maintenance of internal order, so as to make possible the concentration of the regular troops around Peking; but it is apparent, from the wording of the decrees, that she also hoped the reorganized Tuan might prove a valuable auxiliary to the regular forces in case it ever became necessary to resist a foreign invasion.[7]

The "Righteous and Harmonious Bands," as I-ho Tuan should properly be translated, were, therefore, perfectly legitimate and customary bodies for local defense, and were, after November 5, 1898, expressly authorized and encouraged by special decrees. Unfortunately this official encouragement of militarism led to undesirable results of a sort which were only too natural in China. It has already been noted that military forces in China are habitually recruited from the bandits, smugglers, and other disorderly elements of society, and, in the case of the I-ho Tuan, the tendency to absorb the desperado and the ne'er-do-well became early manifest. Moreover, since it was popularly understood that the bands were being officially encouraged in order that they might aid in resisting further foreign aggression, the militia soon received into their ranks the members of various unauthorized bodies which had already attracted attention by reason of their anti-foreign activities.

Of the unauthorized bodies which were assimilated into the I-ho Tuan, the most prominent was the "Ta Tao Hui," the "Society of the Big Knife" or "Big Sword." While the earliest references to the "Boxers" or "I-ho Chuan"—including the report of the "Ihonokinen"—were subsequent to the *coup d'état*, the "Ta Tao Hui" made its definite ap-

[7] On July 17, 1900, Mr. Ku Hung-ming, at that time secretary to Chang Chih-tung, in an interview with the British consul at Hankow, "confessed that Her Majesty had thought that the Boxers would constitute a species of 'landwehr' against invasion, but denied that at that time they had announced any hostility to foreigners and missions." See *British Blue Books, China No. 1 (1901)*, document no. 261.

pearance considerably earlier. Dr. Porter wrote from Pang-chuang, in May, 1898, that "within two years a Big Knife Society has been formed, whose concealed purpose is some form of rebellion. The Roman Catholic missionaries have had many contests with this sort of people." A few months later Mgr. Anzer, the bishop of Southern Shantung, wrote concerning the murder of Fathers Henle and Nies, which had taken place on November 1, 1897: "The mystery which has shrouded the circumstances of their glorious death begins to clear away; it has finally been discovered that the authors of this double crime are members of the Big Knife Society, and the same who, two years ago, organized the persecution in Kiangnan and Shensi."[8]

By April, 1900, Dr. Porter had modified his opinion, or had added to his information, concerning the Ta Tao Hui. In his annual report for Pang-chuang station for the year that had just closed, he gave a careful history of the rise of the Boxers and of the Big Sword Society; in this account he placed the first appearance of the Big Swords *after* the occupation of Kiaochow, and declared that the organization was a patriotic body which had been formed in consequence of this event and for the purpose of resisting further invasion.

A most valuable first-hand report of the early activities of the Big Sword is to be found in a letter by Père Gouveneur, S. J., written June 15, 1898, from Hien Hien, Chihli. "About the end of April," he writes, "a messenger reached us from Tai-ming-fu, coming from Père Wetterwald, who is stationed at Weitsun, 180 'li' to the north. During the night, a band of brigands had attacked one of the Christian villages a few 'li' from Weitsun. These fellows—who are very probably part of a sect formerly called the "Pa-lien-kiao," or Society of the White Lotus, and now desig-

[8] *Annales de l'Association de la propagation de la foi,* vol. 71, p. 206.

nated by the name of "Chi-pa-cheou," the "Eighteen Chiefs," or perhaps, also, the "Ta-tao-hui," the "Big Knives"—these fellows, I say, had come during the night. . . ."

While Père Gouveneur here describes the disturbers as probably a part of the White Lotus Society, the latter part of the same letter seems to disprove that conjecture, and also contains evidence that the disturbance was not primarily religious in its inception.

On the seventh day of the third moon (April 27, 1898) during the baccalaureate examinations which bring together in the prefectural city thousands of candidates, always very turbulent, a placard was posted at the four corners of Tai-ming-fu. Our people told us about it and we sent our catechists to take down the placard and bring it to the notice of the proper authorities. Behold the tenor of this bit of Chinese literature, which has at least the virtue of being quite clear (which is a rare quality in Chinese).

"Notice:—The patriots of all the provinces, seeing that the men of the West transgress all limits (literally, over-reach Heaven) in their behavior, have decided to assemble on the 15th day of the fourth moon and to kill the westerners and burn their houses. Those whose hearts are not in accord with us are scoundrels and women of bad character. Those who read this placard and fail to spread the news deserve the same characterization. Enough! No more words are needed."[9]

From this latter portion of Père Gouveneur's letter it is evident that the anti-foreign demonstrations at Tai-ming-fu, of which the attack near Weitsun was probably an incident, were not organized by the White Lotus or any other heretical sect. On the contrary, they were the work of the most orthodox element in society: the Confucian "literati," who were assembled at the prefectural city for

[9] *Chine et Ceylan*, vol. I, pp. 54-55.

the classical examinations. It is also to be observed that the placard which is quoted made no mention of religion, but announced the popular hatred toward the "men of the west" for their actions, which "transgress all limits." The native Christians are referred to only incidentally, in the characterization of those whose hearts are not in accord with the popular will.

To appreciate the motives for this anti-foreign bitterness at the end of April, 1898, it will be useful to recall the dates of a few events. On March 6 after four months of "negotiation," Germany had obtained the lease of Kiaochow. On March 28 Russia had secured, by similar methods, the lease of the Liao-tung peninsula. April 2 had seen the Tsungli Yamen give way to a British ultimatum, and agree to the lease of Weihaiwei as soon as that port should be evacuated by the Japanese. On April 5 the British minister had presented his request for an extension of the British holdings on Kowloon, and "negotiations" on this topic were still proceeding. On April 9 and 10 China had, by an exchange of notes, leased to France the Bay of Kwang-chow-wan which had been forcibly occupied by a French naval detachment.

Most, if not all, of these events were fairly well known to the educated classes in China, while the Emperor's decree of February 4, authorizing the flotation of a national loan, had been widely promulgated and was popularly understood to be an outcome of the Empire's international difficulties. In view of these aggressions, it is not necessary, or reasonable, to assume that the outbreaks were a manifestation of religious intolerance on the part of the Chinese. Aroused by the aggressions of the West, popular fury turned upon missionaries and mission establishments as the only present and tangible representatives of the powers that were threatening to destroy the Empire. Indeed, if foreign enterprise had been represented in China only by railways and moving picture houses, these institutions would, in all probability, have furnished equally satisfactory objects for patriotic destructiveness.

The carefully considered testimony given by Dr. Porter in the spring of 1900, and the evidence to be derived from Père Gouveneur's report, written nearly two years earlier, lead to the conclusion that the Ta Tao Hui, although it was—in many parts of the Empire—a "bandit" body, had, at least in Shantung and Chihli, neither religious nor revolutionary origins. But while the Ta Tao Hui enjoyed the favor of the local officials in a number of districts in these provinces—Yu Hsien, when he was a Taotai in Shantung, was reputed to have been an enthusiastic patron of the movement—it was not regarded as an authorized organization, and the designation "Hui" placed it technically in the category of "unlawful societies." Hence the growing importance and activity of the I-ho Tuan, which was a perfectly legal body, led the Big Knife members to seek admission to this organization in order to acquire for themselves a legal status which they could not otherwise possess. The older name "Ta Tao Hui" continued, however, to be used by foreign correspondents in parts of Shantung, especially in the southern part of the province where the Big Knife movement had developed its greatest force.

If Lao Nai-hsuan's statement, that the I-ho Chuan was a secret and heretical body affiliated with the White Lotus Sect, is to be rejected as contrary to the prevailing evidence, it becomes necessary to find some explanation for those aspects of the movement which later gave it all the appearance of a religious organization. The charms and incantations of the Boxers, their intricate ritual, their belief in certain supernatural powers which would render them invulnerable and invincible, the fact that some of the Boxer leaders were Buddhist priests, and that Buddhist temples were customary places for meeting and practicing their rites; all these are well attested, and give color to the theory that the movement—whatever its origin—had, by the spring of 1900, become religious in character. These facts, however, admit of an interpretation which does not conflict with what has already been proved concerning the nature of the I-ho Tuan; yet, in attempting an explanation on this point, it is necessary to depart, at times, from the firm ground of provable fact and to embark upon some rather daring conjectures.

Western writers on China have been practically unanimous[10] in pointing out that the religious tolerance of the Chinese is especially manifested in a wide eclecticism. Among the uneducated masses, this characteristic makes it possible for nominal Confucianism to exist side by side with many non-Confucian beliefs: Buddhism, Taoism, and the various local superstitions which have been absorbed by these two religions. Even among the educated and official classes, the behavioristic philosophy of the Sage is often supplemented by the spiritual teachings of Sakyamuni or by the lofty mysticism of Lao-tzu. Hence it was not incongruous for even a strict Confucianist to admit the possibility that there might be some virtue in the ritual and incantations of "Boxerism"; natural credulity in regard to the supernatural will go far toward explaining the credit which was given to the Boxer claims.

But if reliance upon miraculous formulae was a normal development in any organization whose members were largely uneducated, there were special reasons for the appearance of this tendency among the "Tuan." The decrees of the Empress Dowager, in which she urged the develop-

10 With the exception of Professor de Groot.

ment and improvement of the local militia, had repeatedly ordered that these volunteer bodies be given modern armament and drill. Since the arsenals of the Empire could hardly produce modern weapons in sufficient quantities to supply the needs of the regular imperial and provincial troops, no modern weapons were, for the time at least, available for the militia organizations, which continued to be armed with swords, spears, and a few firearms of the most primitive sort. But, although it was impossible to furnish the Tuan with Mauser rifles, it was necessary to comply with the commands of the Throne; this could be achieved by drilling the militia according to the manual adopted for the modern armed troops. Squad and company drill, the "goose-step," and the "setting-up exercises," which had been introduced into the training of the Peiyang Army by the German and Japanese military instructors, were, therefore, taught to the Tuan and were diligently practiced by them as a means whereby the defenders of the Empire might become equal in prowess to the forces of the "outside Barbarians." It requires little exercise of the imagination to visualize the metamorphosis by which these physical exercises became, in the mind of the Chinese peasant, magic rites which would confer supernatural strength and invulnerability upon all who religiously performed them.

A considerable part of the Boxer spiritism may, however, be traced, directly or indirectly, to the influence of Christianity. One needs only to read the letters of the devout missionary workers to realize their abiding faith in the constant presence of spiritual forces. The progress of the Kingdom was to them, in a very real sense, a struggle between the true God and the forces of darkness. Cases of demoniacal possession, successfully cured, were reported by Protestant and Catholic missionaries alike, while the latter patiently expected—and occasionally recorded—miracles of a more imposing nature. A belief that there were supernatural powers at the command of the foreigners was also widely held by the Chinese, pagan as well as Christian. Since the foreign invaders, against whom the Tuan might be compelled to fight, were thus popularly supposed to be aided and protected by alien gods, it was to be expected that every effort should be made to mobilize the local deities for service in the patriotic task of defending the fatherland.

There is, indeed, some reason to believe that the Boxers even went so far as to draw upon Christian sources for the phraseology used in their charms and incantations; this would, at least, seem to be indicated by the following placard which appeared in Peking about the end of April, 1900:

In a certain street in Peking some worshippers of the I-ho Chuan at midnight suddenly saw a spirit descend in their midst. The spirit was silent for a long time, and all the congregation fell upon their knees and prayed. Then a terrible voice was heard saying:—

"I am none other than the Great Yu Ti (God of the unseen world) come down in person. Well knowing that ye are all of devout mind, I have just now decided to make known to you that these are times of trouble in the world, and that it is impossible to set aside the decrees of fate. Disturbances are to be dreaded from the foreign devils; everywhere they are starting missions, erecting telegraphs, and building railways; they do not believe in the sacred doctrine, and they speak evil of the Gods. Their sins are numberless as the hairs of the head. Therefore am I wroth and my thunders have pealed forth. By night and day have I thought of these things. Should I command my Generals to come down to earth, even they would not have strength to change the course of fate. For this reason I have given forth my decree that I shall descend to earth at the head of all the saints and spirits, and that wherever the I-ho Chuan are gathered together, there shall the Gods be in the midst of them. I have also to make known to all the righteous in the three worlds that they must be of one mind, and all practice the cult of the I-ho Chuan that so the wrath of heaven may be appeased.

"So soon as the practice of the I-ho Chuan has been brought to perfection—wait for three times three or nine times nine, nine times nine or three times three—then shall the devils meet their doom. The will of heaven is that the telegraph wires be first cut, then the railways torn up, and then shall the foreign devils be decapitated. In that day shall the hour of their calamities come. The time for rain to fall is yet afar off, and all on account of the devils.

"I hereby make known these commands to all you righteous folk, that ye may strive with one accord to exterminate all foreign devils, and so turn aside the wrath of heaven. This shall be accounted unto you for well doing; and on the day when it is done, the wind and the rain shall be according to your desire.

"Therefore I expressly command you to make this known in every place."

This I saw with my own eyes, and therefore I make bold to take my pen and write what happened. They who believe it shall have merit; they who do not believe it shall have guilt. The wrath of the spirit was because of the destruction of the Temple of Yu Ti. He sees that the men of the I-ho Chuan are devout worshippers and pray to him.

If my tidings are false, may I be destroyed by the five thunderbolts.[11]

It is, of course, quite probable that the translator, in his efforts to give a suitable rendition to this interesting bit of literature, resorted unconsciously to the sonorous phrases of the Old Testament and the Apocalypse. Yet there must have been, in the original of the document, considerable resemblance to the language in which those portions of the

[11] *British Blue Books, China No. 3 (1900)*, inclosure in document no. 273.

Bible had been translated into Chinese. In view of the important part which "street preaching" and the distribution of tracts played in the missionary efforts to spread the Gospel, the language of Christianity was, and is, familiar to thousands of non-Christian Chinese; therefore, it is more reasonable to attribute the resemblance to plagiarism than to explain it away as a mere coincidence.

The traditional account of the origins of the I-ho Chuan, either as it was given by Lao Nai-hsuan or as it has been modified by subsequent writers, must be rejected. The so-called Boxers were a Tuan, or volunteer militia; they were recruited, in response to the express commands of the Throne, in precisely those provinces whose loyalty was most to be trusted; in the rebelliously inclined provinces of the Yangtze Valley and the south, the movement was never allowed to spread. The single indirect reference, in an imperial decree, to the suppression of secret societies in the reign of Chia Ching, is far outweighed by repeated statements which are to be found in other decrees, that the volunteer bands were lawful bodies which must only take care that no unworthy members should be allowed to bring them into disrepute. Even the Ta Tao Hui, although it was cursed with a name which rendered it an object of suspicion, was organized for resistance to foreign invasion and had, for this reason, the approval of many of the local officials. Whatever the Boxer movement may have become—or may have threatened to become—by the spring of 1900, it was, in the beginning, neither a revolutionary nor an heretical organization; it was a lawful and loyal volunteer militia, whose existence was fully justified by the reasonable apprehensions of the government and the people.

CHAPTER VIII.

The Boxers in Shantung and Chihli.

Reasons for Early Development in these Provinces—Governor Yu Hsien in Shantung—Yu Hsien Replaced by Yuan Shi-kai —The "Yuan Shih-kai Myth"—Yuan's Treatment of the Situation—Decline of the Excitement in Shantung—The Brooks Murder—Spread of the Boxers in Chihli—Economic Factors—Exaggeration in Current Reports—Local Autonomy and Foreign Interference.

THE Empress Dowager's decree of November 5, 1898, ordering the reorganization and improvement of the local militia, had named Chihli, Shantung, Shansi, and Fengtien (southern Manchuria) as the provinces in which this policy should be immediately carried out. This first decree was, as has been seen, supplemented by a later decree in December and by one in March, 1899, when the Italian demands concerning Sanmen Bay seemed likely to result in hostilities between China and Italy. Of these four provinces, the most ready response to the imperial commands was found in Shantung and in the southern and eastern portions of Chihli; although the spread of the Boxer movement in Shansi and Manchuria, during the summer of 1900, would indicate that some steps toward organizing the militia had also been taken in those provinces. It was in the extreme southeastern portion of Chihli and in the adjacent districts of Shantung that the "Tuan" organizations first adopted the title "I-ho Tuan," a name which, in its corrupted form of "I-ho Chuan,"—commonly translated "Boxers,"—was later to become so notorious.

The greater activity of the militia movement in Shantung and in southeastern Chihli is not difficult to understand. These were the regions which had been most vitally affected by the seizures of "leased" territories during the winter of 1897 and the spring and summer of 1898. These were the regions from which the modern-armed regular soldiers had been withdrawn for the purpose of concentrating them around Peking in anticipation of further aggressive moves on the part of the Europeans. These were the regions in which recruiting for the newly formed bodies of imperial troops was most actively carried on, and into which news of the apprehensions and military preparations at Peking spread with greatest rapidity.

The name I-ho Chuan—or "Ihonokinen," to use the spelling which appeared in the publication of Père Isoré's diary—was first reported from the Jesuit diocese of southeastern Chihli, yet the organization had its most rapid growth in Shantung. The seizure of Kiaochow by the Germans, and the occupation of Weihaiwei, first by the Japanese and subsequently by the British, had, as early as the spring of 1898, resulted in the spontaneous formation of unauthorized bands for local resistance to further foreign aggression—notably the bands of the "Ta Tao Hui." After the *coup d'état* and the decrees relating to the militia system, these unauthorized groups had been absorbed into the "Righteous and Harmonious Militia," whose name and ritualistic gymnastic exercises made a strong appeal to the popular imagination.

The I-ho Chuan activities in Shantung became especially pronounced after March 14, 1899, when Yu Hsien replaced Chang Ju-mei as governor of the province. Chang, who had succeeded Li Ping-heng when that able officer had been dismissed in compliance with the demands of the German minister, appears to have been a complete nonentity, although his removal from office at this juncture was nominally for the purpose of investigation into charges which had been lodged against him in connection with his official conduct at an earlier post. Yu Hsien, on the other hand, was an official of decided ability, and his rapid advancement in office, during the preceding year, had been due to his recognized ability as much as to the fact that he was a Manchu. Yu Hsien was bitterly anti-foreign in his sentiments, yet this can hardly be considered a distinguishing trait at that particular period. Nor can the appointment of an officer who was known to hold such sentiments be imputed to the Empress Dowager as a crime, when it is remembered that war against an outside aggressor was believed to be imminent.

Apart from the general apprehension as to an impending foreign invasion, the spread of the I-ho Chuan and its subsequent activities, in Shantung as well as in Chihli, had important economic causes. The decrees in which Tzu Hsi had ordered the reorganization of the militia system had always coupled this step with the establishment of "reserve granaries." These granaries were intended to serve the dual purpose of safeguarding the local areas against possible famine conditions and of providing sustenance for the militia. As is often the case with government action in China—and elsewhere, this wise precaution had not been ordered until disaster was in sight. A flood of the Yellow River, which had devastated southeastern Chihli and that portion of Shantung extending west of the Grand Canal, had been followed by a severe drought affecting all the northern provinces of China. As a result of flood and drought, and especially in those areas which had suffered from the double calamity, there was an unusually large number of desperate men among whom the militia bands could find recruits, while the inability of the officials to accumulate reserve supplies of grain made these bands dependent, for their support, upon the more or less voluntary contributions of the well-to-do.

The Peking government was not long in discovering the dangers of the situation, as is shown by the following decree, which appeared in the *Peking Gazette* on July 13, 1899:

> We have received a memorial from Yu Hsien, Governor of Shantung, in which he charges two unworthy members of the gentry of that province with grave misdemeanors. It appears that these two notables, namely, Tsang Chi-chen and Tsang Yu-chen, recently organised, on their own responsibility, a corps of volunteers in their native district of Chuchenghsien without first asking for the necessary official sanction, and then taking advantage of the large number of volunteers under them they began to extort from the inhabitants of the district subscriptions of money and contributions of rice and fodder on the pretence that they were needed for the organization of the corps which they had raised to defend their district from outside invaders, etc. To such an extent did the audacity of these self-authorized volunteers proceed that they even defied the local authorities who tried to remonstrate against their illegal actions, brow-beating the authorities and compelling them to give grain from the reserve granaries for the support of the said volunteers. Now such conduct is decidedly reprehensible, especially as it is stated that the whole district in question has become panic-stricken and disturbed through the action of these two notables. We hereby command that the accused gentry be forthwith cashiered of whatever official rank they possess and that they be placed under the strict surveillance of the local authorities of their native city in the future.[1]

While the forced requisitions of the militia—of which the activities of the Tsang brothers were an example—fell

[1] This decree is taken from the *North China Herald* of January 24, 1900, vol. 64, p. 152. Chuchenghsien is southwest of Tsingtao, and just outside the limits of the neutral zone which was provided for in the Kiaochow lease.

upon all the well-to-do in the affected regions, the Chinese Christians seemed, in some localities, to be especially marked out for these unwelcome attentions. These levies upon the Christians in the early days of the movement had much to do with the general belief that the Boxer movement was primarily religious, or rather anti-Christian, but such an interpretation is unwarranted. Not only did the missionaries of all the districts agree in their reports that the wealthy heathen, in order to avoid paying tribute, were leaving those places where the Boxers were especially active; there were also reasons, which had little or no religious significance, which will explain any particular tendency which may have existed to levy upon the Christians. In the first place, the converts were often disliked in their communities because of the fact that foreign influence had been exerted on their behalf in disputes which had come before the local courts; and even where this was not the case, the fact that the converts had, to a certain extent, withdrawn themselves from the life of the community made it probable that the community would not rally to defend them against the extortions of the Boxers. Indeed, it may be presumed that, in the eyes of their fellow townsmen, there was not a little grim humor and poetic justice in compelling the pro-foreign element to support the patriotic bands by which the fatherland was to be defended against foreign avarice. If there was any religious motive in the Boxer attacks upon missionary work, this must be found in the belief that the presence of the foreign spirits had disturbed the local "feng-shui" and so had caused the flood, drought, and famine from which they were now suffering.

In general, the attitude of the I-ho Chuan toward Christianity was dictated by the desire to force the withdrawal of the missionary from the country, not for religious reasons but because he was a foreigner. The stations where the foreign missionaries were in residence early requested, and received, armed guards of provincial troops which insured the missionary against any personal violence and left him exposed only to verbal expressions of popular hostility. Efforts to get rid of the missionaries were thus confined to such activities as would eventually discourage them and force their voluntary retirement. Threats, impositions, and petty persecutions, directed against the native Christians, were expected to result in such widespread apostasy as would convince the objectionable foreigner that his further residence in the country would be fruitless. This program was not the outcome of religious motives. The native Christians were subjected to attack only because of their connection with the foreign missionary, and the foreign missionary was regarded with hostility only in those regions where popular fears had been aroused by the aggressive acts of the European governments.

In formulating their policy with regard to Christianity, the Boxers had failed to take into account the devotion of the native converts or the resolution of the foreigners. A few of the Christian families, where they were isolated from their co-religionists, did abjure their faith and return to heathendom; even under these conditions, however, by far the greater proportion endured threats and persecution with a patient devotion which calls for our sincerest admiration. Where the Christians dwelt in compact groups, and especially where they had the leadership and inspiration of a "foreign teacher," they promptly organized for resistance; thus, in those districts where the activities of the I-ho Chuan came into conflict with well-established missionary work—either Catholic or Protestant, there soon developed a state of actual or potential civil war. "The villages of Kan-fen and those immediately adjoining were in great terror," wrote Dr. Porter, describing the events of

September, 1899. "Most of the Christians hid their goods and fled into the fields. We went at once into camp, unfurled the American flag, gathered a strong force of Christians about us as guards, borrowed native guns, purchased powder in a considerable quantity, and prepared for any emergency that might suddenly come upon us."[2]

About the middle of November, 1899, the plundering and pillaging, which had seemed—during the late summer months—to be subsiding, broke out again with renewed intensity, especially in the districts that lay west of the Grand Canal. This fresh outbreak appears to have been precipitated, or at least intensified, by a clash which occurred between the I-ho Chuan and the provincial troops, and by the subsequent action of Governor Yu Hsien. The clash had amounted to something approaching a pitched battle between the troops and the "Patriots," in which nearly a hundred of the latter had been killed. In response to complaints which were immediately advanced by the Boxer leaders, the governor, on the ground that a number of innocent lives had been lost in the affray, which had been brought on by the bad judgment and hasty actions of the responsible officers, degraded the officers commanding the troops.

The battle and its consequences had an irritating effect upon all parties concerned. The Boxers, finding in the governor's action complete justification of their legal status, were stirred to even greater hostility toward the missionaries and the native Christians, whose complaints to the authorities were considered responsible for the intervention of the troops and for the losses which had been sustained by the militia. On the other hand, the missionaries,

[2] Report of Pang-chuang Station, for the year ending April 30, 1900. *A.B.C.F.M. Reports, North China Mission*, 1890-1900, vol. III, report no. 33.

who persisted in regarding the Boxer movement as a rebellion, could find but one satisfactory explanation for Yu Hsien's conduct in the affair: it could only mean that he was so bitterly anti-foreign as to be willing to pardon rebels and secret society men in order that they might be encouraged to continue the work of breaking up mission stations and driving out the missionaries. To the foreigner in China—missionary, merchant, or diplomat—the only proper way of dealing with the disturbances was by the plentiful use of armed force and by the exemplary punishment of all who were implicated in the disorders.

The position of Yu Hsien was extremely difficult, and, inasmuch as his treatment of the case had been in accordance with Chinese law and practice, he resented the criticisms of the missionaries and the attacks directed at him by the diplomats at Peking. It is undoubtedly true that he was anti-foreign and that he fully approved the Tuan organizations; yet he had supplied guards for those places where foreigners were in residence and had taken all proper precautions to protect the missionaries against any unfortunate occurrence. If the "Patriotic Militia" had troubled the native Christians, this was due to the fact that the converts were disliked by the other members of their communities; moreover, it was even alleged that the Christians had themselves been guilty of attacking the I-ho Chuan, without provocation, on occasions when they had found themselves strong enough to do so. The Tuan were perfectly lawful bodies, which had been explicitly authorized by repeated imperial decrees; they were not rebels, and had, as yet, been guilty of nothing more serious than disorderly conduct. The governor was responsible for the lives of all the people within his jurisdiction, heathen as well as Christian, and the military authorities had been seriously at fault in permitting an "affray" which had caused the death of nearly a hundred "law-abiding subjects" against whom no crime worthy of death had even been charged.

In spite of the legal correctness of Yu Hsien's treatment of this affair, the imperial government soon decided that it would be unwise to retain him at his post. The diplomatic pressure at Peking had not yet reached the point of a formal demand for his dismissal, but it was apparent that such a demand would not long be delayed. To avoid the necessity of choosing between compliance and resistance in such an event, Yu Hsien was, on December 7, summoned to Peking "for an audience," and Yuan Shih-kai, formerly Chinese resident in Korea and now the commander of the most modern corps of the Peiyang Army, was ordered to Shantung as acting governor.

The appointment of Yuan Shih-kai to take the place of Yu Hsien was heartily approved by the missionaries in Shantung, as well as by the foreign communities at Peking and at the treaty ports. Yu Hsien was a Manchu; Yuan Shih-kai was Chinese. Yu Hsien was known to be reactionary and bitterly anti-foreign; Yuan Shih-kai was believed to be progressive and to have an intelligent appreciation of the advantages which China might derive from the introduction of Western ideas and methods. Yu Hsien was a civil official whose troops had consisted of a few "tatterdemalions" armed with obsolete weapons; Yuan Shih-kai was a military officer and had at his disposal a powerful body of modern-armed soldiers against whom the Boxers could offer but a feeble resistance. It was, therefore, confidently expected that this change in the provincial government of Shantung foreshadowed a campaign of extermination against the forces of disorder.

These cheerful expectations were far from being realized, and the Shantung correspondents of the treaty port newspapers soon began to voice their growing disappointment at the failure of the new governor to deal with the Boxers in accordance with the plans which his critics had drawn up for him. After the collapse of the Boxer movement, certain writers created what may be called the "Yuan Shih-kai Myth"; according to this fabulous account, Yuan handled the situation with ruthless severity and speedily swept the Boxer hordes out of his territory into the adjoining province of Chihli. But no sign of any such activity is to be found in the reports from Shantung which appeared in the columns of the *North China Herald* during the first six months of Yuan's tenure of office; on the contrary, these contemporary records are filled with complaints as to the new governor's "criminal inaction."

As weeks, and then months, passed without producing any of the expected battles between Yuan's troops and the Boxer bands, foreign dissatisfaction at the lack of "strong measures" found expression in attributing to Peking the blame which hitherto had been laid at the door of Yu Hsien. Criticism of the Empress Dowager became especially pointed when the ex-governor, after having received a distinguished mark of the imperial favor, was transferred to the neighboring province of Shansi. In the meantime, Yuan Shih-kai was calming the turmoil in Shantung by methods which were entirely different from those that the foreigners had expected him to use, but which were in complete harmony with Chinese conceptions of good government.

Yuan Shih-kai, since he was primarily a military officer and knew something of the facts of modern warfare, did not share his predecessor's belief in the efficacy of the Tuan as an auxiliary force in the event of a foreign war; he had, therefore, little or no sympathy with the movement. Although he had not arrived at his official rank by the customary literary route, he was sufficiently well educated and enough of an orthodox Confucianist to be sceptical with regard to the supernatural claims which the Boxers were now making. He realized, moreover, that the activities of the Boxers, since they threatened to involve China in a conflict with the foreign powers, were a possible source of incalculable dangers for the Empire. Yet he recognized that the situation must be handled with a due regard for existing law, and that any attempt to break up the Tuan organizations by force would merely result in adding fresh fuel to the conflagration. For this reason, Yuan's policy toward the rioters was marked by no greater display of severity than had been showed by Yu Hsien. In view of the success which attended his efforts to restore peace and order in Shantung, especially when compared with contemporary developments in Chihli, the methods by which Yuan dealt with the situation demand some attention.

A threefold problem confronted the new governor at the moment when he assumed the reins of administration. He must, first of all, see to it that no harm should befall the foreigners within his jurisdiction, in order that no pretext might be given for diplomatic demands or for military moves on the part of any foreign government. Almost equally important was the need for quieting the conflict which, in parts of the province, was involving the Boxers and the native Christians. Finally, if permanent peace was to be established, it was necessary to calm the Boxer madness and to restore the Tuan to their customary status of simple country militia, which would confine their energies to protecting their communities against local disorder and leave the management of foreign affairs to the duly constituted authorities.

For the all-important purpose of protecting foreign lives and property, Yuan continued Yu Hsien's policy of supplying soldiers to guard the missionary establishments where foreign missionaries were residing. But the troops which were so employed made no efforts to break up the I-ho Chuan camps or to interfere with their assemblies and drills. As a further protection to the missionaries, and to prevent any possible repetition of the unfortunate Brooks murder, which had occurred almost as soon as Yuan had established himself in the governor's Yamen, instructions were issued that the missionaries were not to come and go as they pleased, but only when it was absolutely necessary to travel on important matters; where travel was absolutely necessary, they would, upon application to the nearest local official, be provided with a competent military escort. This regulation, being obviously justified by the disturbed conditions in the province, received the approval of the ministers at Peking and of the local consular officers; yet many of the missionaries complained that it showed the intention of the Chinese government to utilize the disorders as a means of checking the progress of Christianity. They claimed that, if the governor would only take the proper steps for breaking up the camps and drills of the Boxers, it would not be necessary to restrict in this troublesome manner their tours of preaching and visitation.

In the same document with the regulations concerning missionary travel, the governor had included a provision that the missionaries should report the number of their native converts, with names and places of residence, in order that the local officials might be able to afford them the necessary protection. This arrangement also received diplomatic and consular approval, yet many of the missionaries in charge of stations flatly refused to furnish the required information which, they said, would merely be utilized by the authorities for the purpose of intimidating their converts. Except for this attempt to secure the registration of native Christians, Yuan made little effort to interfere in the troubles between the converts and the Boxers. These troubles were, after all, merely symptoms of the general unrest, and they would disappear as soon as the fears of the common people and the activities of the Boxers began to quiet down.

The positive measures which were employed by Yuan Shih-kai for calming the Boxer disturbances took the form—in foreign eyes criminally insufficient—of an appeal to reason and right ideas. The brochure of Lao Naihsuan, in which the I-ho Chuan was identified with the "White Lotus" and other similar heretical sects, was officially printed and widely circulated as a warning to the people not to join the disturbing element. The most characteristic part of Yuan's campaign against the Boxers can, however, best be described in his own words. In March, 1900, he reported to the Tsungli Yamen, as follows:

> On the 22nd February, I had the honor to receive the Imperial Edict severely denouncing the Society of the "Fist of Righteous Harmony." With reference to this, I have to report that in the month of January last, after my arrival at my post, I had already issued a Proclamation vigorously denouncing Boxer Societies, and published it throughout my jurisdiction. In obedience to the Imperial commands now received, I have, as in duty bound, again issued a trenchant proclamation, and have expressly composed an ode, in verses of five characters, to be posted from village to village. I have also commanded the local authorities to lead the way in this matter with the gentry, elders, and headmen of the towns and villages, and on all market days to expound the ode carefully and truly.

The proclamation, to which Yuan here refers, was couched in the same terms as his report to the Tsungli Yamen, with these additional remarks concerning the ode:

In addition to this, a copy can be issued to every school and college, large or small, and the students directed to chant the ode from time to time. In this way the ode will be published throughout every village community, and even the women and children will know it. The natural disposition of men for good will thus assert itself, and all will be clearly made to understand that they cannot believe in or follow after perverse Societies, and that the Imperial Decree cannot be disobeyed.

It is my most earnest hope that those who are already members of the Societies will tremble for the consequences, and those who are not members take warning from the fate of those in front of you; that both may strive to follow righteousness, and that joy and prosperity may be your reward.[3]

Such were the methods upon which this redoubtable military officer placed his chief reliance; such was the language in which this representative of an Oriental despotism addressed "brigands" and "rebels" in the effort to bring them to a realization of their duty! And it worked! The Boxer movement was practically "reasoned out of existence" in the province of Shantung. By the middle of March, 1900, order had been so far restored, even in the flood-affected district west of the Canal, that the ladies of the Pang-chuang mission—who had withdrawn, in November, to the less exposed station at Lin-ching—were able to return to their regular work. In May, when a clash occurred between the Tuan and the British authorities at Weihaiwei in connection with the delimitation of the leased area, the British reports stated that there was no vestige of

[3] This report from Yuan is found in *British Blue Books, China No. 3 (1900)*, document no. 106, inclosure; also in *Foreign Relations of the United States*, 1900, pp. 114-115. The words of the ode, although they were transmitted by the Yamen to the British and American ministers, are not reproduced in either of these publications; a translation, drawn from the unpublished documents of the State Department, is given in the Appendix. See Appendix A.

the Boxer spirit among the militia. The Tuan continued to exist, but the Boxer fever gradually died out, so, when the storm broke in June, Yuan was able to prevent the movement in Chihli from spreading to his own province.

There is, indeed, much evidence that the whole matter of the Boxer movement in Shantung, during the winter of 1899-1900, was the subject of a good deal of exaggeration, and that this exaggeration has subsequently been accepted at its face value because of the events which occurred during the following summer. On December 2 the American missionaries at Pang-chuang telegraphed to Minister Conger: "Pillage, arson, *murder*,[4] constantly increasing. Unless four legations unite to demand an immediate cessation of all this terrible condition of things, the Americans in Pang Chuang, Lin Ching, and Chi-nan-fu, consider the situation hopeless." Yet Dr. Porter, in the annual report from Pang-chuang Station for the year ending April 30, 1900, wrote: "*No life has been sacrificed*,[5] though there have been frequent threats of the direst character. The death of poor Mr. Brooks[6] was in a certain sense an accident, not fully premeditated." The report of the same date from the neighboring station of Lin-ching says: "The Christians in seven counties were threatened, some looted, others blackmailed, while still others escaped, but only after passing many sleepless nights. . . . About one-third of the Christians suffered loss. The total amount of this was over $430, a small amount except where the poverty of the people is taken into account. *There was little personal violence*.[7] A Christian living at Ching Ping had a

[4] Author's italics.

[5] Author's italics.

[6] Which did not occur until four weeks after the above quoted telegram was sent to Mr. Conger.

[7] Author's italics.

son and a brother-in-law captured by the Boxers, the latter cut off an ear from each captive. . . ."[8]

Allusion has already been made to the unfortunate death of Mr. S. M. Brooks, a young English clergyman belonging to the S. P. G. mission. Mr. Brooks, who was murdered on December 30, 1899, was the only foreigner to lose his life at the hands of the Boxers in Shantung during the entire course of the movement; he was also the only foreigner killed by the Boxers, prior to May 31, 1900, in any part of China.

This crime was, as Dr. Porter stated in his report, to a certain extent accidental. A careful account of the facts of the case, as those facts were brought out at the trial of the murderers, was written by the Rev. Samuel Couling, who attended the trial as secretary to the British consul.[9] According to Mr. Couling's account, the capture and the subsequent murder of Mr. Brooks were the work of a band of six men, three of whom took part in the capture but lost all interest in the proceedings and left the band before the final tragedy. The leader in the affair was bitter against all foreigners because his brother and other members of his family had lost their lives in the recent conflict between the I-ho Chuan and the provincial troops. After Mr. Brooks had been taken prisoner, the band wandered around with their captive for several hours, without having any clear idea as to what they would do next. Finally, at Mr. Brooks's suggestion, they started for a neighboring village, where some native Christians could be found who would be able to ransom him. On the way to this place, the captive slipped his bonds and tried to escape, but was overtaken and cut down in the excitement of the chase.

[8] These two reports are taken from the *A.B.C.F.M. Reports, North China Mission*, 1890-1900, reports nos. 33 and 32.

[9] See the *North China Herald* for March 31, 1900, vol. 64, p. 524.

The actions of the provincial authorities in dealing with the affair were prompt and correct. Yuan, who had only recently taken over the seals of office as governor, dispatched a force to rescue the unfortunate man as soon as the first news of his capture was received, although this was too late to be of any avail. The guilty men were soon hunted down and brought to justice, and a British consul attended the trial in order to see that suitable punishments were inflicted. As a result of the trial, which was completed within three months after the crime was committed, two members of the band were condemned to death, one to life imprisonment, one to banishment for ten years, and one to banishment for two years; the sixth member died in prison before the trial was ended. Four village headmen, within whose jurisdictions various phases of the crime had been enacted, were sentenced to be flogged and dismissed from office forever. The erection of a memorial tablet, costing 500 taels, was ordered, and an indemnity amounting to 9,000 taels was paid. Yet even this rather imposing list of penalties was not fully satisfactory to the British minister, who complained that the headmen of two adjoining villages—within whose limits the band and their captive had not ventured—should have been included in the punishment.

As has been seen, the I-ho Chuan appeared in the province of Chihli at least as soon as in Shantung; indeed, the reference to the "Ihonokinen" in southeastern Chihli considerably antedates any known mention of the Boxers or of the I-ho Chuan in Shantung. As in Shantung, the part of Chihli in which the movement first made itself felt was the section which had been affected by the Yellow River floods; from this region it gradually spread into other parts of the province. But while the earliest manifestations of antiforeignism among the Boxers of Chihli can be traced to foreign aggression in the past and the fear of further aggression in the future, the movement here soon found fresh fuel in the discontent which was caused by the introduction of certain foreign innovations—steam navigation, the railroad, and the telegraph. Thus, during the first four months of 1900, while the excitement in Shantung was gradually subsiding, in Chihli it continued to increase.

The introduction of the railroad was a source of irritation in several ways. In the first place, it threatened the livelihood of the carters and boatmen, who had hitherto found steady employment in the carrying trade. The carters were, for the time, well compensated by the demand for labor in constructing the railways, but the boating population, always a very turbulent element, had already been hard hit by the opening of the Peking-Tientsin line and of the Peking-Paotingfu section of the line which was eventually to connect Peking with Hankow. The building of these lines had also aroused a good deal of discontent among the agricultural population, who sometimes saw their best fields preëmpted for the railroad right-of-way, and who, among other things, feared that the railroad embankments would prevent the storm waters from flowing off during the heavy rains and so cause floods. Finally, the railroads were regarded with a general superstitious fear, differing only in degree from the fears which had been awakened by the first introduction of railways in Europe and America.

The antagonism aroused by the introduction of steam navigation was purely economic in character, and was particularly strong among the boat people. These were especially affected by the development of the coastwise steamship lines, which now transported from the south the "tribute rice"—formerly brought to Peking via the Grand Canal. But, if the decay of the Grand Canal traffic was primarily a blow to the boatmen, it had hardly less serious consequences for the towns and villages along the route, whose prosperity had been to a considerable extent dependent upon the patronage of this element in society. The discontent was more or less general along the entire length of this ancient artery of trade and reached an especially high pitch at the larger cities which, having been centers for the "junk trade," now saw this important industry dead or dying.

The opposition to telegraph lines was purely superstitious, and would, in all probability, never have had any real importance if the northern provinces had not been suffering from a severe drought. The Chinese commonly attribute favorable or unfavorable atmospheric conditions to the harmonious or discordant state of the "feng-shui"—spirits of air and water; any unusual construction, particularly if it extends above the level of the surrounding buildings, is regarded with disfavor since it is believed that this will be resented by the spirits as an invasion of their domains, and will result in some natural calamity. This widely held superstition has been the cause of frequent disturbances in places where foreigners have erected two or three storied houses, or churches with lofty spires, especially when the erection of these buildings has coincided with any local disaster. Thus the people of Chihli quickly began to attribute the long continued drought to the lines of telegraph poles and their connecting wires, which, they claimed, had disturbed the favorable "feng-shui" of their region.

These economic causes for unrest, which were partly responsible for the continuance and spread of the Boxer agitation in Chihli at a time when it was subsiding in Shantung, tended to concentrate the activity of the disturbers along the main waterways and the railways, and especially at the three important cities of Paotingfu, Tientsin, and Tungchow.

Outside of the region around Taimingfu, in the southeastern part of the province, the first alarming reports of Boxer activities in Chihli came from the neighborhood of Paotingfu. This important city, situated about a hundred miles south-southwest from Peking, had formerly been the provincial capital of Chihli, and now shared that honor with the more rapidly growing commercial city of Tientsin, to which the Viceroy's Yamen had been transferred after the "Tientsin Massacre" in 1870. Paotingfu was a headquarters station for much of the mission work in the southern part of the province. It must also be noted that it had a large boating population, and had recently been connected with Peking and Tientsin by rail, through the opening of traffic on the completed section of the Peking-Hankow line. Construction work on the next section of the railroad was being actively pushed, and, if we may judge from reports concerning the character and behavior of their colleagues at the Hankow end of the line, the European construction engineers made little effort to endear themselves to the native population.

Although the more important elements in the anti-foreignism of the "Patriotic Bands" were entirely unrelated to religious questions, this hostility most readily found expression at the expense of the native Christians. In December, 1899, the Boxers were reported to be threatening a Protestant mission station about seventy-five miles from Paotingfu, as well as another station fifteen miles nearer the city. A few days later, the chapel at the first of these stations, which were both under the charge of native pastors, was reported to have been completely ruined. In January it was announced that a large camp of the I-ho Chuan had been established within twenty miles of Paotingfu, and, from that time, the record of the society's operations in this neighborhood closely resembles the earlier records from Shantung. They organized, armed, and carried on their spiritistic drill; they demanded contributions from the officials for the support of their "patriotic" organization; they made threats against the native Christians, and were frequently reported as on the verge of destroying certain Christian villages; but the actual annihilating attack was always mysteriously deferred.

Tientsin, the seaport of Peking and the center of foreign trade for north China, was another fruitful source of news concerning the I-ho Chuan activities in Chihli. The items of news from this point were marked by a wide divergence in tone, and ranged from extreme alarm to utter contempt for the disturbers. In December, at the request of the British community at the port, Sir Claude MacDonald communicated with the British naval authorities, and obtained for Tientsin "the usual marine guard" for the winter months. Despite the presence of this guard, a dispatch from Tientsin, which appeared in the Hongkong *Telegraph* on March 5, described the state of affairs as critical, and reported "apprehension of impending danger among the foreign community." A Reuter's telegram from Tientsin, on March 27, also stated that the Boxers were giving much trouble around that port. On the other hand, the Tientsin correspondent of the *North China Herald* wrote, on March 17, in the most unalarming tone regarding the "droll drill of the Boxers" and of their long ceremony of initiation, with its "flummery and rigmarole"; and the same correspondent, twelve days later, was unable to report any actual Boxer disturbances at a point nearer to Tientsin than Hochienfu, sixty or seventy miles away.

The third important center of unrest and anti-foreignism was Tungchow, which is about twelve miles east of

Peking on the Pei-ho at the head of navigation for the native cargo boats. This city, which is now the site of extensive railway shops and an important industrial center, had been important, in earlier days, as the point of debarkation for all traffic coming to Peking by way of the Grand Canal. Here the tribute rice was formerly unloaded, to be transported by cart the few remaining miles to its destination, and here the officials, coming to Peking from the south, used to leave their boats and proceed to the capital by chair. The life of the city had thus depended upon the Grand Canal traffic, and the townspeople as a whole, as well as the boatmen and carters, saw ruin staring them in the face as a result of the modern developments in transportation. It was not until April, however, that the foreign missionaries located at Tungchow began to complain that the Boxers were drilling in their vicinity and making threats against the foreign religion. In answer to these complaints, the Chinese government stationed soldiers at Tungchow, and also at Tsunhwa fifty miles farther east, as protection for the missionaries and their property.

A glance at the map of Chihli will show that these reports of Boxer disturbances and threats all came from places which lay south or east of Peking. These places were, it is true, centers of missionary work, but it is to be noted that the mission stations lying west of the Peking-Paotingfu line, and—with the exception of Tsunhwa—those lying north of a line drawn from Peking to Shanhaikwan were apparently untroubled by the Boxers until after June 17, 1900. The principal area of disturbance in the province was a rough equilateral triangle, approximately a hundred miles on each side, whose corners were Peking, Tientsin, and Paotingfu, with a detached area in the extreme south, around Taimingfu, from which the trouble had spread northward.

In spite of the alarming reports which were in circulation, the first five months of 1900 passed without any overt act by the Boxers against the missionaries or other foreigners. This fact was generally attributed to the presence of the Chinese soldiers who were assigned for the protection of mission stations whenever complaints were made that the I-ho Chuan had begun to organize and make threats in a locality where foreigners were situated. Yet the native Christians who resided outside these zones of military protection were almost equally immune from actual violence. At the end of March Mr. W. S. Ament of the American Board mission at Peking, accompanied by Mr. Stelle, an English missionary, made a tour of the outlying mission stations to the south of Peking in order to get first-hand information as to the real state of affairs. In the five districts which Mr. Ament visited, he found that, at one place, "the chapel outside the city had been brick-batted by some Boxers on a previous night"; at another, "men with knives and guns had come to the doors of the Christians' homes and reviled them"; but that, in the entire region, "not a Christian had been injured, not a house burned, or animal carried off." His deliberate opinion was that "the Boxer bubble is practically burst and the officials have understood the movement from the first better than the foreigners have."[10]

Mr. Ament's conclusion, that the Boxer bubble was

[10] *A.B.C.F.M. Letters, North China Mission*, 1900-1910, vol. I, letter 63. Mr. Ament subsequently achieved much undeserved notoriety as a result of an article by Mark Twain. It is with pleasure that the present writer is able to bear witness to Mr. Ament's unfailing sympathy for the Chinese, and his impatience with the foreign policy of interference which he considered responsible for the growing complications and for the anti-foreign bitterness among the people. He was distinguished from most of the foreign residents in China, including many of his fellow missionaries, by his repudiation of the theory that "force" was the proper solution for all existing troubles.

practically burst, may appear ridiculous in the light of subsequent events, but his testimony as to the exaggerated nature of current reports is confirmed from an official source. On May 2 Mr. W. R. Carles, the British consul at Tientsin, wrote to Sir Claude MacDonald: "M. du Chaylard (the French consul) informed me on the 22nd April that he had received a telegram from Paoting stating that the Christians of the environs of Lunglu had been killed in great numbers in the village of Chiang-chia-chuang on the previous day. Two days later he told me that the affray had, it was true, been of a serious character, but that only one Christian had lost his life, and that seventy Boxers had been killed. He also informed me that, acting on his advice, the Roman Catholic priests had placed firearms in the hands of their converts."[11]

There had, indeed, been a state of incipient civil war between the Boxers and the stronger Christian communities, in Chihli as well as in Shantung, from the first appearance of the I-ho Chuan organization. Père Isoré, from whom came the earliest report of the I-ho Chuan, or "Ihonokinen," wrote in his journal under the date October 28, 1898:

> I was implored to send a message to the mandarin; to take measures; and to organize the defence. To all these cowards I made this solemn declaration:—"since I find only ill-will among you and since you leave to me all the expense and all the care of the defence, we shall go—Father Lomuller, Father Suenn, and I—pack our belongings, and leave for Weitsun where there is some courage and good sense." "What, the Father will abandon Tchao-kia-tchuang?" "Yes, and we shall take everything with us, even the cannons." My threats produced their effect. The Christians of the four adjoining villages assembled and or-

[11] *British Blue Books, China No. 3 (1900)*, document no. 273, inclosure 2.

ganized a sort of a national guard for the defence of their interests. Mounted scouts, armed with a gun and . . . my benediction, were sent forth to discover the brigands.[12]

Yet even in the region around Taimingfu, from which this early report had come, the conditions a year and a half later were marked by general unrest rather than by actual violence. On April 6, 1900, Père Paul Wetterwald wrote from Weitsun:

> I have found everything in disorder because of these miserable I-ho Chuan, otherwise called Boxers. Since the month of February the northern part of our mission and that of the Lazarists (North Chihli) have been topsy-turvy. The soldiers have quickly gone to work to put things in order, but officers who show too much zeal are punished by the government. The latter seeks to ruin Christianity without being drawn into the affair; hence its see-saw policy. On the one hand it protects, more or less, the missionaries and the mission establishments; on the other, it excites or at least encourages hate toward Christianity and the Christians, whom it accuses of sympathy for the foreigners.[13]

By the end of March, 1900, the Boxer movement in Shantung had begun to show definite signs of subsiding; in Chihli, although it is true that the actual performances of the Boxers were very generally exaggerated, the disturbance was continuing to spread, always in the direction of the capital. As has been pointed out, this difference was partly due to the effect of certain economic causes for antiforeignism, which were more prominent in Chihli than they were in Shantung. There was, however, another important factor in the divergence between the course of events in the two provinces.

From the time of his assumption of office, Yuan Shih-kai had been allowed to handle the situation in Shantung as

[12] *Chine et Ceylan,* vol. I, p. 107.

[13] *Chine et Ceylan,* II, p. 59.

he thought best, and had adopted methods which were in strict accord with Chinese traditions as to the proper means of quieting a popular disorder—so long as the disturbing elements were innocent of actual rebellion. The imperial decrees had been respectfully received, and embodied in suitable proclamations, but Yuan fully recognized the fact that the real responsibility for handling the situation rested on him, and that he was responsible to the Throne for the lives of the Tuan members as well as for the lives of the native Christians. The excited foreign demands for the immediate application of "force without stint" had been completely ignored, and the governor had made use of his soldiers only for the protection of foreign lives and property. Yuan's chief reliance in checking the spread of the I-ho Chuan had been an appeal to reason and the right ideas of the people, but he had also compelled the missionaries to do their share in bringing about tranquillity, by requiring them to refrain from all unnecessary travel through the country in order that the vague popular fears regarding foreign activities might have time to die down.

The authorities in Chihli were not so fortunate as the governor of Shantung. Because of their proximity to Peking and because of the much greater extent of foreign interests in their province, the actions of the Chihli officials were under closer supervision by the foreign diplomats. Neither the provincial authorities nor the Tsungli Yamen could ignore, as Yuan had ignored in Shantung, the suggestions and demands of the Diplomatic Body. In the next chapter, therefore, it will be necessary to examine the diplomatic activities at Peking which contributed to the development of the Boxer disturbance.

CHAPTER IX.

Diplomatic Pressure at Peking.

Mr. Conger and Yu Hsien—Sir Claude MacDonald and the Brooks Murder—The Decree of January 11—The Identic Notes—The Devil and the Deep Sea—Warships for Taku—Effect on the Chinese Government—Yu Hsien and Wang Pei-yu—"Voluntary" Publication of Yu Lu's Memorial—Decree of April 17—May Disturbances—Bishop Favier's Letter—Demands of the Corps Diplomatique—A Revolution against Foreign Control.

DURING the fall of 1899, the foreign ministers at Peking began to make diplomatic representations to the imperial government on the subject of I-ho Chuan and Big Sword activities. On November 11, on the strength of a report from members of the American Board Mission that riots were occurring in the neighborhood of Douchou, Shantung, the first secretary of the United States legation presented a *note verbale* to the Tsungli Yamen. The note requested that the Yamen send telegraphic instructions to the governor of Shantung to "secure to American citizens living in the threatened districts the protection, both in lives and property, to which they are, under the treaties, entitled." Five days later, a similar note was handed to the Yamen in connection with reports of disturbances in the vicinity of Tsinanfu; it was now requested that "those persons who have been engaged in this disorderly affair be promptly arrested and brought to trial and punished." The request in the first of these notes, while perfectly correct, was not entirely necessary as the foreigners had already been enjoying, for nearly two months, the protection of provincial troops; in his second note, the representative of the United States appears to have prejudged the issue.

In a note to the Yamen on November 25, Mr. Conger, the American minister, went somewhat further than these earlier notes. Bringing to the attention of the Yamen certain fresh reports of riots and threats against native Christians in Shantung, he pointed out the necessity of dealing with the Boxers in a firm manner. He therefore expressed the hope that they would "fully appreciate the gravity of the situation and send such imperative orders by telegraph to the governor and other officials as will compel them to instantly use such forceful means as will forthwith disperse these threatening rioters and protect the lives and property of these people." On the twenty-sixth the "hope" became a "demand"; the following day, the Yamen was requested to furnish "immediate information as to what measures have been taken to protect these people"; on December 2 Mr. Conger demanded "that another telegram be at once sent to Shantung, and that measures requisite to the protection of these people be immediately taken as provided for by the treaties."[1]

In this series of notes, Mr. Conger considerably exceeded the rights which were established in the treaties to which he had appealed. His right to demand adequate protection for the lives and property of American citizens is unquestioned, as well as his right to insist upon suitable punishment for anyone who might be guilty of attack upon these; so far, however, there had been no question of American citizens suffering either in their persons or property.[2] It was also the right of the American minister, under the religious liberty clauses, to demand that the Chinese govern-

[1] These notes are to be found in *Foreign Relations of the United States, 1900*, pp. 78-81.

[2] See Secretary Hay's dispatch to Mr. Conger, *ibid.*, pp. 96-97.

ment should neither persecute the native Christians on account of their faith nor allow them to be so persecuted. It did not follow, however, that the American minister had a right to intervene in all cases of injustice to Christians, merely because they were Christians; to demand that the government afford better protection to its Christian subjects than to others; or to interfere in the case of popular outbreaks in which the Christians suffered in common with their pagan neighbors, unless it was proven that the officials had denied to the Christians the protection or the legal redress that was accorded to non-Christians under like circumstances. In other words, the treaties gave Mr. Conger a legal right to protest against religious persecution; they did not give him any right to instruct the government as to the proper means of governing the country.

The Yamen's answer to this volley of notes took the form of forwarding to Mr. Conger, on the first and third of December, two telegraphic reports which had been received from the governor of Shantung. In his first telegram, Yu Hsien reported that he had already taken strong measures to repress the rioters; that, in retreating before his forces, the I-ho Chuan had passed through Pang-chuang where the Christians had met them, opened fire on them, and chased and tried to capture them; and that the I-ho Chuan had then returned the attack and had burned a missionary chapel.[3] Yu Hsien declared that he had always been prompt in attending to the numerous missionary cases which were brought before him, and complained that the American minister, on the strength of missionary reports, had accused him of refusing to obey the imperial commands. He charged the missionaries with reporting rumors which had no foundation of fact, and

[3] See *ante*, chapter VIII, for Dr. Porter's report in regard to arming the Christians at Pang-chuang.

begged the Yamen to tell Mr. Conger not to listen to their one-sided statements but to instruct the missionaries to keep their native Christians in order.

Yu Hsien's second telegram followed the same general line as his first. The I-ho Chuan and the Christians, he said, did not get along together. He had repeatedly admonished them to make peace with each other and the I-ho Chuan, heeding his exhortations, had gradually returned to their homes, but the Christians had set an ambush for them and had opened fire, killing five or more persons.[4] The governor concluded by stating that, as the result of this and similar occurrences, the bad feeling between the two factions was becoming more and more intense every day, and that it would be almost impossible to keep the peace.

Mr. Conger refused to consider Yu Hsien's defense of his administration of affairs, or to balance the governor's statement of facts against the reports which he had received from the American missionaries. On December 5 he replied to the Yamen's latest note by "suggesting, without demanding" the necessity and propriety of Yu Hsien's removal. To this suggestion was added the following warning: "Unless the Imperial Chinese Government take some immediate effective measures to suppress these brigands, the outside world will be justified in the belief that China is purposely trifling with a momentous question, which may lead to the needless murder of foreigners whom she has agreed to protect and to the most serious trouble for herself." Two days later, Yu Hsien was summoned to Peking "for an audience," and Yuan Shih-kai was, as has already been recounted, ordered to Shantung as acting governor.

[4] Mr. Conger later reported to the State Department that he had obtained verification of this statement, with some modifications; see *Foreign Relations of the United States*, 1900, p. 120.

Diplomatic Pressure at Peking

In replacing Yu Hsien by Yuan Shih-kai, the imperial government was apparently moved by the desire to conciliate the American minister and terminate a dispute which might otherwise lead to an open break. This motive for action was probably supplemented by the belief that Yu Hsien's reputation for anti-foreignism and hostility toward Christianity would make it exceedingly difficult, if not impossible, for him to quiet the disturbances in Shantung; his later appointment as governor of Shansi is, however, conclusive proof that the government did not intend his removal from Shantung to be regarded as a surrender to foreign dictation. The anti-foreign activities of Yu Hsien during the summer of 1900 have generally been taken as fully justifying Mr. Conger's suggestion that he should be removed from his post in Shantung; yet there is reason for believing that these subsequent activities in Shansi were, to no small degree, the result of that removal. In the messages which he exchanged with the American minister through the medium of the Tsungli Yamen, Yu Hsien had rather the better of the debate, so far as the accuracy of their facts was concerned; he was, therefore, fully convinced that he had been unjustly demoted at the request of the American representative, and he assumed his new post filled with an increased hatred for all foreigners, especially for the missionaries to whose complaints he naturally attributed the request for his transfer.

The British minister at Peking, Sir Claude MacDonald, had, according to his subsequent dispatches, begun to make "strong representations" to the Chinese government regarding the situation in Shantung and Chihli at about the same time as those which were made by Mr. Conger. His correspondence with the Tsungli Yamen on the subject of the Boxers did not, however, become a part of his reports to the Foreign Office until January, 1900—after the murder of Mr. Brooks.

On January 5, in acknowledging the Yamen's expressions of regret at the unfortunate occurrence, Sir Claude laid stress upon the importance of proving their sincerity by strenuous action in dealing with this case and in guarding against the possibility of similar events elsewhere. At an interview on January 11, he took occasion to warn the ministers of the serious consequences to China which might result from the existing conditions in Shantung, especially in view of the rumors that the I-ho Chuan had been encouraged by secret orders from the Throne. He attributed the troubles primarily to the support which the I-ho Chuan had received from Yu Hsien, and informed the Yamen that the friendly relations between China and Great Britain depended upon the behavior of the local officials and the way in which they executed the commands of the Throne for the suppression of disorder and for the protection of foreigners.

On January 5 there had appeared in the *Peking Gazette* an imperial decree ordering the immediate capture of Mr. Brooks' murderers and the punishment of the officials who had neglected their duty. This decree was heartily approved by the members of the diplomatic body, who regarded it as satisfactorily severe in tone and well calculated to bring about the restoration of order. Six days later, general misgivings were aroused by the publication of the following decree:

Of late in all the provinces brigandage has become daily more prevalent, and missionary cases have recurred with frequency. Most critics point to seditious Societies as the cause, and ask for rigorous suppression and punishment of these. But reflection shows that Societies are of different kinds. When worthless vagabonds form themselves into bands and sworn confederacies, and relying on their numbers create disturbances, the law can show absolutely no leniency to them. On the other hand, when peaceful and law-abiding people practice their skill in mechanical arts for the self-preservation of themselves and their families, or when they combine in village communities for the mutual protection of the rural population, this is in accordance with the public-spirited principle (enjoined by Mencius) of "keeping mutual watch and giving mutual help."

Some local authorities, when a case arises, do not regard this distinction, but, listening to false and idle rumors, regard all alike as seditious Societies, and involve all in one indiscriminate slaughter. The result is that, no distinction being made between the good and the evil, men's minds are thrown into fear and doubt. This is, indeed, "adding fuel to stop a fire," "driving fish into the deep part of the pool to catch them." It means, not that the people are disorderly, but that the administration is bad.

The profound compassion and unbounded favor of our dynasty have blessed the country for over 200 years; the people eat our produce and tread our soil; they have natural goodness implanted in them; how can they, of their own free will, come to adopt bandit ways, and bring down punishment upon themselves?

The essential thing is that the Viceroys and Governors of the provinces should select officers worthy of confidence, who should rule their districts well and give rest to their people. When litigation arises between converts and people, it should be dealt with according to justice, without the slightest partiality for either side. Such conduct serves as a matter of course to fulfil the people's trustful hopes, and to quiet popular feeling in time of trouble, changing serious affairs to trifles and causing trifling ones to disappear. The stability of the country's institutions and the consolidation of international relations alike depend on this.

The Viceroys and Governors of the provinces have received the fullest and weightiest marks of our favor. If they offer their united services in these critical times, they must be able to carry into effect the determination of the Throne to treat the masses with paternal kindness and to regard all men with equal benevolence. Let them give strict orders to the local authorities, that in dealing with cases of this kind they should only inquire whether so-and-so is, or is not, guilty of rebellion, whether he has or has not stirred up strife, and should not consider whether he belongs to a Society or not, whether he is or is not an adherent of a religion.

As for our common people, let them give thought to the protection and security of their native places, their persons, and their homes. Let them not give ear to those who would unsettle their minds and so bring upon themselves calamities and military operations. Nor let them on the other hand presume upon influence and authority to oppress their fellow-villagers.

In this way it is our earnest hope that the hamlets will be at peace, and that thus we may be relieved of our anxious care by day and night.

Let this Decree be published abroad.[5]

As this decree expressly forbade the authorities to take action against the "Society men" unless they had been guilty of some overt act of rebellion, there was much dissatisfaction among the foreign diplomats who had nationals engaged in missionary work in the affected regions.

Isolated diplomatic action, with regard to the disorders, now gave way to joint action. On January 25 the American, French, and German ministers met with Sir Claude MacDonald at the British Legation and decided to send an "identic note" to the Tsungli Yamen.[6] This note, which was sent two days later, called attention to the possible bad effects of the recent decree, since it created the impression that the I-ho Chuan and the Big Sword Society enjoyed the

[5] Taken from the *British Blue Books, China No. 3 (1900)*, document no. 18, inclosure.

[6] In the French diplomatic documents, it is stated that the meeting on January 25 was held "à la suite d'une démarch faite par M. Pichon." By an oversight, the Italian minister, who also had nationals engaged in mission work in the area affected by the I-ho Chuan, was not invited to this meeting; he joined, however, in sending the identic note, and was associated with the other four representatives in all the subsequent discussions on the subject.

support of the government. The note, therefore, requested "That an Imperial Decree be published and promulgated, ordering by name the complete suppression and abolition of the 'Fist of Righteous Harmony' and the 'Big Sword Societies,' and I request that it may be distinctly stated in the Decree that *to belong to either of these societies*[7] or to harbor any of its members *is a criminal offence against the laws of China.*"[7]

The requests made by the five foreign representatives in their identic note of January 27 were based on the erroneous assumption that the I-ho Chuan was a rebellious and unlawful association; to this there may have been joined the equally false assumption that the imperial government possessed autocratic powers of legislation. In view of the fact that the Tuan were, and had been for centuries, perfectly lawful organizations, it is obvious that the request was one which the Peking authorities could not fulfil. If left to their own devices, the Yamen and the officials of Chihli might have succeeded, as Yuan Shih-kai succeeded in Shantung, in discouraging and finally suppressing the Boxer movement; but to state in an imperial decree that membership in the "Patriotic Militia" was "a criminal offence against the laws of China" was impossible. Such a statement would be a falsehood, and all the people of China would know it as such; since all would appreciate the foreign inspiration of the decree, its publication would, moreover, increase the excitement and turn against the government some of the hostility hitherto felt toward the foreigners. The government was "between the Devil and the Deep Sea," and the Devil—the Boxers—had the law on his side.

The representatives of the five powers were not inclined to leave the Chinese authorities free to settle the troubles

[7] Author's italics.

according to their own devices; they had made certain precise demands and intended that those demands should be precisely conceded. Receiving no answer to their identic note, they wrote again, on February 21, pressing for a reply, and, on the twenty-fifth, received notes from the Tsungli Yamen. The notes stated that, on the twenty-first, the Throne had issued a decree to the viceroy of Chihli and the governor of Shantung, ordering them to forbid the rebellious ruffians in Shantung and elsewhere to form societies and create disturbances. This reply was not satisfactory to the five ministers, and, on February 27, a second identic note was drawn up, in which they repeated the original request and added the stipulation that the Decree be published in the *Peking Gazette*. A joint interview with the Yamen was arranged for March 2, at which it was intended that this new note was to be presented.

On the evening before this interview was to take place, the five foreign representatives received from the Yamen copies of a proclamation which had been issued by Viceroy Yu Lu. This proclamation embodied an imperial decree which seemed quite satisfactory in its severity except for the fact that only the I-ho Chuan was mentioned by name —there being no reference to the Big Sword Society. As this decree illustrates the skill with which the imperial government avoided stating that the I-ho Chuan was *an unlawful association*, a translation is given here:

The Tsungli Yamen memorializes requesting our orders for the strict suppression of the "Fist Society." Last year the Governor of Shantung telegraphed that the Society known as the "Fist of Righteous Harmony" in many of his districts, under the plea of enmity to foreign religions, were raising disturbances in all directions, and had extended their operations into the southern part of Chihli. We have repeatedly ordered the Governor-General of Chihli and the Governor of Shantung to send soldiers to keep the peace. But it is to be feared that if stern measures of suppression of such proceedings as secretly establishing societies with names and collecting in numbers to raise disturbances be not taken, the ignorant populace will be deluded and excited, and as time goes on things will grow worse, and when some serious case ensues we shall be compelled to employ troops to extirpate the evil. The sufferers would be truly many, and the Throne cannot bear to slay without warning.

Let the Governor-General of Chihli and the Governor of Shantung issue the most stringent proclamations admonishing the people and strictly prohibiting (the societies) so that our people may all know that to secretly establish societies is contrary to prohibition and a breach of the law.

Evil customs must be rooted out and the people encouraged to be good. Should any obstinately adhere to their delusions and persist in their old ways they must be immediately punished with the greatest severity and without the slightest mercy.

Both converts and the ordinary Chinese are subjects of the Throne and in all cases of lawsuits the local officials must adjudicate with fairness, discriminating only between right and wrong and not between the adherents of foreign religions and others. There must be no trace of partiality. Thus will be supported our supreme desire to treat all with equal benevolence.

Let the high officials named proclaim our words, that all people may know our will.[8]

The complaining diplomats would have regarded this decree as fully satisfactory if it had appeared in prompt response to the first identic note; in view of the long delay, they agreed to adhere to their plan of presenting the second identic note, with its demand for publication in the *Peking Gazette*. It was also decided that a special point should be made of the failure to mention the Big Sword Society in the decree already issued. At the interview on March 2,

[8] Translation taken from *British Blue Books, China No. 3* (*1900*), document no. 32, inclosure 3.

the Yamen strenuously objected to the new demands. They argued that the Big Sword Society had now become merged with the I-ho Chuan, and that it was contrary to all precedent for the government to publish in the *Peking Gazette* a decree which had already been issued directly to the provincial authorities.

On March 7 the Yamen sent notes to the five legations in which it restated its arguments against the demand for publication in the *Peking Gazette*. The response to these arguments was a third identic note, presented three days later, in which the foreign diplomats insisted upon an immediate favorable answer to their demand, in default of which they would recommend to their respective governments the adoption of such measures as they might consider necessary for the protection of the lives and property of their nationals in China. On the same date, the ministers sent telegrams to their governments suggesting that, in case of continued refusal on the part of the Chinese government and if conditions did not materially improve, a few warships of each nation concerned should make a naval demonstration in North China waters.

The proposal for a naval demonstration found the home governments rather less enthusiastic than their representatives at Peking. Lord Salisbury expressed his opinion that naval force should be used only after all other means had failed, and it was not until Sir Claude had informed him of the intended dispatch of American, German, and Italian ships to Taku that two British warships were ordered to that port. Secretary Hay notified Mr. Conger, on March 15, that an American ship would be detailed to Taku "for independent protection of American citizens and interests"; this ship arrived at Taku on April 7 and left on the thirtieth. The Germans and Italians also sent ships to Taku; but the French government, after consulting Russia and sounding its representatives at Washington, London, and Berlin, did no more than wire instructions to Admiral Courrejolles to hold his fleet in readiness.

It was in connection with the third identic note and the proposal for a naval demonstration that it was first suggested that legation guards should be brought to Peking, not as a necessary protection for the legations but as a means of compelling the Chinese government to accede to the foreign demands. "It is believed by all," wrote Mr. Conger on March 10, "that a naval demonstration would make them comply quickly. But in case this fails, if as a last resort a marine guard was landed by each power, to be brought to Peking on the plea of protecting the foreign legations, there would be little doubt of ready compliance, because nothing could chagrin or grieve them more than for word to go forth that they could not preserve order or protection at their imperial capital, and they would do almost anything rather than have this happen again."

The pressure which the foreign diplomats were bringing to bear upon the imperial government produced an immediate response, but of a very different sort from that which was desired. On March 11 a decree was published in the *Peking Gazette*, approving a request by the Board of Censors that a memorial temple be erected in honor of a former "expectant Taotai" of Kweiyang. The reason which was given in the decree for so honoring this deceased literatus was the desire to recognize the loyalty and patriotism that he had displayed in raising and maintaining a volunteer company with which he had rendered valuable service against the Taiping Rebels.[9] Two weeks later, a somewhat similar decree, issued in response to a memorial from Liu Kun-yih, conferred posthumous honors upon one Li

[9] The special significance of this lies in the fact that the Chinese have always regarded the Taiping Rebellion as a Christian movement.

Kuang-chiu for the services which he had rendered in reorganizing the defenses of Chekiang province. The request of the Nanking viceroy, that special honors be shown to this able military officer, may have had but an accidental connection with the diplomatic struggle which was going on at Peking; but, by issuing such a decree at a time when the warships of four European powers were assembling in the Gulf of Pechili, the imperial government gave unmistakable evidence of its desire to emphasize the importance of preparing for national defense against foreign invasion.

Even more significant, as evidence of the government's determination to resist foreign diplomatic pressure, was the appointment of Yu Hsien, on March 14, to the governorship of Shansi. It will be recalled that in November, 1899, Mr. Conger had blamed the inertia of Yu Hsien for the disturbances in Shantung, and, on December 5, had "suggested" that he ought to be removed from his post as governor—a step which was taken two days later. On January 11 Sir Claude MacDonald had informed the Tsungli Yamen that, in his opinion, the primary responsibility for the murder of Mr. Brooks lay at the door of Yu Hsien, because of his encouragement of the anti-foreign organizations. On March 2 the representatives of France, Germany, Great Britain, Italy, and the United States had, in their joint interview with the Yamen, been unanimous in charging that Yu Hsien was the founder of the Big Sword Society, the chief fomenter of anti-foreign activity in Shantung, and the real author of the objectionable decree of January 11. Finally, on March 6, Mr. Conger had filed a formal protest against the future appointment of Yu Hsien "to any post where he would have under his control either missionaries or their work."

In the face of these repeated expressions on the part of

the foreign representatives, Yu Hsien's appointment to be governor of Shansi admits of but three possible interpretations. In the first place, it may be—and frequently has been—argued that Yu Hsien was sent to this new post in order that he might there carry on the campaign of anti-foreign propaganda and organization which had been interrupted by his removal from Shantung. Secondly, the appointment may be considered as intended to assure the "good societies" that they had nothing to fear from any decrees which might, as the result of diplomatic pressure, be promulgated in the future. Finally, there is the possibility that the imperial government wished to show the Chinese people, as well as the members of the diplomatic body, that it would accept no foreign dictation in matters affecting the administration of internal affairs.

The first of these possible explanations, although it has found wide acceptance among those who have written on the Boxer movement, is hardly tenable; the arrival of the new governor in Shansi was not followed by any concerted agitation against foreigners, and the first Boxer disturbances in the province did not occur until considerably after the allied attack on the Taku forts had precipitated an actual state of war. The real motives for the appointment appear to have been a combination of the second and third of the interpretations which have been suggested above. The imperial government, both in the decree of January 11 and in a number of decrees subsequent to the appointment of Yu Hsien, repeatedly gave evidence of its determination to insist on the distinction between "good" and "bad" societies; if the organization of the militia bands in Shantung had been fostered particularly by Yu Hsien, his appointment to Shansi would be popularly regarded as proof that the repressive decrees and proclamations were not directed against these lawful associations for mutual defense. As to the desire to avoid submitting to foreign domination, Sir Claude MacDonald and the French chargé d'affaires, Baron d'Anthouard, had, in their official reports prior to this appointment, independently expressed their opinion that the Chinese government was extremely anxious to avoid any suspicion of such control, and it has already been pointed out that, from her assumption of power a year and a half earlier, the Empress Dowager had made the maintenance of the government's prestige, in this respect, one of the cardinal principles of her policy.

Another appointment which was made at this time is important only because it has been one of the principal bits of evidence to support the charge that the Empress Dowager was conspiring with the Boxer leaders for the extermination of the foreigners. This was the appointment, on March 13, of Wang Pei-yu as governor of Peking, the "Imperial Prefecture." Two months after this appointment was made, an extremely sensational *undated* story, written by a native Peking correspondent, appeared in the columns of the *North China Herald.* According to this account, Wang was promoted from a much lower position, as a member of the Board of Censors, on the day after he had been received in audience by the Empress Dowager. In the course of the interview, the Empress Dowager asked Wang whether he really thought that the Boxers would join the troops, "when the time came," in fighting against the "foreign devils." Wang declared his faith in the loyalty and courage of the organizations, and his willingness to aid them in any way within his power. The Empress Dowager nodded her hearty approval to these sentiments, but expressed her fear lest the Boxers, having no experienced and responsible men to guide them, should act rashly and get the government into trouble with the "foreign devils" before everything was ready. The next morning, Wang was appointed governor of the Imperial Prefecture, presumably in order that he might have an opportunity to organize and advise the Boxers. Even if the story be accepted as essentially accurate, it merely proves that, on March 12—two days after the Tsungli Yamen had received an ultimatum from the representatives of five Western powers, and two days after those representatives had telegraphed to their governments suggesting a naval demonstration in the Gulf of Pechili—Tzu Hsi recognized that the I-ho Chuan was a legitimate and patriotic organization, but felt anxious lest its activities should involve China in international complications.[10]

The identic note of March 10, in which the foreign representatives had reiterated their demand that an imperial decree against the I-ho Chuan and the Big Sword Society be published in the *Peking Gazette*, remained unanswered for four weeks. On April 5 the five ministers again wrote to the Yamen, and on the seventh received a reply which, although not acceding to the demand which had been set forth in the note, was regarded as satisfactory indication of the good intentions of the imperial govern-

[10] In justice to those who have used this story to substantiate their charges against the Empress Dowager, it must be pointed out that they have probably done so on the reasonable presumption that the events therein recounted took place about the first week in May. The story, under the caption "Peking Notes," appeared in the *North China Herald* of May 16, 1900—vol. 64, p. 868; the decree appointing Wang Pei-yu to the governorship of the Imperial Prefecture was published in the *Peking Gazette* of March 13, 1900, but did not appear in the translations of the *North China Herald* until June 6, 1900—vol. 64, p. 1024. Dr. Smith, in *China in Convulsion*, says that the Peking correspondent of the *North China* was a member of the famous Tseng family and that he subsequently lost his life during the Boxer disturbances; Mr. Morse, in *The International Relations of the Chinese Empire*, vol. III, p. 192, note, makes the same statement. Both writers ignore the fact that this correspondent had, during the preceding two years, been the source of numerous sensational stories from Peking, none of which proved to be altogether reliable.

ment. In acknowledging the receipt of this reply, three days later, the foreign representatives agreed to abandon the demand in their last two identic notes; whereupon, as if it had been deliberately withheld until the demand should have been withdrawn, there appeared in the *Peking Gazette* of April 14 a "Supplementary Memorial" from Yu Lu, the viceroy of Chihli, which contained the full text of the imperial decree whose publication in the *Gazette* had been so vainly demanded for the past six weeks!

The significance of the fact that this decree was published as soon as the formal demand for publication had been withdrawn does not appear to have been appreciated by the foreign diplomats; the voluntary action of the Chinese government gave them great satisfaction, however, and some of the warships which had been stationed at Taku for the last month were allowed to depart. Although the enlisting and drilling of Boxer bands still continued, it was now believed that the government was about to take the necessary steps for suppressing the disorders, and, for slightly more than a month after the close of this protracted struggle between the Tsungli Yamen and the foreign representatives, the activities of the I-ho Chuan called for no formal diplomatic representations at Peking and furnished subject matter for no weighty dispatches between the legations and their home governments.

The imperial government had made every effort to avoid submitting to foreign dictation in this dispute, and had, in fact, published Yu Lu's supplementary memorial only after the formal demand of the diplomats had been withdrawn. For the Chinese people, however, contemporary events had given this voluntary publication the appearance of complete submission. A week before the memorial was published, an American warship had arrived at Taku to join the British, German, and Italian men-of-war which were already anchored there; two days after the publication, the assembled warships began to disappear. This circumstantial evidence was enough to create a strong popular suspicion that the government had given way before the threats of the diplomats, supported by a show of naval force.

To disarm this popular suspicion, and to assure the militia that the strong language in the decree which had been quoted by Yu Lu was intended only for the unworthy characters who were bringing the train-bands into disrepute, a fresh decree was published in the *Peking Gazette* on April 17:

The privilege granted by the Throne to the inhabitants of the country towns and villages to form train-bands and village militia was, properly speaking, in order that they may have the means of self-protection in times of emergency. These measures were sanctioned from ancient times, and so long as the people stuck to the principle enunciated above there have never been any obstacles placed in their way by the Government. The only cause for apprehension is that there may be bad and restless characters amongst the villagers, who might take advantage of the means at hand to break the laws of the land and create trouble for the native Christians. But all should know that the Government treats all who are within the borders with equal kindness and impartiality, and never makes any difference in its treatment because people belong to different places. We therefore look to these train-bands and village militia to take to heart the wishes of the Government, and refrain from causing trouble with the Christians on pain of being punished for their deeds. We hereby command all our Viceroys and Governors to exhort the local authorities under them to keep a careful watch over their people and frequently impress the wishes of the Government in this respect upon all. By obeying these commands we can then hope to preserve eternal peace between the inhabitants and the Christians, and we earnestly call upon all to assist the Government, and that each man continues to work at his daily vocation and avoid all evil character.[11]

Reports as to the situation in Chihli at the end of April closely resembled that which had been made by Mr. Ament a month earlier. The Boxer bands still existed, were still recruiting, and continued to perform their drill, but there were few actual disturbances and the danger of a serious outbreak seemed to be disappearing. On May 8 Mr. Conger reported to Secretary Hay, "In no case as yet have the Boxers attacked any American Mission or disturbed any property in the towns or villages where they are stationed." Replying to the secretary's disapproval of his action in coöperating with the other representatives in the matter of the identic notes to the Yamen, Mr. Conger acknowledged that subsequent events proved that joint action had not been necessary.

By the middle of May the disturbances had begun to take on a new vigor, and the situation became less favorable. May has always been considered a bad month for riots in China, and May, 1900, had certain aspects which naturally contributed to foster popular unrest. The drought in the northern provinces had continued throughout the period of the spring planting, and the superstitious hostility of a large part of the people, who saw starvation staring them in the face, turned more and more against the railways, the telegraphs, and the foreign religion. But the rapid spread of the conflagration during the month of May

[11] This translation is taken from the *North China Herald* of April 25, 1900—vol. 64, p. 737. The *North China* labels it "A purposeless decree." It is also to be found, in slightly differing translations, in the *British Blue Books, China No. 3 (1900)*, document no. 107, inclosure; and in the *Foreign Relations of the United States*, 1900, p. 119. Sir Claude MacDonald expressed the belief that it was intended to correct any false interpretation of the decree of January 11.

must, in part, be attributed to the operation of other than natural forces. The repressive measures adopted by the viceroy of Chihli had served to scatter, without suppressing, the Boxer leaders; while the foreign naval demonstration had, by reviving the popular fears of a foreign invasion, greatly facilitated the recruiting of the Boxer bands. The agitation now began to make its appearance in regions which had hitherto been unaffected. On May 16 an American missionary wrote to Mr. Conger from Ling-shan, thirty-five miles east of Peking, that the first threats of open violence against foreign missionaries and native Christians had been made four days before that, while it was only in the last two months that the I-ho Chuan had appeared in the vicinity of Ling-shan.

At Peking, the earliest indication of a renewed anxiety in regard to the situation was given in a dispatch of the French minister on May 14: "In Peking itself, for the first time in a long while, anti-foreign placards have been posted and distributed." Two days later, M. Pichon reported to his government that he had requested Admiral Courrejolles to send to Peitaiho a warship which would be able, if necessary, to disembark a landing party.[12] On May 17 Sir Claude MacDonald reported the destruction of three Roman Catholic villages in the neighborhood of Paotingfu, with a loss of sixty-one lives among the native Christians, and the next day he informed his government that a chapel of the London Missionary Society had been

[12] See *Documents Diplomatiques, Chine (1899-1900)*, p. 20. In these, as in all his dispatches during this period, M. Pichon reports the absolute accord which he is maintaining with his Russian colleague, M. de Giers. It is interesting to speculate as to the influence which this Russo-French accord may have had upon the subsequent actions of the Corps Diplomatique; to what extent, for example, was the judgment of the British minister affected by the fear that Russia and France were planning to derive some special advantage from the situation?

destroyed, and the native pastor killed, at a village forty miles from Peking. At this time, however, the situation did not yet seem alarming to the British minister. In an interview with the Tsungli Yamen, at which he took up the subject of the recently reported outbreaks and urged the immediate necessity for taking strong measures, Sir Claude found the attitude of the Yamen members much changed for the better, and he reported his belief that the imperial government had at last begun to realize the necessity for suppressing the societies.

On May 19—the day following the interview which had made such a favorable impression upon the British minister—the foreign representatives at Peking, now acting jointly and in full force, renewed their efforts to quell the disturbances by means of diplomatic pressure. At the request of M. Pichon, the Spanish minister and doyen of the diplomatic corps—Señor de Cologan—circulated among his colleagues a very alarming letter which the French representative had just received from the Catholic bishop of Peking. Bishop Favier depicted the situation in the darkest colors, and, as he had certain knowledge that the Boxers had already fixed the day on which the Pei Tang Cathedral was to be destroyed, he requested the minister to provide forty or fifty sailors for the immediate protection of the Cathedral. "Peking is surrounded on all sides," he wrote; "the Boxers draw each day nearer to the capital, delayed only by the work of annihilating the Christian villages. I beg you to believe me, M. le Ministre, I am well informed and am making no rash statements. The religious persecution is but a pretext; the principle object is the extermination of Europeans, an object which is clearly written upon the standards of the Boxers."

On the day following the circulation of this letter, the diplomatic body assembled at the Spanish Legation, and the French minister submitted a draft of a joint note which, after some discussion, the doyen was authorized to address to the Tsungli Yamen. This note, which was sent on the twenty-first, demanded:

1. The arrest of every individual who takes part in the drill of this Association (the Boxers), or who creates disturbances in the streets, or who further posts, prints, or distributes placards containing threats against foreigners.

2. The arrest of the proprietors and guardians of the temples or localities where the Boxers assemble, and the assimilation to the Boxers themselves of their accomplices in criminal actions.

3. The punishment of agents of the public force who are guilty of negligence in the measures of suppression with which they have been charged, or are in connivance with the rioters.

4. The execution of the authors of attempts—at murder or incendiarism—against persons or property.

5. The execution of individuals who have assisted and directed the Boxers in the present troubles.

6. The publication in Peking, and in Chihli and the other northern provinces, of these measures, so as to bring them to the notice of the public.

A satisfactory answer to this set of demands was requested at an early date.

In addition to authorizing the dispatch of this joint note, the diplomatic body, at their meeting, discussed the advisability of calling up the legation guards as a means of bringing pressure upon the Chinese government.[13] Most of the representatives were, at this juncture, averse to bringing guards to Peking, and the suggestion which found most favor was that all the maritime powers should unite in a naval demonstration at Shanhaikwan or at the new

[13] On May 19 de Giers, the Russian minister, telegraphed to the Russian Foreign Office his belief that an affirmative decision would be reached on this proposal, of which he thoroughly approved. See *Krasny Arkhiv*, vol. XIV.

port of Chingwantao. If this plan was adopted, it would be possible to hold the guards for Peking in readiness on ship-board in case of emergency. Final action on these proposals was postponed until an answer to the joint note should have been received, but it was decided not to await such an answer longer than five days.

The diplomatic body had reached its important decision in regard to sending the joint note almost entirely on the strength of Bishop Favier's letter. The note had been drawn up by M. Pichon, before the meeting, on the basis of this report and his own impressions as to the Chinese government's lack of good faith. Yet the facts of which the foreign representatives had first-hand knowledge hardly harmonized with the picture which was presented by the Catholic bishop. On the day after the letter was written, a party of French naval officers arrived at Peking and were able to make a trip to the Great Wall—forty miles north of the city—without any unpleasant incident. Sir Claude MacDonald had been impressed, on the eighteenth, by the sincere desire of the Yamen members to put an end to the disturbances; on the twenty-first he made the following official report of his impressions as to the situation: "I confess that little has come to my own knowledge to confirm the gloomy anticipations of the French Fathers. The demeanour of the inhabitants of the city continues to be quiet and civil towards foreigners, as far as my own experience and that of my staff is concerned, although, from the undoubted panic which exists among the native Christians, it may be assumed that the latter are being subjected to threats of violence." Sir Claude explained that he had agreed to the dispatch of the joint note chiefly because he considered that it contained no demands which the government would not be willing to concede.

Diplomatic Pressure at Peking

On May 24 the Tsungli Yamen replied to the joint note. They informed the doyen that there had already been issued, on May 18, a decree ordering the authorities to adopt strict measures of repression along the general lines indicated by the doyen's dispatch, and that they had now memorialized for the issuance of an additional decree on the subject. They expressed the belief, therefore, that the disturbances would soon be suppressed. The diplomatic corps judged this reply to be unsatisfactory, and, at a meeting which was held on the twenty-sixth, decided that a new note should be sent, demanding that the Yamen communicate the terms of the edict which they had mentioned, together with a categorical statement of the measures which had been taken for the suppression of the anti-foreign disturbances. At this meeting, and at one which was held on the following day, the question of legation guards was again discussed, but a final decision was left to a meeting which was to be held on the evening of the twenty-eighth.

In spite of the firm tone that was being adopted in its communications with the Tsungli Yamen, the diplomatic body appears not yet to have appreciated the full gravity of the situation, and there is ample evidence that international rivalries and suspicions frequently overshadowed the purely Chinese aspects of the question. On May 27, before the diplomatic meeting of that date, M. de Giers dispatched the following telegraphic report to the Russian Foreign Office:

> The answer of the Chinese government to the demands of the ministers regarding the Boxers is in vague terms and at yesterday's meeting was declared unsatisfactory. I have been informed by the secretary of the Yamen that permission to adopt the measures demanded by us had just been granted and will be officially confirmed; the Diplomatic Body has postponed until tonight its final

decision. At yesterday's meeting the ministers were deeply impressed by information given by the French Minister, according to which the number of Boxers in the capital has increased, and the defeat of a detachment sent by the government to fight the Boxers is now confirmed. The Boxers were using fire arms. During yesterday's meeting the German Minister declared quite openly that the landing of available troops was not a sufficient measure and that the moment has come for a more active intervention by the powers. I think, however, that he will not succeed in leading his colleagues into this dangerous path, which would threaten the partition of China, and that things will go no farther than summoning the marines.[14]

Sir Claude MacDonald appears to have submitted to the British government a similar version of von Ketteler's remarks, for, on May 31, Count Bülow wired to the German minister requesting an immediate report of his exact words, which "had led to an exchange of views between London and St. Petersburg." In his reply, on June 2, von Ketteler denied that his expressions could be interpreted as threatening a partition of China; but Bülow, on June 5, reprimanded his spokesman at Peking for having overstepped his instructions by voicing sentiments which might be interpreted to mean that Germany was pressing for more drastic action.[15]

Although the compliance of the Chinese government had not been sufficient to satisfy the demands of the diplomatic body, it had already had the effect of drawing upon the imperial authorities some of the popular irritation. In Peking, the proclamations against the I-ho Chuan were torn down by the populace, and an angry clamor was raised against the government for denouncing so patriotic an

[14] *Krasny Arkhiv*, vol. XIV.

[15] For this correspondence between Bülow and Ketteler, see *Grosse Politik*, vol. XVI, pp. 4-6, documents 4512-4514.

organization as the militia. The popular attitude toward the Boxer movement became, indeed, increasingly favorable in proportion as the conviction grew that the government was being controlled by the foreign diplomats. Not only did threats and abuse against the native Christians and their foreign teachers increase with each new proclamation against the patriotic bands; the imperial government, in its efforts to appease the foreigners, was now faced with the danger of turning into a revolution a movement whose leaders had hitherto been loud in their demonstrations of loyalty.

While Yuan Shih-kai—sufficiently removed from diplomatic influence to be allowed to meet the problem in his own way—had been successful in gradually quieting the Boxer disturbances in Shantung without the use of drastic measures, the situation in Chihli had been growing steadily worse. In spite of efforts of the Tsungli Yamen to avoid the appearance of submitting to dictation, the foreign origin of the repressive measures decreed in March had been fully recognized. Any benefit which might have resulted from the increased activity of the authorities in dealing with the I-ho Chuan had been more than offset by the growing popular hostility toward the foreigners. In May this hostility threatened to include the government which had thus shamefully submitted to dictation.

The demand of the five foreign ministers, in the identic note of January 27, that membership in the I-ho Chuan be declared a criminal offense against the laws of China, amounted to a demand that the Throne repudiate its own earlier decrees and make new laws for the Empire to suit the wishes of the foreign diplomats. The demands of the diplomatic body, commencing on May 21, for the adoption of specific measures and the issuance of specific decrees, meant the assumption of sovereignty by the representatives of the Treaty Powers. If, after this point, the Boxer movement threatened to become a revolution, it was a threatened revolution against "government by ultimatum," vested in the diplomatic body, and speaking through the Tsungli Yamen.

CHAPTER X.

The Crisis: May 28-June 20, 1900.

The Outbreak at Fengtai—Legation Guards—"Twenty or Thirty Men"—The Paotingfu Party—Murder of Messrs. Norman and Richardson—The Cossacks—Interruption of the Railway—Imperial Efforts to Restore Order—MacDonald's Telegrams of June 9—The Seymour Expedition—Effect on Conditions at Peking—Capture of the Taku Forts—Peking, June 17-20—Summary.

THE answer of the Tsungli Yamen to the second joint note from the diplomatic body was dated May 27, but it was not received at the Spanish legation until the next morning. Following a formal acknowledgment of the doyen's dispatch, the Yamen gave the wording of the decree of May 17, to which they had made reference in their previous note,[1] as well as two additional decrees which had been issued on May 24 and 25, the first of these in response to a memorial by the Yamen, the second in answer to a report from Yu Lu relating the measures which he had taken against the rioters. The Yamen also communicated copies of the regulations which had been issued for the maintenance of order in the Tartar city, the proclamation of the governor of Peking against the Boxer societies, and the regulations for the Chinese city. They closed their note by begging the doyen to inform them in case there were still any points upon which the foreign representatives were not fully satisfied.

The diplomatic corps, at its meeting on May 27, had

[1] A copy of this decree had been privately communicated to the American legation on May 21 by the secretaries of the Yamen; see *Foreign Relations of the United States*, 1900, p. 134, note.

postponed till its next meeting, which was scheduled for the following evening, a final decision in regard to summoning guards for the legations; but the Russian and British ministers, in the course of interviews with the Tsungli Yamen on the twenty-seventh, had both impressed upon the Yamen members the certainty that guards would be brought to Peking unless the necessary measures were immediately taken by the imperial government. The Yamen's full—almost abject—compliance with the foreign demands now confirmed the opinion, which had been frequently expressed, that the authorities at Peking were willing to go to almost any extreme in order to avoid the humiliation of having the legation guards again brought to the capital.

The gratification caused by the conciliatory attitude of the Yamen was short-lived. The government's surrender to diplomatic pressure was attended by—if it did not actually cause—increased popular excitement. By the evening of the twenty-eighth, when the foreign representatives met to discuss the Yamen's reply, fresh news had been received of such an alarming character that immediate and decisive action was felt to be absolutely necessary. During the course of the morning, the railway station at Fengtai—the junction point of the Peking-Paotingfu and the Peking-Tientsin lines—had been attacked and destroyed by a mob, which then proceeded to loot and burn the residences of the foreigners attached to the railway administration. As all the foreigners had left for Peking before the mob began its work of destruction, no lives had been lost, although M. Pichon reported that one Frenchman had received personal injuries at the hands of the rioters. Especial alarm was caused by the news that soldiers at the scene of the disorders were fraternizing with the mob and refusing to protect foreign property.

Immediately after receiving reports of this fresh outbreak, and without awaiting the decision of the meeting which was to be held that evening, the French minister telegraphed to his naval commander at Taku for a detachment of marines.[2] At the subsequent meeting of the diplomatic body, it was unanimously decided that the guards should be summoned at once; the doyen was authorized to inform the Tsungli Yamen of this decision and to request that facilities be provided for transporting the detachments to Peking. On the following morning the Yamen replied to this notification and request by begging the ministers to reconsider their decision, if only to the extent of postponing for a few days the arrival of the detachments; if, after three or four days, the measures which were being taken by the government for the restoration of order proved successful, the coming of the guards could then be stopped altogether.

On the twenty-ninth the alarm in regard to the railway was considerably abated, since it was discovered that the train service between Peking and Tientsin was functioning normally. In spite of this improved aspect of the situation, the meeting of the diplomatic body, which was held at noon on the thirtieth to consider the Yamen's objections to summoning the guards, decided to ignore the objections which had been raised by the Chinese government and to bring up the detachments, if necessary by force. After the close of this meeting, M. Pichon, Sir Claude MacDonald, M. de Giers, and Mr. Conger, all of whom expected contingents of marines on the following day, called in a body upon the Tsungli Yamen and informed the Chinese offi-

[2] It is probable that the Russian minister took similar action at the same time; on the morning of the thirtieth, 100 Russians and 100 French marines approached the landing at Taku, but returned to their ships because of the threatening aspect of the forces at the forts.

cials of the decision which had been reached. The members of the Yamen were assured that the only result of a refusal on their part would be that the guards would come up without permission, and, no doubt, in larger numbers than would otherwise have been the case.

This interview was concluded about four o'clock in the afternoon, and, at two o'clock the next morning, a note from the Yamen was received at each of the four legations; the Chinese government agreed that the guards should be brought up, on the condition that the number for each legation should not be more than twenty or thirty men, and with the understanding that these guards would be charged only with the task of protecting the legations and would not be allowed to interfere in other matters. The condition upon which the government gave its consent was completely ignored; the first detachment, comprising the American, British, French, Italian, Japanese, and Russian contingents, consisted of 337 men, of whom the British, French, and Russians each had seventy-five. In spite of this disregard of its wishes, the Chinese government, by moving the troops of Tung Fu-hsiang out to the Imperial Hunting Park—south of the city, gave evidence of a real desire to avoid any clash between its own forces and the foreign guards, and the detachment, which reached Peking by special train about seven o'clock on the evening of May 31, entered the city without the occurrence of any unpleasant incident.

At the moment when the diplomatic body reached its decision to summon the legation guards, the Boxer disturbances had resulted in no loss of foreign life since the murder of Mr. Brooks, five months earlier, in Shantung; in Chihli, the only foreigner who had suffered personal injuries of any sort was the French railway official at Fengtai. By the time the first detachment of marines arrived at Peking, however, additional foreign lives had been lost. On the morning of May 31, a party of French and Belgian railway engineers, making their way by boat from Paotingfu to Tientsin, came into conflict with bands of armed Chinese about twenty miles from Tientsin; in the fight which ensued, four of the Europeans were killed and several of the party were wounded.

The circumstances attending this first clash between armed Europeans and the I-ho Chuan are of considerable importance. According to an account which appeared in the *North China Herald* of June 13, the chief engineer in charge of construction work at Paotingfu decided, on May 28, to leave immediately for Tientsin with his entire staff. This decision had been reached because news of the riot at Fengtai had been followed by rumors that an attack was about to be made upon the foreigners at Paotingfu. The departure was postponed, however, until the following afternoon, when the party, which consisted of thirty-three men, seven women, and one child, embarked upon a dozen boats and started for Tientsin with their Chinese servants and with a number of Chinese soldiers as an escort. The Europeans were armed with revolvers and a few rifles, but the fact that they were divided into small groups—three or four on each boat—gave them a general feeling of insecurity, which was intensified by warnings from "friendly Chinese" that they were certain to be attacked on the trip.

For the first twenty-four hours of the journey, the party was accompanied by an official from Paotingfu; but on the afternoon of the thirtieth this official returned to his post, leaving his interpreter to act as commander of the expedition. Several times during the first day the foreigners had been ordered down into the boats and the hatches had been closed while the boats were passing certain localities which were said to be dangerous. Strenuous objections had been raised against this procedure, and the commands of the mandarin had been obeyed only when supplemented by the orders of the chief engineer; the air inside the boats was terribly hot, and, as the members of the party had no confidence in their military escort, they were afraid of being caught "like rats in a trap" in case the anticipated attack was made upon them.

About sunset on the thirtieth some members of the party felt certain that an attack was about to take place, but nothing happened. At midnight, after anchoring for a few hours, the flotilla resumed its journey; all the Europeans were again sent below and the hatches were closed, in spite of the usual protests. About 6 A.M. on the thirty-first, the sound of rifles was heard, and the Europeans immediately forced open the hatches and came up on deck. All jumped ashore; as soon as they had arrived there, they formed into groups and began to return the fire which was being directed at them. The boats were pushed away from the bank, either by the boatmen or by the enemy, and from this point the little party fought their way into Tientsin, where they arrived on the second of June.

Accepting this account as accurate—and there is no reason for suspecting that the Tientsin correspondent of the *North China Herald* would distort it in favor of the Chinese—the actual responsibility for the origin of the conflict remains undetermined. The position of the Europeans—divided into small groups on a dozen boats, shut in below the decks, continually expecting an attack, and having no confidence in the loyalty of their escort—makes it unreasonable to suppose that they would wait, after hearing the sound of shots, to find out whether the shots were actually being fired at them. Such inaction might have resulted in their being slaughtered without any chance of escape. On the other hand, the sudden and unexpected appearance of thirty or more armed foreigners in the midst of a Chinese town would, in the existing state of popular excitement, have been quite sufficient to start a fight even if the original attack had not been made by the townspeople. Finally, since the Europeans were divided into groups of three or four on the different boats, it was obviously impossible for any one of them to say whether or not the people on boats other than his own had appeared on deck before the first shots were fired.

The "battle" between the Paotingfu party and the I-ho Chuan threw the districts west and northwest of Tientsin into an uproar, to which the news that foreign armed forces, the legation guards, were proceeding to Peking probably contributed. On the morning of June 1 a band of Boxers invaded the village of Yung Ching—some twenty-five miles to the north of the point at which the battle had started—and killed two missionaries of the S. P. G. mission, Messrs. Norman and Robinson. There had already been some friction between the militia organization and the Yung Ching mission; on May 2 the British consul at Tientsin had reported that the author of some placards attacking the English mission there had been forced to apologize to the Rev. Mr. Norman, but that the hostility of the people had since apparently died away. The earlier friction was probably a fundamental cause of the double murder, but there is hardly any question that this attack, which was the only fatal attack upon missionaries—or upon *unarmed* foreigners of any description—between the murder of Mr. Brooks and the bombardment of the Taku forts, was precipitated by the events of the previous day.

The excitement among the villages west of Tientsin was given no opportunity to subside. When the Paotingfu refugees finally reached Tientsin, during the afternoon of June

2, it was discovered that several members of the party were missing. A party of twenty-five or thirty Cossacks was, therefore, sent out during the night to scour the countryside and bring in the stragglers. This rescue party returned the following evening, but with their officer and two men badly wounded; they had come upon a large body of the I-ho Chuan and a severe battle had been fought, in the course of which heavy losses had been inflicted upon the Chinese. A few hours before the return of the Cossacks, seventy-five additional marines, comprising the contingents for the German and Austrian legations, had gone up to Peking by rail. That night—the night of June 3-4—the railway line between Tientsin and Peking was attacked at several points; rails were torn up and attempts were made to destroy some of the bridges. From this moment, rail communication between the capital and the coast was at an end.

The interruption of traffic on the Peking-Tientsin railway was known to the foreign legations on June 4, and a meeting of the diplomatic body was immediately called to consider this new turn of events. At the suggestion of M. Pichon, it was unanimously decided that the representatives of all the powers having warships in Chinese waters should at once telegraph to their governments and request that their naval commanders be given instructions to take any necessary measures for the relief of the legations in case telegraphic communication should also be cut. These telegrams were promptly sent, and the commanding officers at Taku received the requested instructions.

Despite the fact that every show of force on the part of the foreign powers and every repressive step taken by the imperial government in response to foreign dictation had served only to intensify the popular excitement, the foreign diplomats were practically unanimous in the belief that there was but one satisfactory method to be employed in dealing with the situation. They considered that their several governments should take such combined action as would compel the Chinese authorities either to utilize sufficient military force to put down the disturbances or to acknowledge that they were no longer capable of governing the country. There was a growing disbelief in the willingness, or ability, of the imperial government to adopt the measures which the foreign representatives regarded as suitable. There was no faith at all in the efficacy of such measures as the Chinese were willing to adopt, and no inclination to await the outcome of those measures. At the same time it seems to have been recognized, by some of the foreign representatives, that, if the imperial government did attempt to adopt extreme measures, this might very possibly result in a formidable revolution in the north which would immediately be echoed by an anti-Manchu outbreak in the Yangtze Valley and the south.

The Chinese authorities gave the diplomats repeated assurances that the troubles would soon be quieted, and took immediate steps to restore the railway service on the Peking-Tientsin line. General Nieh, with 6000 troops, was ordered from Lu-tai—to the east of Tientsin—and was assigned to the task of dispersing the bands who were obstructing the railway. The troops, however, did not employ violence against the Boxers, but merely attempted to secure their departure by means of persuasion. Indeed, it may be conjectured that the real purpose of the government, in bringing troops to the obstructed portion of the line, was to calm the minds of the people by convincing them that there was no more danger of further "foreign invasions" of the capital.[3] Reporting an interview which he

[3] The *North China Herald* of June 20, 1900, contains what purports to be the translation of an official account of a conflict, on June 5, between

had with the Tsungli Yamen on June 6, Sir Claude MacDonald said it was evident that Prince Ching doubted whether the troops "would be allowed to fire on the Boxers except in defence of government property, or, if authorized, whether they would obey."

At this interview, and at one which he had on the preceding day, the British minister was impressed by the apathetic and pessimistic tone of the Yamen; he was convinced that the Yamen had ceased to represent effectually the ruling power of China, and that it was no longer of use as a lever for moving the Chinese government. Sir Claude accordingly requested the doyen to call a meeting of the diplomatic body for the afternoon of the sixth, to consider the advisability of demanding a collective audience with the Throne in order to explain to the court the extreme gravity of the situation. The suggestion that an audience might be demanded had been unofficially communicated to the Tsungli Yamen before the meeting was held; this greatly perturbed the members, who begged the foreign ministers not to make this demand until the authorities had had a few days in which to show their good faith and their ability to restore the railway communications. At the meeting, the diplomatic body decided to wait until the ninth before making a formal demand for an audience, but, in the interval, the various representatives were to obtain

some of General Nieh's troops and the I-ho Chuan. According to this report, the troops first tried to disperse the mob good-naturedly and were reviled by the mob, who accused the soldiers of being bribed by the foreigners; shots were fired at the soldiers, and the popular captain of one company was killed, whereupon his soldiers attacked the I-ho Chuan and killed a great number of them. It is noteworthy that, according to this report, the mob was not destroying the railroad, but merely blocking it. Admiral Seymour's account of his first conflict with the Boxers, on June 11, also indicates that they were merely trying to obstruct the line.

from their governments the necessary authority to make such a demand.

On the same day, the Russian minister, acting independently of his colleagues, addressed a letter to the Empress Dowager in which he warned her of the dangers which she was bringing upon China, and demanded that immediate action be taken against the "insurrection." This letter was committed to the hands of Prince Ching for presentation to his sovereign, and M. de Giers personally informed Prince Ching that, if the telegraph line was destroyed, Russian troops would at once be brought to Peking.[4] Even before this threat by the Russian minister, the air had been filled with rumors in regard to the movements of Russian troops; one report was that a large Russian force had already been landed at Peitaiho, another was that several transports loaded with Russian soldiers had arrived at Taku and were preparing to land their men. On June 7, therefore, six battalions of the Peiyang forces under General Sung Ching were ordered to Lu-tai, a position from which they would be able to oppose any military movement along the railway from Taku or Peitaiho toward Tientsin and the capital. It was also reported, on the same date, that General Nieh had been ordered to move his army corps from the Peking-Tientsin railway to the same defensive position.[5]

While the disturbances along the railway had effectively stopped traffic between Peking and Tientsin, the situation

[4] M. de Giers' letter and his conversation with Prince Ching were reported in a dispatch from M. Pichon to Delcassé on June 6; see *Documents Diplomatiques, Chine (1899-1900)*, p. 32.

[5] The report as to General Nieh's troops appears to have been unfounded; as late as the morning of June 11 these troops were still endeavoring to quell the disturbances along the Peking-Tientsin line. No precise information is available concerning the movements of General Sung Ching's forces at this time.

inside the capital, so far as the behavior of the Chinese toward foreigners was concerned, remained perfectly quiet. The missionaries from remote parts of the city, who had moved to the legation quarter for safety, made daily visits to their "compounds" for the purpose of bringing back valuables, necessary clothing, and food; these reported that a spirit of vague apprehension prevailed throughout the city, but that there were, as yet, no demonstrations of hostility against the foreigners. It would almost seem as though the only centers of excitement in Peking, during the week that followed the interruption of the railway service, were the offices of the several foreign legations, and there the excitement was feverish.

This continued quiet in Peking was regarded as a justification of the decision to summon the legation guards, to whose presence was attributed the fact that no attacks were made upon the foreign residents. Yet the foreigners did not confine themselves to the legation quarter, where they would be under the protection of the guards; they did not even confine themselves to the city. The requests of the Chinese authorities that parties from the legations should not venture into the surrounding country lest they be attacked by lawless bands, were completely ignored, and rides outside the city gates continued to be a popular form of recreation as late as the ninth of June. On this date, a party of student interpreters from the British legation came into conflict with a band of the I-ho Chuan outside the city, and, after shooting one of the Chinese, had to beat a hasty retreat. In consequence of this incident, the British minister issued an order forbidding British subjects to ride outside the city, and this form of diversion was abandoned by the entire foreign community.

The imperial government, in the meantime, continued its efforts to quell the disorders by conciliating, rather than crushing, the disturbing element. In a decree published on June 6, the distinction was again made between the good members of the I-ho Chuan and those disreputable characters who, by their lawless acts, were bringing disgrace upon the organization. This decree pointed out that responsibility for the general disorder rested partly upon the Christian converts, among whom there had recently come to be many of bad character; partly on the local officials, who had not governed properly, or had failed to decide promptly the disputes between the Christians and non-Christians; and partly on the bad characters who had gotten into the I-ho Chuan. The decree announced that the Grand Councillor Chao Shu-chiao had been appointed imperial commissioner for the purpose of restoring order and sending the people back to their homes. If any should continue disobedient to these commands, the good members of the I-ho Chuan must hand over the guilty ones to the authorities for punishment; should the I-ho Chuan refuse to coöperate with the government in this way, they would be declared rebels and lawbreakers, and the imperial troops would then be sent to exterminate them.

There are, of course, no means of proving that the Empress Dowager issued this decree in perfect good faith, and there has been a general tendency to dismiss it as having been obviously insincere; yet the efforts made by the Chinese government for the restoration of order deserve more respect than they have usually received. The foreigners especially resented those passages in the decree which attributed some of the blame to the bad elements among the Christians; this was regarded as a gratuitous attack upon the Christian religion, and as an attempt to arouse popular hatred against the native Christians. Only by a frank statement of the facts, however, could the government hope to secure respect for its commands; the people knew that the attitude of the Christian converts had been responsible for some of the friction, and any decree which ignored this fact would have been regarded with contempt. On the other hand, the decree of June 6 might have made it possible, if no fresh complications were introduced by the foreigners, for the government to utilize against the Boxers the military force which the foreigners had been demanding. If the I-ho Chuan refused to obey a decree which the people generally recognized as reasonable—a decree which was free from any suspicion of foreign dictation—they would put themselves in a position of open defiance against the lawful authorities, and it would then be possible forcibly to dispel the bands without stirring up a popular revolt. The possibility of this outcome depended upon the forbearance of the diplomatic body as much as upon the sincerity of the Empress Dowager. The absence of fresh cause for popular alarm was an essential condition for the restoration of order, and this condition was not granted.

On June 4 the Austrian chargé d'affaires at Peking had expressed the opinion that the number of the guards that had been brought up for the legations would be exaggerated tenfold in the reports which circulated among the Chinese; this fact would, he believed, do much to quiet the disturbances.[6] Whatever may have been the effect of such exaggerated reports within the city of Peking, the effect outside the city was quite different from that which Herr von Rosthorn had so hopefully anticipated. On June 8 all the American missionaries from Tungchow came in to the capital, bringing reports of attacks upon the native Christians in Tungchow. The next day the race course pavilion, outside the west gate of Peking, was burned by the Boxers, and the clash between a band of these rioters and the stu-

[6] See Winterhalder, *Kämpfe in China*, p. 48.

dent interpreters from the British legation showed that the I-ho Chuan were now at the very gates of the city. So far, however, none of the Boxer bands had gained access to Peking, although there had been frequent reports that the ritual and drill were being performed by sympathizers inside the city.

On June 6 Sir Claude MacDonald had wired to Admiral Seymour, asking him to send an additional guard of seventy-five men for the British legation, and, on the eighth, some of his colleagues had made an unsuccessful attempt to secure, from the Tsungli Yamen, permission to bring up extra guards. On the ninth a meeting of the diplomatic body was called for the express purpose of deciding whether the ministers who had naval forces at their disposal at Taku should telegraph for reinforcements. Shortly before this meeting took place, Sir Claude, because of various alarming rumors which had come to his ears, sent off an independent telegram to the British admiral saying that, unless reinforcements were sent immediately, it would be too late.

When the diplomats assembled to consider the situation, the other representatives, especially M. Pichon, took a much more reasuring view of conditions, and it was decided not to send for any reinforcements until two o'clock the following afternoon. In accordance with this decision, Sir Claude telegraphed again to the admiral, and countermanded his earlier request. Still later, however, the British minister learned from a Chinese source, which, he said, he had hitherto found trustworthy, that the Empress Dowager had openly expressed her desire to rid the capital of the foreigners, and that the soldiers of Tung Fu-hsiang were only waiting for the word to begin the attack. He therefore again wired to the admiral, at 8:30 P.M., requesting that troops be landed and arrangements be at once made for an advance on Peking. Mr. Conger dispatched a similar telegram, at about the same time, to the commander of the American naval force.[7]

The council of naval commanders at Taku had already agreed that, in case the dispatch of an expedition for the relief of Peking became necessary, the combined forces should be under the command of the British admiral, with a Russian colonel as his chief-of-staff. When the telegrams of the British and American ministers were received, the ships at Taku immediately began to land their men, and by 5 A.M. on June 10 an international force of some 1500 men, with field guns, machine guns, and rations for three days, had been disembarked and was entraining at Taku. This force reached Tientsin by half past seven in the morning, and by nine o'clock the first train had started for Peking,

[7] This account of MacDonald's telegrams of June 9 is drawn from his own detailed report, which is printed in the *British Blue Books, China No. 4 (1900)*, document no. 1. One—almost farcical—passage in this report deserves passing notice: Sir Claude attributes his first telegram, asking for reinforcements, partly to an interview which he had with Lien Fang, one of the interpreters of the Tsungli Yamen, in the course of which interview he was particularly impressed by *what Lien Fang did not say!* When a presumably well-poised British diplomat was making momentous decisions on the basis of such vague impressions, it is difficult to criticize the Chinese people very severely for their acceptance of all sorts of wild rumors. It must be borne in mind, however, that the British official publications are carefully edited, and that the real reasons for MacDonald's decision have probably not been made public; it is not unreasonable to suspect that his independent action in summoning the reinforcements was influenced by other considerations than the reported attitude of the Chinese court, *e.g.*, the rumored activities of the Russian forces. It should be noted that, some time on June 9, de Giers wired to St. Petersburg: "In my judgement, the rôle of the diplomats has come to an end and the admirals must take charge of the situation. Only the prompt arrival of a strong detachment can save the foreigners at Peking."—*Krasny Arkhiv*, vol. XIV. Mr. Conger's dispatches give no explanation of the coincidence between his own decision and that of the British minister; as he was under definite instruction to act independently, this is not surprising.

carrying about 800 men with artillery and machine guns. A second detachment of 600 men, with additional supplies, left Tientsin later in the day, and reinforcements on the eleventh and twelfth brought the total strength of the expedition up to about 2100.

Owing to the damaged condition of the railway, the forces under Admiral Seymour were compelled to proceed slowly, repairing the line as they went, and, in their first day's advance, were able to cover only thirty miles of the eighty which separated Tientsin from the capital. On June 11 their progress was even less rapid and they advanced only about ten miles, but it was not until the afternoon of this second day that they had their first contact with the Boxers. Near Lang-fang, about halfway to Peking, the advance guard came upon the bands engaged in blocking the railway, and drove them off after a skirmish in which thirty-five of the Boxers are reported to have been killed. On the twelfth the column advanced only three miles, but no fighting took place. The first attack made by the Boxers upon the advancing foreigners was on the thirteenth, three days after they had left Tientsin; this attack was repulsed with heavy losses to the Chinese and no casualties among the Europeans, but, from this time, the expedition was able to make no further progress. The railway was now impassable behind, as well as in front, and all communication with Tientsin had been destroyed.

For two days, in the face of constant attacks by the Boxers who were repeatedly driven off with heavy losses, efforts were made to repair the railway. On the sixteenth it was decided that the expedition should abandon the railway and attempt to reach Peking by advancing along the river. On June 18—the day after the seizure of the Taku forts by the allied naval forces—the column was attacked by imperial troops acting in coöperation with the

I-ho Chuan, and the foreign officers realized that there was no alternative but retreat. Almost out of food, hampered by their sick and wounded, continually harassed by a galling rifle fire, the little army finally succeeded, on June 23, in reaching and capturing the imperial arsenal of Hsi-ku, a few miles northwest of Tientsin. Here they were besieged until the twenty-sixth, when a relief party of fresh troops from Tientsin rescued them, and brought them safely back to the shelter of the foreign settlements.[8]

The news of foreign military activity at Taku, which was received by the imperial authorities—perhaps in exaggerated form—during the night of June 9, brought an immediate response. The meetings of the sovereign with the Grand Council of State are regularly held at daybreak; a meeting was, therefore, in session at the moment when the Seymour expedition was entraining at Taku, and the *Peking Gazette* of June 10 published the following decree, which had been approved at that meeting:

> Let Prince Tuan be appointed President of the Tsungli Yamen. Let Chi Hsiu, President of the Board of Rites; Pu Hsing, Junior Vice-president of the Board of Works; and Na Tung, sub-chancellor of the Grand Secretariat and holding the brevet rank of Vice-president of the Board of Rites; be appointed members of the Tsungli Yamen.
>
> At the present time we are confronted with difficulties and troublesome questions, and it is absolutely necessary that the said prince and ministers should sincerely apply their minds to the performance of the duties of their post so as to aid us. They will not be permitted to decline appointment.[9]

All four of these newly appointed members of the

[8] The casualties of the expedition amounted to 62 killed and 228 wounded.

[9] This translation is taken from *Foreign Relations of the United States*, 1900, p. 147.

Tsungli Yamen were Manchus, and were known to belong to the conservative party. Prince Tuan, especially, who was father of the heir apparent, was looked upon as the leader of the extreme anti-foreign clique and the avowed patron of the I-ho Chuan; his appointment to the position of joint president—with Prince Ching, the old president—of the Yamen was, therefore, generally regarded by the members of the diplomatic body as presaging grave dangers for the foreigners at Peking. Mr. Conger expressed the belief that this appointment would mean closer harmony, in the future, between the Yamen and the throne, but was of the opinion that it "ought not to be recognized or permitted." These appointments unquestionably indicated that power at Peking was beginning to pass into the hands of the war party, but it is necessary to bear in mind that they were the result of apparent foreign invasion, and do not prove a determination, on the part of the imperial government, to assume the offensive against the foreigners.

Even after the appointment of Prince Tuan and his fellow conservatives to the Tsungli Yamen, the moderate party still retained, for a while, a controlling influence in the affairs of state. The old president of the Yamen, Prince Ching, and three other prominent members—Yuan Chang, Lien Yuan, and Hsu Ching-cheng—were still in favor of a conciliatory attitude toward the outside world; while Jung Lu and Li Shan, in the Grand Council, continued to throw their influence on the side of peace. On June 12, when the Seymour expedition was already halfway to Peking, four members of the Yamen called upon several of the legations and endeavored to obtain assurance that the reinforcements would come no farther than the railway terminus. Failing to secure any promise on this point, they eventually announced that the government would not oppose their entry into the city if their numbers did not exceed 1200.[10]

The moderates still exerted an influence in the councils of the Empress Dowager, and their voices were still heard in the cause of peace, but the storm was rapidly gaining strength and threatening to sweep them away. The first effect of the Seymour expedition was to rouse the entire population along the Peking-Tientsin railway; the second was to focus upon the capital the activities of the Boxer organizations. A few hours after the first detachment of the relief force left Tientsin, the telegraph line between Tientsin and Peking was cut; for the next four or five days, the legations were able to send telegrams to their home governments by way of Kiachta, and to get messages through the Boxer lines by means of native messengers, but, by the fifteenth, the foreigners at Peking were completely cut off from communication with the outside world.[11] On the night of the tenth the Boxers burned the British "Summer Legation" at the Western Hills; on the eleventh Mr. Sugiyama, the chancellor of the Japanese legation was killed at the gate of the city, while on his way to the railway station to meet the expected reinforcements; and on the thirteenth the first Boxer bands appeared within the walls of the capital.

Upon entering Peking, the Boxers immediately began to loot and burn the outlying abandoned residences of the foreigners who had taken refuge in the legation quarter, to burn the churches, and to attack the native Christians—the "secondary devils." Conflicts also began to occur, al-

[10] See *Foreign Relations of the United States, 1900*, p. 154; *British Blue Books, China No. 3 (1900)*, document no. 126, and *ibid., China 4 (1900)*, document no. 3.

[11] It has been asserted, but not definitely proved, that a military wire from Peking to Taku was in working order at least as late as June 17, but this wire was not at the disposal of the foreign diplomats.

most immediately, between the rioters and the armed guards of the legations.

It is difficult to determine to what extent the clashes between the legation guards and the Boxers were, for the first day or two, the outcome of a purely defensive attitude on the part of the guards. The British minister, in a review of this period which he wrote on September 20, says that preparations were made, on June 13, to resist an attack upon the legation quarter, but that there was no attack of any importance until the following night, when several attacks—all easily repulsed—were made upon the pickets. On the other hand, the Rev. Roland Allen, in his diary of the siege, states that on the afternoon of the thirteenth a party of German and Italian guards raided a near-by temple in which the Boxers were said to be drilling; the Boxers had, however, received warning of the intended attack, and the foreigners succeeded only in capturing a few weapons and a quantity of red cord, which the Boxers customarily used as part of their uniform. The same witness also reports that, on the next evening, German marines on the city wall near their legation opened fire on a Boxer mass meeting which was being held in the southern, or "Chinese," city. Mr. Conger, in his dispatch of June 15, says: "We are simply trying to defend ourselves until reinforcements arrive, but nearly 100 Boxers have already been killed by the various legation guards. If we had been feeling at all safe with our present guards, many hundreds would have been already punished." This passage suggests that the foreign diplomats were inclined to ignore the Yamen's stipulation—that the guards were to be charged only with the task of defending the legations—or that they had put rather a broad interpretation upon the idea of defense.

On and after the fifteenth rescue parties were sent out

through the city to bring in to the safe refuge of the legation quarter such of the native Christians as had managed to escape the Boxer fury. These parties, which were composed partly of guards and partly of civilian volunteers, turned, at times, from their humanitarian purpose to the more exciting sport of hunting down and exterminating bands of the I-ho Chuan. The rescue parties, and even the legation guards while on picket duty, also fired occasionally upon bodies of regular Chinese troops, apparently under the mistaken impression that these were Boxers. A collision of this sort occurred, on June 17, between a small German outpost and a body of Kansu soldiers, and resulted in two or three of the Chinese being killed. Both Sir Claude MacDonald and Mr. Conger regretted this incident because it increased the danger of the situation; the American minister, however, expressed the belief that "these exhibitions of skill and courage on the part of the foreign troops are good object lessons."

"Audacity," rather than "courage," would best describe the act of firing upon the troops of a friendly country within the very walls of its capital city, and the "skill" which was required to hit—with modern military rifles at a hundred yards or so—two or three men of a company marching in column formation does not appear excessive. Nor is it entirely possible to agree with Mr. Conger's estimate as to the benefits which were to be derived from such exploits. That a sergeant of the regular forces shot and killed Baron von Ketteler on the morning of the twentieth and that the greater part of the imperial troops coöperated in the attacks upon the legations after that date must, in part, be attributed to the activities of the legation guards during the week which followed June 13.

The testimony of the British and American ministers, in regard to the collision on June 17, agrees in the statement that the officers of the Kansu soldiers controlled their men and prevented their replying to the shots which had taken effect among them. Yet these were a part of the turbulent and undisciplined hordes of Tung Fu-hsiang; these were the men whose reported readiness to exterminate the hated foreigners had caused MacDonald, on the night of June 9, to summon the Seymour expedition! Because of contemporary happenings on the coast, the restraint displayed by the Kansu troops on this occasion must be regarded as especially important. During the morning of that day the combined naval forces at Taku had bombarded the Taku forts and had taken them by storm. It therefore becomes necessary to examine the events which had been taking place in the vicinity of Tientsin and Taku since the departure of the Seymour expedition.

On June 11 General Nieh, whose forces were still engaged in the task of restoring order along the railway, sent the following two telegrams to Viceroy Yu Lu at Tientsin:

I previously telegraphed asking that the foreign envoys might be requested by the Yamen to order the foreigners at Tientsin to postpone going up to Peking.

Besides, I have issued repeated proclamations, all to the effect that the railway is State built. Now, when the foreign troops suddenly come and begin to repair the railway, alarm and suspicion are aroused among the people, and I am afraid that they may be excited into a rebellious movement, when it would be difficult for my troops to escort and protect them. I accordingly send you this telegram, and request you to inform the different foreign envoys and consuls. This is my earnest request.

This day at noon over 1000 foreign troops armed with quick-firing guns and stores were proceeding straight to Peking in the train; I was just going to stop them when I received your message in reply from the Railway Office Telegraph, saying that the special train to convey the foreign troops to Peking was provided by the Viceroy's orders.

It seems to me that, if foreign troops are coming in such numbers, coast defence is important, and, as there is absolutely no use in my troops remaining at Yang Tsun, I had better order the officer in command of the cavalry to return to Lu-tai to guard against eventualities. I humbly beg you will give instructions in compliance with this.[12]

On the twelfth and thirteenth the messages and telegrams of Viceroy Yu Lu were almost equally concerned with the protection of the foreign missionaries in the outlying districts, and with the proper disposition of the troops for defense against "possible eventualities along the coast." The second of these two concerns soon came to occupy his entire attention; on the fifteenth, the viceroy received imperial commands directing that the forces at his disposal be concentrated for the defense of Tientsin against possible foreign attack. From this time Yu Lu appears to have abandoned his efforts to maintain the peace, and to have thrown himself into the work of preparing for war.

A similar "drift" toward war was taking place on the foreign side. On June 14, immediately after it became known at Taku that Admiral Seymour's communications with Tientsin had been destroyed, the foreign naval commanders held a council to consider the necessity of taking over the Taku forts and the railway station at Tangku in order to insure the maintenance of communications between the fleet and Tientsin. On the fifteenth the station at Tangku was occupied by a detachment of marines, and, on the following morning an ultimatum, demanding the surrender of the forts, was drawn up. This ultimatum—

[12] These translations are taken from *British Blue Books, China No. 1 (1901)*, document no. 229.

in which the American commander, Admiral Kempff, refused to participate on the ground that no act of war had yet been committed by the Chinese government—fixed the time limit for the surrender of the forts at 2 A.M. on the seventeenth, and copies were communicated to the commander of the forts and to the viceroy at Tientsin.[13]

During the afternoon and evening which followed the delivery of the ultimatum, landing parties were set on shore by the larger warships, and the gunboats were moved up into the shallow waters of the Pei-ho within easy range of the forts. The Chinese made no efforts to prevent these warlike preparations, but, a few minutes before 1 A.M.—about an hour before the ultimatum was to expire—the forts opened fire upon the ships which were anchored in the river. The foreign ships immediately replied to the fire; the landing forces moved up to the attack; and, by 6:30 A.M., the forts were in the hands of the allied forces. At three o'clock that afternoon, the imperial troops at Tientsin began to bombard the foreign settlements, and, on the next day, the Seymour expedition was, for the first time, attacked by Chinese regular soldiers.[14]

[13] The surrender of the forts was demanded on the ground that hostile preparations were being made, at Taku and along the railway, which endangered the communications with Tientsin, but Baron d'Anthouard, first secretary of the French legation, in *La Chine contre l'Étranger*, pp. 37 ff., describes conditions on the afternoon of June 15 at Taku and Tangku as quite normal. Baron d'Anthouard and his wife landed at Taku on the fifteenth with a party of eighty French marines who were being sent up to Tientsin as reinforcements; he did not observe any unusual excitement until after reaching Tientsin.

[14] During the attack on the forts, a number of shots from the Chinese guns were fired in the direction of the U.S.S. *Monocacy*, which was lying at anchor near Tangku; in consequence of this hostile act, Admiral Kempff considered that a state of war existed, from that time, between China and the United States, and felt justified, therefore, in coöperating with the other senior naval officers in their subsequent operations. See the *Boston Evening Transcript* of July 25 and 27, 1900, for Admiral Kempff's reports.

It has been rather generally assumed that, even after telegraphic communication between Tientsin and Peking was destroyed, a military wire still existed between Peking and the Taku forts, and that the imperial government was, by this means, promptly informed as to the ultimatum of the naval commanders and the capture of the forts.[15] The existence or non-existence of this wire would, however, have made but little difference in the time at which the imperial government received news of this act of war. The news that the forts had been taken was published in Shanghai by the *Tungwen Pao*—a Chinese paper—at 3 P.M. on June 17, having probably been telegraphed from Tientsin by way of Tsinanfu. From Shanghai, it must have reached Peking, by way of Hankow and Paotingfu, some time during the course of the afternoon. Whatever the exact moment at which the information was received, events at Peking, during the seventeenth and eighteenth of June, indicate that the councils of the imperial government were still strongly influenced by the party which favored the maintenance of peace with the outside world.

The following imperial decree, published in the *Peking Gazette* of June 17, had been approved by the Empress Dowager at a meeting of the Grand Council which took place while the fighting at Taku was actually in progress:

Lately the people and the Christians have sought means to stir up enmity, and bad language has arisen on every side. Vagabonds have taken occasion repeatedly to burn and rob. All foreign ministers ought to be really protected. Jung Lu is ordered to detail his soldiers at once and energetically use his authority and go imme-

[15] This assumption may be questioned. On and after June 11 the viceroy at Tientsin was sending messages by carrier to Tungchow, for transmission to Peking; if a military wire had been in operation between Peking and Taku, it would have been more expeditious to telegraph his dispatches to Taku and have them transmitted to Peking from that point.

diately to East Legation Street and vicinity and with all his power protect those ministers. He must not be in the least careless. If the ministers and their families wish to go for a time to Tientsin, they must be protected by the way; but the railroad is not now in working order. If they go by cart road, it will be difficult, and there is fear that perfect protection cannot be afforded. They would better, therefore, abide in peace as hitherto, and wait till the railroad is repaired and then act as circumstances render expedient.[16]

This decree was immediately communicated to the foreign diplomats by the Tsungli Yamen, and the officers to whom Jung Lu delegated the task of guarding the legations consulted with the commanders of the foreign forces with respect to the most desirable disposition of the Chinese soldiers. The behavior of the troops assigned to this duty was perfectly satisfactory, and, as late as the afternoon of June 19, foreigners walking on the city wall found the Chinese officers and soldiers friendly and peaceable.

There is considerable possibility that the decree ordering Jung Lu to provide protection for the legations was issued while the Empress Dowager and the members of the Grand Council were still in ignorance concerning events at Taku. At 9 P.M. on the same day, however,[17] Li Shan, the president of the Board of Revenue, and two members of the Tsungli Yamen, Lien Yuan and Hsu Yung-i, called at the American legation for an interview with Mr. Conger. All three of these officials belonged to the peace party, and

[16] This translation is taken from *Foreign Relations of the United States*, 1900, p. 168. Morse, in his *International Relations of the Chinese Empire*, vol. III, p. 218, incorrectly gives the date of this decree as June 16; as Mr. Morse is among those who assume the existence of telegraphic communication between Taku and Peking, the importance of this error in date is obvious.

[17] *I.e.*, six hours after the news that the forts had been taken was published at Shanghai.

it may be mentioned, in passing, that they were later put to death as traitors for having opposed the declaration of war. They stated that they had come, under express orders from the Empress Dowager and the Emperor, to give assurance that every means would be devised to give full and adequate protection to the legations and to all foreigners and their property in Peking. The visitors then endeavored to secure information as to the number and whereabouts of the additional guards—the Seymour expedition—and the time when they were expected to arrive at Peking. They explained to Mr. Conger that the presence of the guards who were already in the capital had excited the populace, and they hoped, for this reason, that no more would be sent.

Mr. Conger very naturally pointed out that, as telegraphic communications had been destroyed, he knew nothing as to the movements of the reinforcements. He then proceeded to lecture the delegation in regard to the shortcomings of the Chinese government, and to voice some rather ill-advised threats. He asked "why the Chinese troops did not fire upon the Boxers; nothing but killing them could ever bring about order. . . . American soldiers were now on their way from Manila, and as many as it was thought necessary to protect life and property of Americans would be brought here. . . . If he had 1000 American soldiers, he could kill every Boxer in Peking." He did not know the number of troops that were coming to Peking. "The first detachment here numbered about 400; the second—on their way—about 900; but, as the telegraph is cut and as the foreign admirals knew the situation here, and having (*sic*) plenty of troops at command, thousands may be on their way. . . . If any member of his family, or member of the United States legation, was injured, the American troops would destroy Peking, and it would be very serious for the Chinese government if any of the foreign troops, on their way to Peking, were attacked by Chinese soldiers."[18]

Mr. Conger was, of course, not aware of the warlike measures which had been adopted by the admirals at Taku; he was probably ignorant of the fact that his visitors represented the party at Peking which was striving to prevent the outbreak of hostilities—although ignorance of this sort is a serious diplomatic blunder. The only reasonable explanation of the language which he used at this interview is that he still believed it possible to frighten the imperial government into suppressing a popular movement which was itself the outgrowth of fear, and which, because of fear, found increasing support among the highest officials at Peking. At all events, the moderates in the Grand Council, in their opposition to those who favored an immediate declaration of war, could find little comfort or support in the sentiments expressed by the American minister.

There is a third, and perhaps even more significant, piece of evidence to support the belief that the Empress Dowager had not yet surrendered herself absolutely to the guidance of the war party, or was not yet convinced that peace was no longer possible. On the seventeenth or eighteenth of June, the aged Li Hung-chang, viceroy of the Liang Kwang, received telegraphic instructions to come immediately to Peking for an audience with the Throne. Once more Tzu Hsi was turning, as on so many previous occasions in the past thirty years, to her one successful diplomat for aid in straightening out the tangled web of international affairs.[19]

[18] This summary of the interview is taken from Mr. Conger's official memorandum, the parts in quotations being verbatim extracts. See *Foreign Relations of the United States*, 1900, pp. 152-153.

[19] It has not been possible to fix, beyond question, the precise date of

Popular knowledge of the bombardment and capture of the Taku forts travelled slowly, but its gradual spread from the point of origin was everywhere followed by immediate outbreaks against the foreigners. On the afternoon of June 17 the news reached Tientsin. Acting in conformity with the earlier instructions of the Empress Dowager, that the high provincial officials and military commanders should not wait for detailed orders when war had actually broken out, the local military commanders immediately began an attack upon the foreign settlements, where, in addition to the civilian population, there were some two or three thousand foreign marines and soldiers who had arrived too late to join the forces under Admiral Seymour. On the following day the news was received by the officers in the vicinity of Yang-tsun, where, as has already been mentioned, the Seymour column now found itself opposed by imperial troops as well as by the Boxers. On the nineteenth the news that war had broken out on the coast was received by the people of Peking, and, from this time, the war party in the Grand Council had the support of the general public in addition to that of the I-ho Chuan.

At 5 P.M. on June 19 the foreign community, still ignorant of the capture of the Taku forts, was thrown into the utmost confusion by the receipt, at each legation, of identic notes from the Tsungli Yamen. The foreign representatives were informed that, in consequence of the commencement of hostilities by the naval forces assembled at Taku, it would no longer be possible to guarantee protection to the ministers and their families at Peking. They were, therefore, requested to prepare to depart from Pe-

this summons. The earliest report that Li had been ordered to Peking is found in a dispatch, dated June 18, from the French consul at Canton; see *Documents Diplomatiques, Chine* (1899-1900), p. 43.

king within twenty-four hours, and were notified that an escort would be provided to accompany them to the coast.

The diplomatic body immediately held a meeting, and a note was sent to the Yamen protesting that it would be impossible for the representatives to leave Peking at such short notice. This note also requested that an interview be granted to the foreign ministers the next morning at nine o'clock, and that the princes—Ching and Tuan—be present for this interview. On the morning of the twentieth no answer had been received to this note, and the diplomatic body met again, at eight o'clock, to decide what action should be taken. All but one of the ministers considered that it would be useless to proceed to the Yamen in the face of the probability that no one would be there to receive them. The one dissenting voice was that of the German minister. Unmoved by the arguments and apprehensions of his colleagues, Baron von Ketteler set out for the Yamen office, accompanied by his secretary and two outriders, and had almost reached his destination when he was shot and killed by a Chinese soldier.

Some hours after the murder of the German minister, the legations received a new note from the Yamen. This note made no reference to the murder, although the writers could not have been in ignorance of it, but expressed regret that it would not be safe for the foreign ministers to come to the Yamen for the interview which had been requested. The Yamen also stated that, as it would now be obviously unsafe for the ministers and their staffs to attempt to leave Peking, there would be no objection to extending the twenty-four time limit which had been fixed in the former note. Notwithstanding this concession, at 4 P.M.—*i.e.*, promptly on the expiration of the time limit—the Chinese troops opened fire on the legations. Thus commenced, on the afternoon of June 20, the siege of the legations which was to continue, in varying degrees of intensity, until August 14.

The foreign ministers at Peking had, from the first appearance of the Boxers, been at fault in their judgment regarding the nature and extent of the popular agitation, as well as in their conception of the powers which could be legitimately exercised by the imperial government. Considering the I-ho Chuan to be primarily an anti-Christian and rebellious secret society, the foreign diplomats reached the conclusion that the authorities at Peking were condoning rebellion in order that the foreign religion might be extirpated. The diplomatic body therefore attempted, by frequent recourse to threat and ultimatum, to frighten the central government into taking immediate and drastic measures for suppressing the disturbances. Each successive display of force on the part of the foreign powers served, however, only to increase the popular agitation, while each apparent surrender on the part of the imperial government tended to lessen the popular respect for its authority.

The decision to summon the legation guards was reached in the face of strenuous objections from the Chinese officials, who gave warning that such action could not fail to increase the apprehensions of the already disturbed people. The government gave its reluctant consent to this step only after an ultimatum had been received from the diplomats, and the conditions which were attached to this consent were promptly violated by the foreigners. It is, of course, possible to argue that the Chinese authorities would have made no bona fide attempt to suppress the rioters if the legation guards had not been brought to Peking; it is even probable that the arrival of the guards would not have led to increased disorders if it had not been for the unfortunate clash between the Paotingfu refugees and the militia bands; but the coincidence of these two occurrences, followed by the Cossack expedition in search of the Paotingfu stragglers, created, in the districts between Peking and the coast, a new and infinitely more dangerous situation than had existed hitherto.

On the evening of June 9 the American and British ministers, without consulting their colleagues or the Chinese government, dispatched telegrams to the fleet which resulted in the invasion of China by an international force of 2000 armed men. Mr. Conger's reasons for sending his telegram have not been published; those of Sir Claude MacDonald—so far as they have been published—were, to say the least, hardly adequate grounds for so momentous a decision. If the Chinese government had desired war with the outside world, the landing of the Seymour expedition would have furnished it with a suitable pretext. This pretext was not utilized; the railway authorities were instructed to furnish transport for the reinforcements; the imperial troops along the railway line did not offer any opposition to their advance; and, on June 12, the Tsungli Yamen consented that a limited number of additional troops should enter Peking.

The ultimatum demanding the surrender of the Taku forts, and the subsequent capture of the forts were natural consequences of the situation created by the advance of the force under Admiral Seymour After the destruction of the admiral's communications with Tientsin and with the ships at Taku, the decision to seize the forts and to occupy the railway was a military precaution which was considered absolutely necessary by all the naval commanders, with the exception of the American admiral. The contention that hostilities were actually precipitated by the Chinese—inasmuch as the forts opened fire an hour before the ultimatum had expired—does not merit serious consideration. The ultimatum, followed by the landing of storming parties and by the movement of warships into positions suitable for attack, was, in itself, an act of war; and the Chinese commander of the forts would have been guilty of betraying his trust had he failed to seize whatever advantage was to be gained by being the first to open fire.

Each of the decisive steps taken by the diplomats at Peking, or by their naval commanders at Taku, was taken on the strength of rumors which have never been substantiated; each has been justified only by appealing to subsequent events as evidence of the wisdom and necessity of the act. Each step was followed by an increase of popular hostility toward the foreigner; by a growing fear that the invasion and partition of the Empire were about to begin, or had actually begun; and by a weakening of the peace party among the officials at Peking and throughout the northern provinces. The final step, the attack on the Taku forts, precipitated a state of war, and the Peking government led the Boxers—or was forced by the Boxer leaders—into a course of action which violated the principles of Confucius as well as those of the Law of Nations.

CHAPTER XI.

The I-ho Chuan in the Provinces.

Spread of the Movement in Chihli—Shansi—Early Activities of Boxers—First Attacks—Taiyuanfu, July 9—Shensi, Honan, and Shantung—The Yangtze Provinces—"Conditions" of the Yangtze Viceroys—Situation in the South and West.

ON June 17, when the foreign attack upon the Taku forts precipitated a state of war between China and the outside world, the activities of the I-ho Chuan were still strictly localized. At Peking the presence of the Boxer bands had thrown the entire city into wild confusion; at Tientsin, the militia bodies were dominating the native city; between these two points, the country was much excited, and thousands of armed Boxers along the railway line were successfully blocking the advance or retreat of the Seymour column. Outside of this limited area, the disturbance, even in Chihli, was potential rather than actual. After the seventeenth of June, however, the movement spread into the other parts of the metropolitan province and into the regions to the southwest, west, north, and northeast.

The spread of the Boxer disturbances, outside the area originally affected, corresponded, to a remarkable extent, with the time required for the spread of news from Taku and Peking. Even where telegraphic means of communication still existed, the attacks upon missionaries or upon other foreigners did not, in general, take place until sufficient time had elapsed to allow the news of hostilities to spread among the common people by non-telegraphic methods. As soon as it became commonly known in any locality that the Empire was actually being invaded by foreign forces, the popular apprehensions immediately gave vent to anti-foreign or anti-Christian activity, and the ranks of the I-ho Chuan were filled with numerous and enthusiastic recruits.

The popular prestige of the patriotic militia received a tremendous impetus from the official recognition of its loyal services in the following imperial edict, which was issued by the Empress Dowager on June 24:

> We have received from Yu Lu a Memorial reporting that the foreigners had started trouble and suddenly seized a pretext for acts of war, but that in successive battles, lasting for several days, victories had been obtained.
>
> The reading of this Memorial greatly rejoiced and comforted us. China had lived in peace and harmony with all countries for years, but, after all, affairs have come to an open rupture owing to the hatred between the people and the converts to Christianity.
>
> Relying on their strong iron-clads and powerful armies, the foreigners attacked the forts of our port of Taku, and issued from Tzu-chu-lin [*i.e.*, the foreign quarter of Tientsin] in all directions to fight. But Yu Lu was everywhere at once, offering resistance; and also our Boxer troops aided him with all their heart and strength, opposing the rampart of their bodies to the assailing cannon and bayonets.
>
> On the 21st, 22nd, and 23rd [of June], our forces destroyed two war vessels and killed many of the enemy. The people's resolution had become like walls to protect their country, and the firmness of their minds raised the spirit of the troops.
>
> The Boxers who helped the troops so much in these actions are men of the people; with them, the State need not use a soldier nor spend a dollar. Even the little children wielded arms in defence of their altars and fields. In all their dangers, the spirits of their ancestors, of the gods, and the sages, protected them. The myriads of the people are actuated by one ideal.
>
> We hasten to publish this Edict in praise of the patriotic Boxers, and to assure them that those of their number who are in distress

will be cared for. When these troubles are over we intend to bestow on them special marks of our favor. Let these people's soldiers only still continue, with united hearts and utmost efforts, to repel aggression and prove their loyalty, without failing, to the end. This is our earnest desire.[1]

Yu Lu's memorial, which furnished the occasion for this enthusiastic tribute to the patriotic Boxers, had obviously reported the military situation at Tientsin and Taku in terms that were optimistic, rather than accurate; and the Empress Dowager, for the time at least, had completely discarded any doubts which she may have felt concerning the efficacy of the militia as an instrument for national defense.

The effect of this edict upon the status of the I-ho Chuan can hardly be overestimated. Instead of being treated as an auxiliary force of questionable military value, they were now officially recognized as the first line of defense against invasion. This new military importance was quickly reflected by an assumption of dictatorial powers in local affairs. By the first of July—two weeks after the capture of the forts—the Boxers were in complete control of the situation throughout the metropolitan province of Chihli. The few officials who continued to advocate peace, or to oppose the activities of the patriots, were killed, intimidated, or driven from their posts, and the loyal defenders of the Empire displayed their patriotic hatred toward the foreign invaders by an indiscriminate slaughter of missionaries and native Christians.

The decree of November 5, 1898, in which Tzu Hsi had first ordered the reorganization of the local militia, had specified Shansi as one of the four provinces in which this

[1] This edict, in substantially the same form, is reported from several sources; the above translation is taken from the *British Blue Books, China No. 1 (1901)*, inclosure in document no. 289.

plan should be put into immediate operation. It was to Shansi that Yu Hsien, the reputed founder of the "Big Knife Society" and patron of the Boxers, had been sent as governor, in March, 1900, after his removal from Shantung; and it was in this province that the Boxer outbreak resulted in the heaviest loss of foreign life. For these reasons the development of the Boxer movement in Shansi is of especial importance.

Because of the interior position of their province, the people of Shansi had almost no first-hand knowledge of Europeans other than missionaries, and they had displayed little or no hostility to these foreign teachers or to their doctrines. Unlike the mission workers in Chihli and Shantung, the missionaries in Shansi reported that the *coup d'état* of September, 1898, had produced no change in the attitude of the people toward the preaching of the gospel; indeed, mission letters, during the year 1899, are filled with references to the pleasant relations between the missionaries and the educated Confucianists in those cities where mission work was established.

During the winter of 1898-1899 Shansi first became acquainted with non-missionary foreigners. A few engineers connected with the Peking Syndicate entered the province and began to make preliminary surveys for the railway concession which had recently been granted. The appearance of these strangers, whose actions were extremely mystifying to the simple countrymen, coincided with the beginning of the great drought which affected Shansi in common with the other provinces of North China. The year 1899 was a bad one for the farmers, while the winter of 1899-1900 was so dry that no crops could be planted in the spring and the winter wheat died in the ground. This calamity was popularly attributed to the mysterious strangers who had recently wandered through the country pointing their "magic tubes" at the hills and villages and across the planted fields, and the Shansi people soon began to show unrest and anti-foreign feeling.

Yu Hsien was appointed governor of the province on March 14, and took over the seals of his new office before the end of the month. In view of his notorious hostility toward foreigners, attempts have been made to prove that the governor was responsible for the entire Boxer movement in Shansi, by establishing a connection between his arrival at Taiyuanfu and the earliest appearance of the Boxers in the province. Even this point, however, has failed of proof, as the testimony regarding the first appearance of the I-ho Chuan is marked by a wide divergence. Some of the witnesses state that the Boxers followed close upon the heels of Yu Hsien, if they did not actually precede him into the province, while others say that the first Boxers did not appear until the end of May or the beginning of June, and that Boxer placards were not posted until nearly the middle of June.

Whatever may have been the date on which the activities of the Boxers were first observed—and it probably differed in the various parts of the province—there is complete agreement as to the time when the disturbances first became a matter for alarm. In general, the missionaries did not begin to regard conditions as dangerous until the first week in July; up to that time, the unrest was attributed to famine conditions, resulting from the drought, and there had been no open display of anti-foreign hostility. Not until the fifth and sixth of July did the missionaries in various parts of the province commence to flee southward into Honan, on their way to the Yangtze River, or westward into the less hostile province of Shensi.

The first loss of foreign life in Shansi was on June 27. On the evening of that date the Shouyang mission in Taiyuanfu was attacked by a mob; the mission premises were pillaged and burned, and one missionary—a Miss Coombs—was killed. Miss Coombs's companions succeeded in escaping to the home of another missionary, where they were protected by the governor's soldiers until July 9. The governor was in no way implicated in this disturbance, and the attack seems to have been due, in part, to the desire for plunder.[2] Two days after this riot in Taiyuanfu, ten members of the Swedish mission were massacred at Soping, just north of the Great Wall.

For twelve days following the attack on the Shouyang mission, the missionaries in the provincial capital were protected by the governor's soldiers. On the ninth of July, however, Yu Hsien ordered, or invited, all the missionaries in Taiyuanfu to appear at his Yamen. When the foreigners had assembled, the governor informed them that, as a result of the invasion of China by their troops, war now existed between their countries and China; after giving this information, he ordered their immediate execution. From this moment, the unfortunate missionaries in all parts of the province were ruthlessly hunted down and put to death. Except for those who succeeded in escaping from the jurisdiction of Yu Hsien before the date of the Taiyuanfu massacre, few of the Shansi workers survived to tell the story of the Boxer movement, and the history of the tragedy must be compiled from the accounts of native Christians and from the last writings of the victims.

The wholesale massacre at Taiyuanfu, and the subsequent extermination of missionaries throughout Shansi

[2] Miss Bird, of the American Board Mission, entered in her journal, under the date of June 28, the current report that one of the mob had attempted to snatch a bag of money which Miss Coombs was carrying; that Miss Coombs, who was armed with a revolver, shot the man and was then struck down and killed.

have been almost universally attributed to Yu Hsien's bitter hatred for all things foreign, and for the teachers of Christianity, especially. Yet the first three months of Yu Hsien's governorship were not attended by any manifestation of this bitterness, and, when attacks upon foreigners did take place, they could, in many instances, be traced to causes for which the governor was not accountable. The first loss of life in the province did not occur until ten days after the bombardment of the Taku forts; the actual reign of terror did not begin until July 9, three weeks after hostilities had commenced, and just a month after the Seymour column had started to force its way to Peking. It appears, moreover, from the accounts of the survivors and from the journals of the victims, that the attacks upon the foreigners were not exclusively the work of Boxer bands, but were often the act of unorganized mobs. These mobs were sometimes actuated by the desire for plunder, and almost always gave evidence of the belief that the missionaries were responsible for the drought.

Some writers, while holding Yu Hsien criminally responsible for the Boxer atrocities in Shansi, have adopted an explanation for these atrocities which would, in strict logic, exculpate the governor and throw the full responsibility upon the Empress Dowager, or whoever was in control at Peking during the last week of June. According to this explanation, a secret edict, issued on June 24, commanded that all missionaries and other foreigners throughout the Empire be immediately put to death. It is further alleged that two members of the Tsungli Yamen—Yuan Chang and Hsu Ching-cheng—so altered the wording of the edict that it became a command to protect, instead of to slay, but that Yu Hsien, suspecting the authenticity of the command, telegraphed an inquiry; this resulted in his receiving the correct form, which he then proceeded to execute.[3]

The authenticity of the alleged edict of June 24 is decidedly shadowy; but the following commands, of a diametrically different nature, appear in a decree published in the *Peking Gazette* on July 2:

> . . . As hostilities have now broken out between China and foreign countries, the missionaries of every nationality must all be driven away at once to their own countries, so that they may not linger here and make trouble. *But it is important that measures shall be taken to secure their protection on their journey.*[4]

Even in the absence of telegraphs, this decree would have reached Yu Hsien at Taiyuanfu, about 300 miles from Peking, in four or five days at most, that is to say, not later

[3] This explanation rests upon a very shaky foundation. *The Martyred Missionaries of the China Inland Mission* gives, on page 9, what purports to be the wording of the command to slay, and, in a note, tells of the alteration. Dr. Smith, in *China in Convulsion*, vol. II, p. 594, also gives the wording of the alleged edict and states that "twice, at least, the original despatch was seen by foreigners"; but he neglects to cite these important witnesses by name. The *Diary of H. E. Ching Shan*—entries for July 4, July 29, and August 1—tells the story very circumstantially. Morse, in *The International Relations of the Chinese Empire*, vol. III, p. 237, says that the edict appears to have been issued on June 24, and, "although no copy is available, yet its authenticity is well established." In support of this he cites Smith and the Ching Shan *Diary;* but Ching Shan, in his entry for July 29, states that an edict on July 14 reprimanded Yu Hsien for executing the missionaries without asking imperial sanction, and asserts that Yu Hsien's action resulted from private letters from his son-in-law, by whom Yu was informed that Prince Tuan and Prince Chuang were supporting the Boxers. On January 22, 1901, the diplomatic body decided to demand rehabilitation for Yuan Chang, Hsu Ching-cheng, and three other high officials who had been put to death for their opposition to the declaration of war; at the same meeting, Sir Ernest Satow cited the case of two officials in "a southern province" who had been put to death for having weakened the force of a proclamation against foreigners by modifying two characters; but these were quite distinct affairs.

[4] *Foreign Relations of the United States*, 1900, p. 171. Author's italics.

than July 7; it probably reached him by telegraph on the date of publication.

The attempts to prove that the Boxer atrocities were primarily the work of Yu Hsien, of the Empress Dowager, or of any other high official, are based upon a common fallacy: that of regarding the Chinese government as highly autocratic. Only by recognizing the popular nature of the Boxer agitation and the extreme dependence of Chinese officials upon the popular will, is it possible to understand either the development of the movement in Chihli and Shantung, or its spread into Shansi and the other parts of the country. Throughout the entire northern part of the Empire, the rising popular hatred toward foreigners closely followed the diffusion of popular knowledge that China was being invaded by foreign armies. In some localities, where an anti-foreign spirit had already been engendered by active work on behalf of preparedness, the dates of the outbreaks indicate that news of the invasion had spread by telegraph; in some, even, there is evidence that the news was given out by the local officials. In general, however, there is every indication that the news spread among the people by slower methods of communication, and that the attacks did not occur until some time after it had become known in the officials' yamens. The guilt of Yu Hsien, like that of many other officials within whose jurisdictions massacres took place, lay in the fact that he made little effort to quell the agitation, but put himself, all too willingly, at the head of the popular movement to exterminate the hated "barbarians."

In Manchuria and in Mongolia the first attacks upon missionaries took place even later than in Shansi; in no district did the first murder occur before the first of July, and, in some cases, the attacks did not commence until the end of July or well on in August. In southern Manchuria the first foreigners were killed on July 3, at Mukden. In northern Manchuria a Roman Catholic priest was killed at Iu-tsing-kai on July 16, and a second at the same place four days later. In eastern Mongolia a priest was burned alive on July 24, but it was reported, on August 2, that the officials in this region were making efforts to protect the foreigners. In southern Mongolia Bishop Hamar, the only foreign victim among the Catholic missionaries, was killed on July 24. In central Mongolia, two priests were put to death on August 15, and three more on the twenty-second.[5] The order in which these five Roman Catholic dioceses suffered from the uprising corresponds quite well to their closeness of non-telegraphic communication with Peking, and confirms the belief that the attacks on foreigners resulted from the spread of popular knowledge that China was at war with the outside world.

To the southwest and south of Shansi, in the provinces of Shensi and Honan, the anti-foreign outbreak was much less severe. In Shensi, Governor Tuan Fang showed no sympathy with the Boxer movement, and gave all possible assistance to the unfortunate refugees who fled into his territory. In Honan there were attacks upon foreigners, beginning about the seventh of July, but, although the missionaries were often in fear for their lives, the actions of the Honanese mobs were confined to plundering and destroying mission property, and committing acts of personal violence which fell short of murder. At the subsequent peace settlement, the foreign diplomats demanded the suppression of official examinations—as a penalty for cruel treatment to foreigners—in only two towns in Honan. The Boxer "war of extermination" against foreigners

[5] These details are drawn from the *Missions Catholiques* for August and September, 1900, *passim*, and from *Annales de l'Association de la propagation de la foi*, vol. 73, *passim*.

was, indeed, limited to the two provinces of Chihli and Shansi, and the outlying dependencies of Manchuria and Mongolia. Where disturbances occurred in Shensi and Honan, they took the form of banditry or of harrying the unpopular intruders as they withdrew from the country.

In Shantung, where the Boxers and the Big Swords had originally been so turbulent, the patriots—with the connivance of some of the local and provincial officials—took advantage of the prevailing unrest to persecute and intimidate the native Christians. Yuan Shih-kai was, at the time, severely criticized for his failure to take vigorous measures against these persecuting elements, but he was able to furnish adequate protection to the foreign missionaries in their hasty retreat to the coast, and no foreign lives were lost in the province.

In the other maritime and Yangtze provinces, and even in the extreme southwestern provinces of Yunnan and Kweichow, the Boxer movement did not take root. There were, indeed, sporadic outbursts of anti-foreign feeling at various points in the central and southern part of the Empire, but there was no general popular movement against the foreigners in these regions. The most serious of these isolated outbreaks took place in Chekiang province, where the Italian demands, during the preceding year, had aroused so much local apprehension. On July 21, 22, and 24 eight adults of the China Inland Mission and three children were massacred at Chuchow, in the interior of the province. This massacre was the work of the local trainbands, and was undoubtedly an echo of the disturbances in the north, but the general excitement in Chekiang was partly due to the arrival, during the first weeks of July, of large numbers of refugees from Shanghai, who brought with them the most alarming rumors as to the purposes of the foreign nations.

The fact that the war in the north did not spread into the Yangtze Valley was due, primarily, to the circumstance that the I-ho Chuan was never allowed to establish itself in this region. Tzu Hsi had authorized the development and extension of the train-band system only in those provinces upon whose loyalty she had perfect reliance, and she did not feel sufficient confidence in the Yangtze provinces to be willing to see these organizations established there. Nor did the Yangtze viceroys desire to see the growth of the I-ho Chuan within their jurisdictions. Chang Chih-tung and Liu Kun-yih had little or no faith in the efficacy of the volunteer militia, and were content to rely upon their regular troops for the successful defense of their provinces against any possible foreign invasion. Having no sympathy with the movement, Chang and Liu looked with disapproval upon the developments in the north which threatened to involve the Empire in war against the entire outside world, and both repeatedly warned the Empress Dowager against the dangers which were impending. When the catastrophe which they had foreseen finally occurred, these two powerful officials jointly decided to declare their neutrality with respect to the "rebellion" in the north, a decision in which they were followed by most of the other central and southern viceroys and governors.

The avoidance of a general outbreak, involving all the central and southern provinces, was also due, in part, to the efforts which were made by the foreign naval and consular officers to localize the disturbance. On June 20 the senior naval officers at Taku issued a joint proclamation assuring the people of China that their forces were, and would be, directed only against the Boxer "rebels" and those who opposed the rescue of the diplomats and other foreigners at Peking. This proclamation, which gave evidence that the foreign admirals had at last begun to appreciate the nature and causes of the excitement in the north, had little beneficial effect in Chihli; but it was copied and reissued by the consular officers at Shanghai and the other treaty ports as a means of dispelling the suspicion that the military events in the north indicated the approaching partition of the Empire. The declaration of policy made by the American State Department, on July 3, and similar declarations on the part of the other governments were also given wide publicity at the treaty ports.

By far the most important factor in preventing the spread of hostilities into the Yangtze Valley, however, was the stand which the Yangtze viceroys took in regard to foreign naval and military operations within the areas under their jurisdiction. On June 27 the "Taotai" at Shanghai was instructed to submit to the consular body at that port a list of articles which, in the opinion of Liu and Chang, were the only measures that could insure the maintenance of tranquillity in the Yangtze. The viceroys assumed full responsibility for the protection of foreign life and property within their viceroyalties, and agreed that the foreign authorities should take reasonable steps for the protection of Shanghai, but declared that "the Viceroys shall not be held responsible for the consequences of any disturbances which the entrance of foreign ships of war into the Yangtze may occasion, unless such entrance shall have been sanctioned by them." The articles submitted to the consular body also included strict prohibitions against foreign warships anchoring, or maneuvering, near any of the forts, arsenals, or powder magazines in the Yangtze, and demanded that the measures which might be taken for the defense of Shanghai "be conducted in the least obtrusive manner possible, and so as to avoid exciting the fears of the populace."

A week later the conditions of Liu Kun-yih and Chang Chih-tung were stated more concisely in the following joint telegram, which was sent to the Chinese ministers at the various foreign capitals: "We, the viceroys of the Liang Kiang and the Liang Hu provinces, undertake to hold ourselves responsible for the security of foreign life and property within our respective jurisdictions, as well as in the province of Chekiang, so long as the treaty powers do not land troops either in the Yangtze Valley or in the province of Chekiang." Liu and Chang had no sympathy with the Boxer movement, and had denounced the disturbances in the north as a "rebellion"; but their refusal to accept responsibility for the consequences which might result from a foreign military or naval demonstration in mid-China throws a reasonable doubt upon the sincerity of this characterization. Their determined stand on this point is convincing evidence that they feared a similar rebellion in their own provinces in case the foreign powers should repeat there the policy of intimidation which had been followed in the north.

The foreign community at Shanghai had little confidence in the ability of the viceroys to maintain order, and was insistent in its demand that foreign troops and warships be sent to protect the port; but the conditions of the Yangtze viceroys were at least tacitly accepted by the treaty powers. The native authorities were consulted in regard to all movements of warships in the Yangtze, and when, on August 18, troops were finally landed at Shanghai to satisfy the demands of the international community, this was done only after formal "permission" had been received from Liu Kun-yih. The lead taken by viceroys Liu and Chang in this matter was followed by the provincial authorities of the other maritime provinces. The viceroys and governors adopted an attitude of neutrality with respect to the struggle in the north, and undertook to prevent the spread of the disorders into their own administrative areas on condition that the foreigners avoid all military or naval demonstrations which might arouse popular apprehension and lead to an outbreak.

By the stand which they took in regard to the hostilities in the north, the Yangtze viceroys and their colleagues were able, not only to prevent the spread of the disturbances, but also to protect the Empress Dowager against subsequent humiliation at the hands of the victorious powers. Having repudiated the Boxer movement on the ground that it was a rebellion, they were in a position to demand assurance that the powers would not hold their sovereign personally responsible for the consequences of the outbreak. This assurance the powers were compelled to give; without it the "neutral" viceroys and governors would have had no justification for continuing—and few of them would have continued—to hold themselves aloof from the struggle.

In the extreme southern provinces of Kwangtung and Kwangsi, there was never any real danger of a Boxer uprising. Here the danger was that the anti-dynastic secret societies, with which many of the native Christians were associated, would take advantage of the disturbances in the north and start a revolution for the purpose of overthrowing the Manchus. In view of this danger the Empress Dowager countermanded the order that Li Hung-chang should come to Peking, and, until the middle of July, Li was retained at Canton for the purpose of crushing any incipient revolutionary movement. Here, also, the powers took extreme care to avoid any step which might alarm the people and which, by weakening the authority of the viceroy, might enable the revolutionary elements to recruit their strength among a populace aroused to fears of foreign aggression.

The foreigners in the western province of Szechuan, far beyond the possible scope of foreign military operations, were naturally much alarmed by the news which reached them during the month of June and by the disturbing rumors of local origin. They immediately began to withdraw down the Yangtze, and, by August 2, M. Bons d'Anty, the French consul at Chungking, and the missionaries of the Roman Catholic mission were the only foreigners in the province. In his official reports M. d'Anty expressed his satisfaction at the behavior of the provincial officials, and his confidence that they would be able to deal with the situation. Instead of advising the missionaries under his protection to take refuge in the chief towns of the province, he advised that they simply retire to the walled towns of their respective districts, and there place themselves under the protection of the local officials. This arrangement not only resulted in safety for the missionaries, but also, by preventing any unusual amount of foreign travel through the province, greatly simplified the task of calming the excitement of the people. The only circumstance which, according to the reports of the French consul, might render dangerous his position at Chungking would be a foreign naval or military demonstration in the Yangtze Valley.

This brief survey of conditions in the various provinces, after the commencement of hostilities, effectively supplements the earlier evidence as to the nature of the Boxer Movement and the causes which led to the actual outbreak. Outside of Chihli, concerted attacks on foreigners occurred only in those provinces which, largely by reason of their nearness to the capital, had long been agitated by fears of an impending foreign invasion. The slow spread of the disturbances, after the seizure of the Taku forts, weakens, if it does not actually destroy, the theory that there was a carefully planned conspiracy for the annihilation of the foreigners. The failure of the movement to gain a foothold in the rebelliously inclined provinces of central and southern China is hardly compatible with the charge that the movement was originally anti-dynastic; the contemporary rebellious movements in those regions were avowedly dissociated with the I-ho Chuan and even hostile to it. The powerful viceroys of the Yangtze, with all their military strength, and in spite of the fact that the I-ho Chuan did not exist in their provinces, refused to accept responsibility for the consequences which would result if the powers should adopt, with respect to these provinces, a policy similar to that which they had followed in the north. The foreign acceptance of the conditions upon which Liu Kun-yih and Chang Chih-tung were willing to guarantee the tranquillity of the Yangtze was the one thing which prevented the so-called "rebellion" from becoming a nation-wide "war of liberation."

CHAPTER XII.

The Reckoning.

Delay in Relief of Legations—Peking Occupied, August 14—Flight of the Court—Bases of Negotiations—Dominating, and Conflicting, Policies—The Collective Note of December 22—Nature of the Proposed Settlement—The Final Protocol, September 7, 1901.

MORE than six weeks elapsed, after the capture of the Taku forts, before the international army was ready to start from Tientsin for the relief of the beleaguered legations at the capital; not until the end of July did the foreign commanders in North China feel able to order an advance upon Peking.[1] This period was not spent in utter idleness. The first two weeks were occupied in relieving the besieged settlements at Tientsin, in rescuing the little army of Admiral Seymour, and in routing the combined forces of Boxers and imperial troops which held the native city of Tientsin and the neighboring forts and arsenals. But after these preliminary tasks had, by dint of hard fighting, been accomplished, a number of considerations combined to delay the next move in the campaign.

The first of these considerations was military. The belief which, since the close of the Japanese war, had been so commonly held—that 10,000 modern armed troops could

[1] During this period of inactivity, there was much telegraphic debate over a proposal—originating with the consular body at Tientsin—that the powers threaten the Chinese ministers with the destruction of the Imperial Mausolea in case any harm was done to the foreign ministers at Peking. This suggestion was later revived, when it was feared that the approach of the relief force would result in a final, and successful, attack upon the legations.

march at will through the length and breadth of the Empire—had now been discarded. The military experts now considered that 20,000 men would be required merely to hold the Taku-Tientsin base of operations, and they estimated at from 50,000 to 100,000 the number that would be necessary for an advance upon Peking. The only country in a position to furnish any considerable portion of such a force on brief notice was Japan, and Japan was not anxious to assume a disproportionate share in this venture. The expense of the undertaking would have been heavy, and extreme activity on the part of Japan might serve to draw upon the Japanese the concentrated hostility of the Chinese people.

These military considerations were complicated by uncertainty as to the possible course of developments in the rest of the Empire. The circular telegram sent out by Secretary Hay on July 3 had been utilized to convince the officials and people of the southern and central provinces that the powers were not contemplating the partition of the country, yet there was danger that an advance upon the capital might force the neutral viceroys and governors to abandon the policy which they had hitherto adopted. Hence it was felt that it would be unsafe to commence the advance until the foreigners in the interior had been withdrawn to the treaty ports, where they would be under the protection of the warships, or until a force should have been assembled sufficient to overawe the other parts of the Empire while the movement on Peking was taking place.

A final cause for delaying the advance of the international force lay in the continuance of mutual suspicion among the chief powers. All the governments had been profuse in their statements that the sole purpose with which they were actuated was the desire to rescue their diplomatic representatives and other nationals at Peking, yet each suspected the others of having some ulterior motive, not entirely in harmony with their diplomatic professions. This mutual distrust—of which the Chinese plenipotentiaries were later able to make considerable use—was intensified by the general uncertainty as to the precise nature of the proposed advance upon Peking; no one knew whether it would prove to be a relief or a punitive expedition. For just a month, following the twentieth of June, but one direct communication had been received from the foreigners at Peking; on the twenty-ninth a brief message from Sir Robert Hart, dated five days earlier and urging the utmost haste, was received at Tientsin—after that, silence. In the absence of any further messages, the reassuring reports given by China's representatives abroad were regarded with growing scepticism, and the Western world readily accepted the circumstantial accounts which were telegraphed from Shanghai, describing, in lurid detail, the annihilation of the legation community.

On July 20—as the result of an effort which had been made by Minister Wu Ting-fang to establish communication between the American government and its representative at Peking—the State Department at Washington received a code telegram from Mr. Conger. Mr. Conger's message conveyed the information that the foreign community at Peking still existed, but was in desperate straits and was forced to defend the legation quarter against constant attacks by the Boxers and the imperial troops. This news, the authenticity of which was, for a while, questioned in some official circles, put an entirely new aspect on the situation. Now that there was good reason for believing that the foreigners at Peking were still holding out, public opinion in Europe and America demanded that the powers lay aside their jealousies and take effective steps for the relief of the legations before it should prove to be too late.

Purposeful activity immediately began to be displayed at Tientsin, and on August 4 the expedition at last moved out on its march to Peking. On August 6 the Chinese forces were routed in a battle at Yangtsun; on the twelfth Tungchow was taken; on the fourteenth the relief forces entered Peking, and the eight-week siege of the legations was ended.[2]

The occupation of Peking by the international forces was immediately followed by the flight of the Imperial Court from the capital. Almost exactly forty years before, Tzu Hsi, at that time the young mother of Hsien Feng's infant heir, had fled from Peking in company with her lord and master to avoid the advancing armies of France and Great Britain. On that earlier occasion the flight had been northward to Jehol, beyond the Great Wall; this time, however, the court fled southwestward. Accompanied by the Emperor and a small retinue, the old Empress Dowager proceeded first to Taiyuanfu and then to the more distant refuge of Sianfu, the capital of Shensi province. Not until January 7, 1902, four months after the final arrangement of the terms of peace, did the imperial household reënter the capital.

[2] The advance on Peking had been made without any commander-in-chief, each national force proceeding under the separate command of its own senior officer. On August 7, the Kaiser—who was convinced that the foreign community had been destroyed, and that no advance on Peking would be possible until the end of September—instituted negotiations to secure the international acceptance of Field-Marshal Count von Waldersee as commander-in-chief of the combined forces in North China. This proposal was ultimately accepted, and the Field-Marshal left Berlin for the Far East on August 20, six days after Peking had been occupied. Baron von Eckardstein, in his *Lebenserinnerungen und politische Denkwürdigkeiten*, gives an amusing "inside" story of the manner in which the German Emperor labored for the appointment of von Waldersee. In von Waldersee's own *Denkwürdigkeiten*, vol. III, there is an account of the Kaiser's bitter disappointment at the receipt of the news that Peking had been taken, and that the foreign diplomats were alive.

The allied forces were now in possession of Peking—a capital without a government—together with a line of communications running to Tientsin and the coast. The rest of the province of Chihli, and the other northern provinces in which the I-ho Chuan had gained a foothold were still dominated by the Boxer bands, somewhat subdued in their claims to invincibility but bitterly hostile toward the foreigners. Under these circumstances, the problem which confronted the military and diplomatic representatives of the powers was extremely complicated. On the one hand, there was the question of maintaining order in the area under foreign military control, and of restoring order throughout the entire north. On the other hand, there was the task of negotiating a satisfactory settlement with the government of China. In regard both to the military and the diplomatic aspects of the situation, there were wide differences of opinion and divergence of interest between the leading powers. The brief period of united action was succeeded by a reappearance of the old antagonistic groups, each of which aimed at the attainment of its own aims by its own methods.

For nearly two months after the relief of the besieged legations the allied governments sought to evolve a satisfactory "formula" upon which to base the negotiation of a settlement. At the end of August Russia proposed that—inasmuch as the international expedition had advanced on Peking for the single avowed purpose of rescuing the beleaguered foreign community—the powers should now withdraw their troops and their legations to Tientsin, and should postpone all attempts at a settlement with China until the return of the Imperial Court to the capital made possible the reëstablishment of normal diplomatic relations. This proposal was approved only by the French; and the Russian minister, who had moved to Tientsin, was eventually instructed to return to Peking. On September 18 the German government suggested that the powers should make it a preliminary condition to entering upon diplomatic intercourse with the Chinese government that the real instigators of the offenses against international law, which had been committed at Peking, should be surrendered for punishment at the hands of the powers. The majority of the powers were in favor of this suggestion, but its acceptance was prevented by the opposition of Russia and the United States.

To preserve even the outward appearance of unity—and no power now dared trust its recent allies in separate negotiations with China—it was necessary to find some middle ground between the unaccepted proposals which had been advanced by Russia and Germany. It was also necessary to adhere to the diplomatic fiction that the recent disturbance had been a "rebellion." The allied advance on Peking would have been impossible except for the neutral stand which had been taken by the Yangtze viceroys and by the other provincial authorities in central and southern China; the military forces of these powerful officials were still intact, and there had been repeated demands for assurance that the sovereignty of China and the persons of the imperial family would be respected. Any attempt to treat China as a conquered country might involve the allies in a real war—a war in which China would probably not find herself again opposed by the united outside world.

A satisfactory formula was finally produced by the French. In a circular dispatch, on October 4, the Paris government submitted the following six points as bases for deliberation among the powers, and for negotiation at Peking:

1. Punishment of the principal culprits, to be designated by the representatives of the powers at Peking.

2. Maintenance of the prohibition of the import of arms.
3. Equitable indemnities for states, societies, and individuals.
4. Establishment of a permanent legation guard at Peking.
5. Dismantlement of the forts at Taku.
6. Military occupation of two or three points on the road from Tientsin to Taku, which would thus be always open in the event of the legations wishing to reach the sea, or for forces coming from the sea with the object of proceeding to the capital.

These six "bases" were accepted, with reservations, by the several powers, and, on October 26, the representatives of Austria, Belgium, France, Germany, Great Britain, Italy, Japan, Spain, Russia, and the United States—the minister from the Netherlands did not arrive until later—entered upon the task of drafting a collective note which should conform to these general principles and, at the same time, respect the policies and interests of the various governments.

Throughout the subsequent negotiations, as during the period which had already elapsed since the taking of Peking, Russia was the leading advocate of mild treatment for the Chinese government.[3] The reasons for this policy are not difficult to discern. In Manchuria, especially along the Amur River and in the railway zones, Russia was taking full advantage of the disturbances as an excuse to establish her complete military control, but at Peking M. de Giers was to be the apostle of benevolent moderation. By coming to the aid of their secret ally and obtaining a modification

[3] On September 6 Nicholas II made the following note upon the margin of a document submitted for his perusal: "There is still one very delicate question to be taken up with France, namely: the question of missionaries. I consider these persons the root of the evil; they, together with the merchants, have aroused the wrath of the Chinese against the Europeans. This should be mentioned somehow, in order to prevent the shameful exploitation of the Chinese people by means of the holy name of Christ." *Krasny Arkhiv*, vol. XIV.

of the terms which should be imposed at Peking, the Russians hoped to secure—as they had secured, by similar methods, in 1860—China's assent to certain important "readjustments" in the north.[4] Apart from these special aspirations with regard to Manchuria—which became generally known, shortly after the New Year, through the disclosure of a proposed Russo-Chinese agreement respecting Manchuria—the Russian government had no desire to see the Boxer settlement utilized by Russia's Western rivals as a means for increasing their financial control over China, or the scope of their commercial activities in the Empire. For these reasons M. de Giers consistently opposed every suggestion to incorporate in the preliminary note, or in the final protocol, clauses which would effect the extension of foreign commercial privileges, or the alteration of China's political system.

The efforts of the Czar's representative to secure moderation in the penalties imposed upon China were usually seconded by the representatives of the Mikado, Baron Nissi and, during the later period of the negotiations, Baron Komura. In anticipation of their approaching conflict with Russia—a conflict which shrewd observers of Far Eastern affairs had come to regard as inevitable—the Japanese government had every reason for assuming a conciliatory attitude toward the government of China, and for endeavoring to make a favorable impression upon the Chinese people. Even in the advance on Peking, the Japa-

[4] On December 16, 1900, Kuropatkin, minister of war, reported as follows to the Foreign Office: "I have received a secret telegram from Giers, dated November 28 (Dec. 11), in which he says that an agreement can be signed now between the legation and the Chinese ministers in order to get exclusive rights for a concession to explore mines and construct a railway in Manchuria. Giers says that we should stipulate now the rights we want to secure in Manchuria, for it will be difficult to secure them later." *Krasny Arkhiv*, vol. XIV.

nese troops, who did rather more than their share of the real fighting, distinguished themselves by their humane treatment of non-combatants and by their respect for private property. After the occupation of the capital, the population suffered less violence in the part of the city placed under Japanese control than in the sections which were occupied and policed by the troops of the Christian powers.[5] The Japanese did, it is true, take part in the looting, and it is credibly reported that they displayed more system and thoroughness in this direction than was shown by their Western colleagues, but their attitude toward the Chinese people was unmarked by the racial, religious, and cultural antipathies which characterized the Westerners. The spirit shown by the Japanese soldiers reflected the considerate policy of their government. Although it would be rash to assert that the Japanese government felt sympathy for the Chinese in their effort to resist the domination of the West, Japan at least gave repeated evidence, during the negotiations, of her unwillingness to see that domination extended.

In direct opposition to the Russian and Japanese advocacy of moderation, was the vigorous policy of Germany, whose influence was consistently exerted on the side of extreme severity. On every debatable point Baron von Mumm, Germany's new minister at Peking, argued and

[5] The German expeditionary force, which the Kaiser had dispatched with his exhortation to treat the Chinese as Attila and the Huns had treated their enemies, did not arrive in the Far East in time to share in the relief of Peking; the troops of the other Western nations, however, displayed toward the Chinese a ruthless vengefulness which closely accorded with the spirit of the Kaiser's injunctions. Most of the Western correspondents who accompanied the expedition, in reporting the looting and the acts of violence, excepted only their own fellow-nationals and the Japanese from criticism; the few who differed from this general rule did so to the extent of excepting *only the Japanese* from the charge of excessive and disgraceful cruelty.

voted in favor of drastic punishments and the widest possible extension of the provisions by which China was, in the future, to be kept under control. From the date when the murder of Baron von Ketteler had become known to the outside world, Germany had assumed leadership among those powers that demanded condign punishment for the "treacherous Chinese." Except for this heinous offense, however, Germany had rather less ground for bitterness than any of the other Western powers which were interested in China. German economic interests were almost entirely confined to Shantung and to those provinces which were little affected by the outbreak, and, of the 242 missionaries and civilians who were murdered by the Boxers, only one was a German.[6]

Germany's policy with regard to China, throughout the Boxer period, was very largely the personal policy of the Emperor William. Field-Marshal von Waldersee, during the two weeks prior to his departure for the Far East, spent several days at the foreign office in Berlin, where he was allowed to read everything which would enable him to acquaint himself with the Chinese situation. "It thus became clear to me," he writes in his *Memoirs*, "that our policy, apart from the punishment of the Chinese, followed no definite purpose. The Kaiser had, it is true, vague ideas in regard to the partition of China. The chief factor was, however, the desire to play a part in world politics, without any clear understanding as to the consequences of this activity."[7] In this somewhat pointless, but decidedly vigorous, policy, Germany was able to count on the support

[6] Among the victims of the Boxers there were 112 British, 79 Americans and Swedes—so grouped in the official list—26 French, 6 Belgians, 5 Dutch, and 1 Swiss. Classified as to occupations, there were 190 Protestant missionaries—including 61 children—46 Catholic missionaries, and 6 non-missionary civilians.

[7] Von Waldersee, *Denkwürdigkeiten*, vol. III, pp. 3-4.

of Austria and Italy, whose representatives at Peking usually voted in harmony with Baron von Mumm.

The British government, from the beginning of the Boxer disturbances, had maintained a close understanding with Berlin, and Sir Ernest Satow—who replaced MacDonald at Peking—coöperated with the German minister on almost every point that arose during the negotiations. Unlike the rather vague policy of the Kaiser, however, British policy had certain very definite objects. The chief of these objects was to prevent any increase of Russian influence in North China, and, for the attainment of this end, the British government hoped to derive material assistance from the presence of a strong German force in that part of the world. Indeed, as the negotiations dragged on through the winter and spring, von Waldersee repeatedly expressed the conviction that Satow was deliberately prolonging the discussions in order to retain the German force in China as a potential ally against Russia. Great Britain was quite ready to fall in with the German schedule of punishments and penalties, but firmly opposed the Kaiser's dreams of a possible partition of the Empire. For the rest, the British were in favor of any use which could be made of the Boxer settlement to improve the existing commercial conditions in China.

France, although an ally of Russia, supported Russia only in her opposition to such proposals as would result either in the extension of commercial privileges, or in any serious modification of China's political organization. On the points which related to the imposition of penalties or the establishment of guarantees, the French minister, like the representatives of the three minor European treaty powers—Spain, Belgium, and the Netherlands—usually voted for severity.

The government of the United States maintained its

traditional independence of action, and, like the governments of the other countries, considered the interests and opinions of its own public. This resulted in a policy which, on most points, practically reversed that of France. Mr. Conger and, later, Mr. Rockhill usually favored any stipulations in the settlement which would extend the opportunities for commercial enterprise, or which might improve the diplomatic machinery through which China had intercourse with the outside world; but, on the questions of punishments, penalties, and guarantees, the American representative was usually to be found supporting the ministers of Russia and Japan in their advocacy of moderation. American trade in the Far East was, at this time, not very extensive, but the recent acquisition of the Philippines had aroused fresh interest in the Orient, and it was generally believed that the time had come when America should regain the important position which, prior to 1860, she had held in Far Eastern trade. In view of these expectations, American interest was clearly in favor of any changes which would throw open new fields for enterprize, and opposed to any step which might lead to the partition of China, or to the establishment of a form of international control that might be manipulated to the disadvantage of American commerce.[8]

The question of exemplary punishment for the Boxer leaders was one on which America, at an early date, ranged herself with the moderates. During the height of the Boxer movement, and for the first few weeks after the relief of

[8] The "Open Door" negotiations, to which reference has already been made, were an early manifestation of this newly awakened interest. The debates in both houses of Congress, during 1900 and 1901, supply additional evidence as to the hope of a new era for American trade in China and the Far East. It may also be noted that the low rate of return on investment, during the late '90's, constituted a powerful motive for seeking new fields of activity for American finance.

the legations, the outbreak in China had been widely employed to discredit those who criticized the administration's policy in the Philippines. The I-ho Chuan and the Filipino "insurrectos" were consistently coupled in the newspapers, and the wildest possible reports of the horrors in China were utilized—with more success than logic—to convince the American voter that the Philippine rebellion should be vigorously suppressed. With the close of the presidential campaign, the excitement in the United States rapidly abated. With less imperial experience than the Europeans, the American people had yet to learn the necessity of executing a suitable number of "natives" in order to establish the supremacy of the white race, and newspaper reports of the treatment which the Chinese had suffered at the hands of the allied forces soon produced a decided revulsion of feeling. The government of the United States supported demands for the execution of those who had been chiefly responsible for massacres, where that responsibility was beyond question, and where the infliction of suitable punishment could be carried out by the Chinese government, but refused to support demands that were beyond the power of the Emperor.[9]

The six "bases" which had been proposed by the French government dealt with punishments, indemnities, and certain definite guarantees against any possible recurrence of the danger which had recently threatened to destroy the foreign legations. During the course of the preliminary negotiations, a number of additions were made to these original points. Some of these new proposals were merely reasonable extensions of the principles which had been set forth in the French circular, but some were, as has already been indicated, concerned with matters which had no vital

[9] *E.g.*, the demand that Tung Fu-hsiang, who was still in command of his Kansu troops, be put to death.

connection with the recent disturbances. In the two years which had elapsed since the Empress Dowager's *coup d'état,* the powers had met with little success in their efforts to secure imperial assent to any new concessions, and the foreign representatives who had been vainly endeavoring to obtain satisfaction on various outstanding topics wished to use the present situation as a means for achieving their objects. There was also a rather general desire to see some change made in the constitution and personnel of the Tsungli Yamen, which, especially after the Empress Dowager inaugurated her policy of extreme decentralization, had enjoyed little influence and had been an altogether unsatisfactory channel through which to communicate with the imperial government. It was decided, therefore, to include the following among the "irrevocable conditions" of the preliminary note:

> Art. 11. The Chinese government will undertake to negotiate regarding amendments to the treaties of commerce and navigation considered useful by the powers, and also other subjects connected with commercial relations with the object of facilitating them.
>
> Art. 12. The Chinese government shall undertake to reform the office of foreign relations, and modify the Court Ceremonial with reference to the reception of foreign representatives in the manner which the powers shall indicate.

In consequence of the growing opposition between the policies which were advocated by the several leading powers, the incorporation of these new points, as well as the precise formulation of the original French proposals, necessitated long discussions on the part of the diplomatic body and frequent reference to the home governments for authority to accept the various modifications. On December 20 the note, in its final form, was accepted and signed by ten of the foreign representatives; Mr. Conger

—whose signature was delayed by the unwillingness of the American government to approve the term "irrevocable" —later received the necessary permission, and signed the document on the twenty-second.

The note opened with a summary of the principal "crimes against the law of nations, against the laws of humanity, and against civilization" which had been committed in China during the recent outbreak. Since China had now recognized her responsibility, had expressed her regrets, and had manifested a desire to terminate the situation created by these disturbances, the Powers had decided to accede to this request, upon certain "irrevocable conditions" which they deemed indispensable for the expiation of the crimes and for the prevention of their recurrence.

The Chinese government was to make honorable reparation to the German government for the murder of Baron von Ketteler, and to the Japanese government for the murder of Mr. Sugiyama. The severest punishment, in proportion to their crimes, was to be imposed upon the high officials who had been responsible for the attacks upon the legations or for the massacre of Europeans in various parts of the Empire; these officials, and the punishment considered suitable for each, would later be designated by the foreign representatives.[10] All official examinations were to be suspended, for a period of five years, in the towns

[10] It was originally intended to demand "the punishment of death" for certain enumerated officials, but the note was modified on this point. The diplomatic body felt that the name of Tung Fu-hsiang could not be omitted from such a list, but, in view of the fact that Tung Fu-hsiang was still in command of his Kansu troops—who were devoted to him—the American, Japanese, and Russian ministers argued that it was highly improbable that the imperial government would be able, at this juncture, to inflict upon him the penalty of death.

where Europeans had been massacred or cruelly treated, and monuments were to be erected in all the foreign cemeteries which had been desecrated by the Boxers. China was to pay an "equitable indemnity," and was to adopt such financial arrangements as would be acceptable to the powers for the purpose of guaranteeing the payment of this indemnity and for the service of her outstanding loans.

Partly as punishment, and partly as insurance for the future, the powers were to prohibit, under conditions which they were to settle among themselves, the importation of arms and munitions, as well as of materials serving exclusively for the manufacture of arms and munitions. The foreign powers were to have the right to maintain permanent legation guards, in such numbers as they might consider desirable, and to put the legation quarter in a "condition of defense." The Taku forts, and other forts which might impede communication between Peking and the coast were to be razed; and foreign military forces were to occupy such points as the powers should consider necessary to insure the maintenance of free communication between the capital and the sea. The government of China was to cause to be posted, throughout the Empire, an imperial decree enumerating the penalties inflicted upon persons and communities in consequence of the Boxer outrages, and prohibiting, under pain of death, membership in any anti-foreign society. There should also be issued, and posted in every part of the country, an edict declaring all provincial and local officials to be personally responsible for the occurrence of any anti-foreign disturbance or other treaty infraction within their jurisdiction.

The last two of the enumerated conditions were those which have been cited above, relating to the revision of treaties and the modification of the Tsungli Yamen, and the note closed with the warning that, "until the Chinese government have complied with the above conditions to the satisfaction of the powers, the undersigned can hold out no expectation that the occupation of Peking and the province of Pechili by the allied forces can be brought to a conclusion."[11]

Immediately after the preliminary note had received the signatures of the entire diplomatic body, the doyen invited the Chinese plenipotentiaries—Prince Ching and Li Hung-chang—to present themselves, on December 24, at the Spanish legation in order to receive from his hands the formal demands of the powers. The Chinese representatives were also instructed to bring with them, on this occasion, their diplomatic "full powers," which should be submitted for the inspection of the foreign representatives. Owing to the illness of his colleague, Prince Ching appeared alone at this meeting; he received the note and assured the ministers that he would immediately communicate its terms to his sovereign and would inform the doyen as soon as a response had been obtained. After depositing eleven copies of his own and Li Hung-chang's "full powers," Prince Ching caused some embarrassment by requesting that the foreign representatives reciprocate by displaying their own credentials. With the exception of Baron von Mumm, the foreign diplomats had not considered the possibility of such a demand and had failed to bring their commissions with them; the meeting was,

[11] This final clause was inserted in the note, at the instance of Sir Ernest Satow, on December 19, the day before the note was signed. Satow's original suggestion was that, in the official French version, "complied with" should be translated by "rempli." M. de Giers objected that this would still further increase the harshness of the note, and proposed that it be translated "accepté." Baron Nissi was willing to agree to the new clause if "accepté" was used, but could not agree to "rempli." An acceptable compromise was found in "se soit conformé à . . .," which was proposed by M. Pichon.

therefore, hurriedly adjourned without complying with Prince Ching's request.[12]

The Chinese plenipotentiaries acted with uncommon promptitude, and, six days after they had received the collective note, were able to communicate to the doyen the terms of an imperial decree, dated December 27, by which the twelve articles were accepted in their entirety. In notifying the doyen of this acceptance, Prince Ching and Li Hung-chang requested that a date now be fixed for the discussion of details, and they expressed the hope that, inasmuch as China had already agreed to the articles, no further expeditions would be undertaken by the foreign troops.

More than eight months were to elapse between China's acceptance of the "irrevocable conditions" and the withdrawal of the international forces. A considerable portion of this time was necessary for assembling detailed information with regard to the injuries—in person and property—which had been suffered by foreigners in various parts of the Empire. Much additional time was required for studying the financial condition of the country, in order to determine how large an indemnity China could be made to pay without having a disastrous effect upon the development of foreign commerce. Some of the delay was also occasioned by prolonged debates among the foreign representatives—or between the foreign representatives and those of China—concerning the precise punishments which should be inflicted upon the high officials whom the diplo-

[12] Prince Ching's request to see the credentials of the foreign ministers is reported by Sir Ernest Satow, in his dispatch of December 24; see *British Blue Books, China No. 6 (1901)*, document no. 91. No mention of the episode is found in the official minutes of the meeting, *Négociations de Pékin*, pp. 51-55, but at the meeting which was held immediately after the retirement of China's representative there was considerable debate as to the response which should be given in case of such a demand.

matic body had pointed out as notoriously guilty of anti-foreign activity. Over and above these considerations, however, the long-continued military occupation of Peking and the province of Chihli was caused by the nature of the expedient which had been adopted by the powers as a means of obtaining satisfaction from China.

The allied powers were not demanding a new treaty settlement from China; they were endeavoring to force from her the actual performance of certain definite acts of reparation and reform. It was not sufficient that the imperial government should assent, in principle, to the conditions which had been set forth in the note of December 22. It was not even sufficient that the signatures of Li and Prince Ching, and the impress of the imperial seal should be affixed to documents wherein these conditions had been worked out in elaborate detail. It was necessary, before the powers would consider that China had, to their satisfaction, complied with the conditions, that these demands should, as far as was practicable, be actually fulfilled, or at least in the process of fulfilment. The missions of apology and reparation to Berlin and Tokyo must actually be sent; the punishments must be actually carried out, and the decrees and edicts actually posted; the land for the new legation quarter must be handed over, and the designated forts in the process of destruction; the modifications in the treaties, and the transformation of the Tsungli Yamen must be accomplished facts. Then, and not till then, would the powers consider that China had sufficiently expiated her crimes of the past, and furnished satisfactory guarantees against a future possible recurrence of her offenses; then, and not till then, would the international occupation of the capital and the metropolitan province be brought to an end.

There were obvious reasons why the foreign powers,

especially those which were determined to make full use of the situation for the purpose of modifying China's relations with the outside world, should favor a settlement of this nature. The experience of more than half a century had convinced them that only the pressure of foreign military force would compel the imperial government to make any essential changes in its administrative or economic policies; but it was believed that, when these changes had once been effected, the natural inertia of the Chinese would combine with a growing appreciation of the substantial benefits from the innovations to make the changes permanent. The method of settlement was also desirable in that it offered the Chinese little opportunity for playing off one power against the others. Opposition by a minority could, indeed, delay the proceedings, but it would not serve to lessen the pressure of military occupation, and the retirement of one or more of the foreign representatives from the deliberations at Peking would merely allow those who remained to dictate the terms upon which their own troops would be withdrawn. A final advantage for all the governments involved—except, possibly, those of Russia and Japan—lay in the fact that this form of settlement required no ratification; the terms imposed upon China might become the subject of interpellation and partisan attack, but the governments were under no necessity of submitting the final settlement to their respective legislative bodies for approval.

The two most debatable matters for detailed arrangement, after China's acceptance of the collective note had been established, were the amount of the indemnity and the nature of the punishments which were to be pronounced against the provincial and local officials within whose jurisdiction massacres had occurred. On the first of these points, the United States, opposing the majority of the powers, made efforts to limit to a maximum of 40,000,000 pounds sterling the amount which should be demanded from China, and, on June 8, formally proposed that the entire question of the indemnity be submitted to the Hague Tribunal. The figure suggested by the United States and the proposal that the amount be decided by arbitration were equally unacceptable to the other powers, and the total amount of the indemnity was ultimately fixed at taels 450,000,000—equivalent to 67,500,000 pounds—an increase of slightly less than 70 per cent over the American proposal. On the question of punishments for the provincial and local officials, M. de Giers completely dissociated himself from the demands of his colleagues. As a result of the efforts made by the ten remaining representatives, three officials were eventually sentenced to decapitation, ten were sentenced to death and the punishment commuted, and about a hundred and twenty others received punishments ranging from perpetual exile to simple reduction in rank.

On September 5, 1901, the doyen of the diplomatic body received from the Chinese plenipotentiaries copies of the two decrees which were still wanting to complete the evidence that China had satisfactorily complied with the demands of the collective note. The first of these was a decree of August 19, which imposed suitable penalties upon the provincial and local officials; the second was an edict, of the same date, proclaiming the suspension of official examinations, for a term of five years, in the localities in which foreigners had been murdered or otherwise cruelly treated. At the meeting of the diplomatic body, on the sixth, the dates of these decrees, and the dates for the withdrawal of the foreign forces were entered in the final protocol, and the following day was fixed for the formal signing of this important document.

On September 7, 1901, the Chinese representatives met the plenipotentiaries of the eleven treaty powers, at the Spanish legation, to sign the protocol. The Chinese government having, to the satisfaction of the powers, complied with the conditions enumerated in the note of December 22, 1900, the powers now acceded to the desire of China that the situation which had been created by the disorders of the summer of 1900 should be brought to an end. Except for the permanent legation guards, the international troops were to be withdrawn from Peking by the seventeenth of September, and, except for the forces which—in accordance with the terms of the settlement—were to be left at Tientsin and at other points between Peking and Shanhaikwan, the province of Chihli was to be evacuated by September 22.

After the signatures of the foreign and Chinese plenipotentiaries had been affixed to the twelve copies of the protocol, the doyen of the diplomatic body read a brief discourse to the representatives of China. He expressed the hope that, as a result of a loyal attempt by China to fulfil the terms of the settlement which had just been signed, the unhappy memories of recent events would become more and more enveloped in the mists of time. To this discourse Prince Ching replied in a few carefully chosen words. With these brief diplomatic formalities, China accepted the new humiliations imposed upon her, and once more acknowledged defeat in her efforts to resist the overpowering West.[13]

[13] A number of the more important documents relating to the settlement are given in the Appendix.

CHAPTER XIII.

Conclusion.

Four Centuries, East and West—Essential Opposition—Avoidable Irritation—The Doctrine of Force, and China's Answer—A "Tragedy of Errors"—China's Crimes, and the Punishment—Consequences.

THE final protocol of the Boxer settlement marks an epoch in the four centuries of direct contact between China and the nations of Western Europe. Four centuries of progress had produced many changes in the West; new nations and new empires had arisen to dominate the lands made accessible to Europe by the voyages of Columbus and Vasco da Gama. By one of the ironies of fate it was the Spanish minister who, as doyen of the diplomatic body at Peking, announced to the Chinese plenipotentiaries that the powers were now willing to see the memory of recent events shrouded in the mists of time. Yet Spain had ceased to be reckoned as a "power" and had, in the last three years, seen the few remaining fragments of her once great colonial empire fall from her weakening grasp; Portugal, under whose flag Vasco da Gama had opened the highway to the East, was not even represented at the Peking negotiations.

Four centuries is a much longer time in the life of the restless West than in that of the contemplative East, but even in the East some change had taken place. Japan had been forced from her safe seclusion, and, in self-defense, had adopted many external features of Western civilization. Western methods of government and finance, and Western machinery of warfare had enabled the Mikado, at the close of the nineteenth century, to succeed where

Hideyoshi, at the close of the sixteenth, had failed; and Japan had secured, in Korea, that foothold on the continent of Asia which had long been the dream of her rulers. Soon the clash of "manifest destinies" between the Island Empire and the Muscovite was to furnish proof to the world that one, at least, of the Eastern peoples had finished its term of apprenticeship under the nations of the West.

China alone had remained essentially unchanged; in China alone did the innovations of the West and the ever-increasing needs of Western commerce meet with stubborn resistance. The pride and complacency of a nation whose civilization was already old at a time when Rome and Athens were still but country villages were rendered the more obdurate by an instinctive feeling that the methods and theories of the West were incompatible with the social institutions evolved by the sages. Along the seacoast, and along the great rivers where the foreign gunboat could pass, the West had gained a footing; the Russian, in the north, and the Briton and Frank, in the south, had succeeded in tearing away some of her dependencies and outlying provinces; but China, in 1900, was still the unreconstructed East. After the humiliating war with Japan, a hasty effort was made by the Emperor—with the support of a small party which had adopted the ideas of the West—to modernize and Westernize the Empire; but the brief reform effort was quickly followed by an attempt to restore the full force of ancient tradition in all the functions of the state.

For China, as for all countries and all ages, the way back to tradition was closed. Across the path stood the West, stronger now than in the days when its merchants had submitted to Chinese control and regulation; stronger, even, than in the days when China had been compelled to sign the treaties of Nanking and Tientsin. If the West was now stronger, richer, and more populous, so also were its needs greater for those things which could be found in China: raw materials and potential consumers for the products of a million factories. For China, the preservation of sacred traditions demanded a return to the conditions of the past; for the West, the maintenance of its growing institutions—the preservation of life itself—demanded that China should not turn back. Out of this conflict arose the chain of events which culminated in the Boxer movement.

In the fundamental conflict between the West and the East, there can, of course, be no attempt to apportion blame. The causes of conflict were inherent in the wide divergence between two civilizations which had grown up separate and independent, but which, with the mechanical progress which was taking place in the West, could no longer remain isolated. The West was not at fault in following its natural tendency toward progress and expansion; nor can it legitimately criticize China for desiring to maintain those traditions which past experience had proven to be good. Not even the insistent aggression of the West, or the obstinacy with which China opposed all foreign innovations can be imputed to either party as evil-doing; the governments of China and of the West merely expressed, in their respective policies, the natural aspirations of two dissimilar worlds.

The Boxer outbreak was not, however, a necessary outcome of this essential conflict. Only on the assumption that misunderstanding, arrogance, and stupidity are inevitable factors in human relationships can the Boxer movement be regarded as an unavoidable occurrence. Neither China nor the West was wholly free from blame in these respects; but the chief responsibility for the conditions which led to the tragedy of 1900 must be laid upon the Western powers, and upon their official and non-official representatives in China.

Throughout the nineteenth century, the West, by reason of its growing economic needs, was constantly pressing for modification in the conditions of its intercourse with China; during the last half of the century, their superiority in mechanical—especially military—development gave the nations of the West the power to force their will upon China. The fact that the West was the active party in the relationship imposed the greater responsibility upon its statesmen; the power to force changes carried with it the duty of understanding—or of attempting to understand—the consequences which those changes would entail. Let it be granted that commercial expansion was of vital interest to the nations of the West; let it even be granted that intelligent self-interest is, for a political organism, the highest form of morality; the peace of the world still demanded that such self-interest should be intelligently pursued. This condition was not fulfilled. With every increase in the power which enabled them to impose their will on China, the governments of the West felt themselves increasingly absolved from any necessity of considering how their policies would react upon China and—eventually—upon the world. To the formula that the Chinese, like all other Orientals, would respect no argument but force, there was added the belief that the Empire was an inert mass upon which the Western nations could work their will without fear of protest or resentment. The careful consideration for Chinese susceptibilities, which, at the end of the eighteenth century, had characterized the embassy of Lord Macartney, gave way, in the closing years of the nineteenth, to the brusk methods of von Heyking, MacDonald, and Martino.

The Chinese were as arrogant as the West, and, although

they treated the earliest European arrivals with respect, soon came to regard the swelling tide of Western visitors as barbarians, whose only claim to consideration lay in the superiority of their death-dealing instruments of war. Unable to resist the powers of Western arms, China was compelled to undertake treaty obligations which the government was neither able nor willing to fulfil. The people and the local officials refused to regard these treaty stipulations as binding, and the treaty powers had frequent cause for complaint at the impunity with which their solemn covenants were set at naught. The Chinese knew little, and cared less, for the code of international law which had been evolved among the European countries; they considered that a question could be finally settled only when it had been settled in accordance with equity and propriety. The West knew and cared equally little about the Chinese standards of propriety, and merely saw in China's attitude toward treaty obligations conclusive proof that force alone could secure from China the fulfilment of promises.

So completely had the foreign powers, during the summer of 1900, become convinced of China's helpless inertia, that the significance of the *coup d'état* in September was wholly disregarded. Instead of recognizing that the Empress Dowager and her advisers were brought into power by the growing determination to resist the extension of Western domination, the foreign diplomats dismissed the affair as a mere passing incident of Oriental palace intrigue, or, at most, as a reaction against the recent progressive efforts of the Emperor and Kang Yu-wei. The concentration of imperial forces for the possible defense of Peking attracted attention only in connection with the episode concerning the troops of Tung Fu-hsiang—an episode in which the Chinese were given fresh cause for irritation and alarm by the summoning of the foreign legation guards. The decrees relating to the local militia, and those which provided for the decentralization of diplomatic responsibility passed unnoticed; the decree of March 15, 1899, was generally attributed to the successful intrigue of the Catholic hierarchy. Even the stubborn resistance to Italy's belated demands, during the spring and summer of 1899, brought no appreciation of the new spirit which was developing in the people and government of China. Goaded into activity by recent humiliations, and pushed forward by the growing popular unrest, the Chinese government was abandoning its reliance upon diplomatic finesse and was preparing to resist, by force, if necessary, all further acts of aggression.

These signs of approaching trouble—now so obvious in the light of subsequent events—were ignored by the West. The statesmen of Europe felt no concern for the national aspirations of the Chinese people, and had no fear that the "sick man of the Far East" would be able to offer serious opposition to the partition of his possessions. The governments of the interested powers discussed the approaching partition, and endeavored to reach a satisfactory adjustment of their rival claims; the United States, which was not in a position to participate in such proceedings, took steps to obtain assurances that, in any eventuality, existing treaty rights in China would be respected. Such was the status of the "Problem of China" when, in the closing months of 1899, alarming rumors began to be received concerning the activities of the I-ho Chuan.

The efforts of the diplomats at Peking to secure satisfactory government action against the Boxers were marked by ignorance or misunderstanding with regard to every important factor of the situation. Perhaps their most essential error lay in a total misapprehension as to the nature of the Chinese government and the powers which it legally possessed. The traditional belief that the Chinese Emperor was clothed with autocratic and unlimited authority led the diplomatic body to make demands whose fulfilment lay outside the actual competence of the government; when those demands were not fulfilled, recourse was had to ultimatum—supported by naval demonstrations and other displays of force—in the effort to compel compliance. Almost equally important was the error in regard to the nature and causes of the disturbance. Ignoring the many outstanding causes for popular hostility toward foreigners, the diplomats accepted the erroneous report that the I-ho Chuan was primarily a rebellious secret society. From this premise, they reached the conclusion that the imperial government was deliberately condoning incipient rebellion in the hope of seeing the extermination of all missionary enterprise. Finally, the foreign representatives accepted, without verification, exaggerated accounts of the Boxer depredations and of the sufferings which were being inflicted upon the native Christians. These accounts, which were sent in by the missionaries—usually in perfect good faith—and were based upon the tales of frightened converts, were later contradicted by some of the missionaries who had reported them. If the accounts had been true, they would have justified many of the foreign demands; the Chinese government, accepting the contradictory—and frequently more accurate—reports of its local officials, was convinced that the foreign powers were merely seeking pretexts for the further humiliation of the Empire.

Upon this foundation of error and misinformation the foreign representatives at Peking built up a policy which was uniformly disastrous. From the dispatch of the first identic note, in January, down to the summoning of the Seymour expedition, on the evening of June 9, every step which was taken by the diplomatic body—either as individuals or collectively—served to intensify the disorder and to hasten the final catastrophe. The diplomatic pressure and the threats of force, by which the supposedly autocratic government was forced into partial compliance with demands for specific performance, weakened popular respect for the constituted authorities at a moment when the foreign demonstrations were arousing fresh popular fears of invasion. The growing disorder in the districts between Peking and the coast was seriously complicated by the conflict, on May 31, between the Paotingfu "railway party" and the Boxers, a conflict for which the foreign diplomats were—of course—not responsible; but, until the morning of June 10, there was always a chance that the final tragedy might be averted. From the moment when Admiral Seymour left Tientsin, in his attempt to reach Peking, the situation passed definitely beyond the control of the imperial government and of the foreign diplomats. The eventual outbreak of war was now inevitable, and there was, from this time, merely the question how far the disturbance would spread. The localization of the conflict to the northern provinces was due to the energy and determination of the great Yangtze viceroys, and to the fact that—for once—the foreign governments allowed their actions to be limited by Chinese demands.

During the months which followed the seizure of the Taku forts, the Chinese people, with the approval and leadership of the more reactionary elements among the official class, poured out upon the helpless missionaries and native Christians their accumulated store of bitterness and rage. At Peking a foreign diplomat was shot down in the street, and the legation quarter was subjected to a long and desperate siege. For these atrocities, over which all friends of China would gladly draw the veil of oblivion, there can be no excuse. Yet these crimes were not, as has been so often charged, the result of a deliberate conspiracy; they were the work of an infuriated people, whose fury had been roused to the breaking point by a long series of foreign aggressions. The concession-hunting governments of the West and their diplomatic representatives at Peking must share, with the people and officials of China, the responsibility for the atrocities of Boxer year—even for those atrocities which were actually committed by the Chinese.

The governments of the world, in the collective note of December 22, 1900, indicted China for "crimes against the law of nations, against the laws of humanity, and against civilization." This indictment did not refer merely to the events of the past few months; China's chief offense against "civilization"—as that term was understood in the West—had been her long-standing resistance to progress, and for this unbending obstinacy she must now make satisfactory amends.

China's crimes against international law and against humanity could be easily punished. The lives of a few high officials, in addition to the many thousands of "mere people" who had already been killed, and an indemnity of some twenty million taels a year, over a period of thirty-nine years, could be made to balance that account. Any possible tendency toward a fresh outbreak of anti-foreignism was to be prevented by stringent prohibitions against membership in any anti-foreign organization—except, of course, the regular army—and by nation-wide publication of the penalties which had been imposed for this past outbreak. In addition to these guarantees for the future, a fortified legation quarter and eight or ten thousand foreign soldiers, posted along the railway from Peking to Shanhaikwan, would serve to remind the Chinese that "right makes might," and that they should never again dare to challenge the power of the West—until they had become strong enough to have hope of success.

While the clauses relating to China's punishment for these more obvious crimes occupied the greater part of the preliminary collective note and of the final protocol, those which were calculated to end her obstinate resistance to progress deserve considerable attention because of their far-reaching consequences. The stipulation that China—in order to guarantee the payment of the new indemnity as well as her earlier debts—should adopt financial measures which were acceptable to the powers placed the administration of the Empire's finances, for the next thirty-nine years, completely under foreign control. Until the Boxer indemnity had been fully paid, no modification could be made in China's tariff or other financial arrangements without the approval of the treaty powers; and only by manifesting an intention to adopt progressive policies could the government of China hope to obtain such approval. In addition to accepting foreign control of her finances, China was forced to undertake the immediate revision of her existing commercial treaties, where such revision was desired by the foreign governments; this arrangement resulted in the rapid introduction of further Western innovations into the economic life of the nation. Finally, through the abolition of the Tsungli Yamen and the creation of the "Wai-wu-pu"—Board of Foreign Affairs—which was given seniority over the six original "boards," China was forced, in diplomatic affairs, to bring her political organization into harmony with Western ideas. For more than a century, the absence of any centralized administration of foreign affairs had been a constant cause for foreign dissatisfaction with China. That shortcoming was now rectified; Tzu Hsi's recent step in the direction of even greater decentralization was definitely reversed, and China had, henceforth, a responsible Foreign Office with which the foreign diplomats could effectively negotiate.

The imperial government of China did not long survive the humiliating and disruptive effects of the Boxer settlement. Ten years and a month after the protocol was signed at Peking, there began the revolution which forced the abdication of the Manchu emperor and ushered in the Republic. Yuan Shih-kai, as first president of the Chinese Republic, was able to maintain some semblance of national unity, but even before his death, in 1916, the Republic had entered upon a stage of rapid disintegration.

The subsequent condition of semi-anarchy in China has been variously attributed to the general corruption and inefficiency of the old official class, to the outbreak of the World War, and to the aggressions and intrigues of Japan. All these factors undoubtedly contributed to the growing disorder, but the temporary break-up of China must be traced to more fundamental causes. The West, after a century of conflict, reduced the reigning dynasty to a state of humiliating dependence upon foreign power, and, at the same time, imposed upon the Chinese Empire a degree of centralization which was utterly alien to traditional theory and practice. The first result of this arrangement was the fall of the dynasty—its "Mandate from Heaven" had been exhausted. But the movement which overthrew the Manchus was also accompanied by a wave of reaction against centralization, and the attempt to establish a unified republic along Western lines—although supported and approved by foreign interests—has failed to secure any real support among the great mass of the people.

Something more than twenty-one centuries ago the Emperor Shih Huang Ti commenced the construction of a great wall along the northern frontier of his Empire, a wall which was intended to shield the country against the devastating incursions of the northern barbarians. The Great Wall failed of its purpose; the invasions from the north continued; and China has, on several occasions, been subjected to Tartar rule. Yet each successive inundation from the north has been slowly assimilated into the Chinese race, and China still exists.

The same mighty ruler—whom some have termed the "Napoleon of China"—also decided to sweep away the old system of local autonomy and to establish a great centralized Empire, with all the power in his own hands. In pursuance of this policy, he ordered the destruction of all the ancient classics and attempted to exterminate the Confucian "literati"; but, with the end of his dynasty—which was one of the shortest in Chinese history—the old literature, the old traditions, and the old system of government resumed their accustomed places. More than once, since the days of Shih Huang Ti, changes have been made in the organization of the Chinese state. Sometimes these changes have been in the direction of greater centralization; sometimes China has broken up—for short periods of time—into a number of rival and warring parts; yet each time China has returned to a system closely resembling that which has existed since before the days of Confucius.

Like the Great Wall of Shih Huang Ti, the Boxer movement was a futile—although quite explainable—effort to find relief from the pressure of the outside world. The Boxer movement failed, and the Chinese people are faced once more, as they have been on so many occasions in history, with the task of assimilating troublesome foreign influences. The fact that these new invading elements are ideas and machines, rather than a race of men akin to themselves, makes the problem more difficult, perhaps, but not impossible. The greatest problem confronting

China is that of adjusting these new machines and ideas to the organization of society. In the face of this difficulty, the old machinery of the state has, for the time, broken down; but the past record of the Chinese people holds every reason for believing that the adjustment will eventually be made—and that the reorganized Chinese social system will be found to bear a close resemblance to that which has existed for more than three thousand years.

Appendices.

A

Yuan Shih-kai's "Ode" Against the Boxers.

THE Court loves the people,
The people should obey the Court.
The superior and the inferior will thus become attached to each other.
Earthly conduct should be allied with Heavenly principles.
Shantung is a state known for its civilization;
The ancient customs of the town of Tsao, in the state of Lu, are still in existence.[1]
The highest education should be taught in the schools;
The manners and customs of the people will then be pure-minded and honest.
The gentry and retired officials should assist in leading and directing the people as to the proper course to follow.
Who would have thought it?
That corrupt and evil teaching should have been started and circulated about.
The roads connect with Kiangsu and Anhwei,
The ocean communicates with Tientsin,
The wandering banditti are daily becoming very numerous.
Strange and magical tricks cause wrangling.
In former years there were the teachings of the "White Lily Sect,"
Also the society called the "Gate of Righteous Harmony."
These societies spread to all departments and prefectures;
Their adherents increased in numbers with the result that serious calamities occurred;

[1] The ancient state of Lu was in the southern part of the modern province of Shantung; the town of Tsao was the birthplace of Confucius.

They were exterminated and further complications stopped.
This happened several tens of years ago.
The evil acts of former years have now recommenced.
The name of "Righteous Harmony" still remains.
The calamities caused by the "Fist Society" have been very great.
There is the "Divine Fist" and the "Red Fist";
And there is the "Big Sword Society."
There is a difference in the names of these societies;
Their object is, however, the practice of sorcery.
Supernatural manifestations are not worth relying on.
These societies put out notices summoning pupils to join them;
They teach them that a magic spell will fly to them;
They can call the spirits and then they can escape the fire of guns and cannon;
Further, they can withstand the weapons of war.
Blood and flesh are thinner than metals and stones,
Their reasoning is certainly not true;
In point of fact they are a treacherous and guileful class of persons.
These societies are formed for the purpose of gathering in money.
Outlaws from abroad seize the opportunity to join them;
They have, for a long time, unexpectedly broken out in open rebellion.
Previous warnings were given them, but it was a long time ago.
Here are the facts concerning the recent troubles.
In the summer of the 22nd year of Kuang Hsu, the "Sword Society" suddenly sprang into existence.
Yen-chow-fu and I-chow-fu connect with the Hwei and Su region;[2]
At all these places there are many outlaws.
The rebel leader Liu Shih-tuan took the lead in the teaching of magical arts.
In addition to him there was Tsao Te-li.
The members of the society took the oath.
The students reverently submitted;
They received their orders as though coming from the Gods.

[2] Anhwei and Kiangsu.

One morning the leaders were arrested;
They suffered death by decapitation.
Afterwards the "Fist" society started.
The chief leaders were still more numerous;
One was named Yu Ching-shui,
Another named Chen Hung-teng.
These men were in league with Yang Chao-shun.
Then there was the uncanny priest, styled Hsin Cheng.
Each of these men brought adherents to the society;
They numbered hundreds and thousands.
They began by plundering first the foreign missionaries;
This was followed by robbing the native Christians.
They first resisted the train-bands, or militia,
Afterwards they resisted the soldiers.
They burned houses and killed people in the villages and market-places;
They plundered; they even stole chickens and pigs.
Numerous sparks at first were not extinguished,
Until finally a blaze occurred which aroused action.
Three outlaws were in due order arrested;
They were decapitated and their heads exposed in Chih Ping.
Hsu Ta-hsiang was killed;
The bullet entered his breast.
Many other cruel outlaws were killed,
And their corpses were cast away in the country.
Since this society speak of charms and spells,
How is it that they fail to show the efficacy of this supernatural spirit?
Since they say their bodies can withstand the fire of guns and cannon,
How is it that they are killed?
It is evident that false or heretical doctrines have created suspicion in the minds of the common people.
Once their minds are excited with doubts and fears, they find it difficult to get rid of them.
The Governor, on assuming office, hearing this, felt compassion for the people;

He was unwilling at first to use armed force
For fear the good and the bad would perish together.
The duty of the department and district magistrates is to make arrests.
The responsibility of protecting the country rests with the army.
Orders have been repeatedly issued to prohibit (the societies).
This has been clearly made known to all villages and hamlets by proclamations.
The "Sword Society" must be put an end to;
The "Boxing" establishments must be closed up;
Those who have been coerced to join these societies must be dispersed.
There are those who connive at the "Boxers" and know what they are doing.
It is now about three months, and several tens of outlaws have been arrested.
Deputies were appointed to investigate judicially their cases;
Having got at the facts of each case, still the Governor pitied them for wrong doing.
The punishment to be inflicted is heavy or light,
Extreme penalty of the law or an admonitory hint;
Still the Governor hopes that the outlaws will really reform and mend their ways.
If they are able to do this, all will be right.
The Court loves the people;
The Imperial admonitions have been repeatedly given.
It is to be feared that you people will follow the old groove leading you astray;
Trouble will overtake you,
And you may be killed.
Beware: you should show a friendly feeling towards your village neighbors.
The Imperial Mandate is truly generous and liberal;
In studying it one feels like shedding tears.
If you people remain obstinately fixed in delusion,
How can you answer the Emperor?

Our Court has shown unbounded favor
And great kindness to the people;
The Governor makes this known to you.
The taxes on land are not increased;
The poll-tax is not increased;
The employees on government works have not been increased;
The people are not harassed by being called upon to render increased labor.
The Yellow River rushes to the Eastern Sea;
The great work on this river rests with the Board of Works.
A large sum of money is provided to conserve this water-way,
Amounting to millions of taels.
The Emperor is informed when calamities happen;
The collection of the land-tax is postponed,
Grain is given to relieve the poor,
Money is appropriated to save the sufferers from the flood.
Receiving such unbounded kindness from the Emperor,
The people should be grateful.
The Governor of Shantung reverently desires to make known to the people the Emperor's benevolence.
He hates the wicked like an enemy;
He loves the good and virtuous like his relations;
He only considers who is right and who is wrong.
No distinction is made between Christians and non-Christians;
The Christians and non-Christians are all the people of the Empire;
The Governor would strive to comfort and pacify all.
You all reside together in villages,
So you must avoid being hateful and quarrelsome.
What do you gain by being hateful and quarrelsome toward each other?
To cherish an evil feeling is the same as seeking or picking a quarrel.
The treaties provide for Christian teaching;
Protection is also provided for.
Partiality must not be shown.
The Imperial Decree ought to be reverently obeyed.

China and the Occident

In obedience to the Imperial Decree the Governor makes it clearly known to all,
So as to enable everyone to hear.
You all have mothers and fathers,
You also have brothers.
Labor and trade are possible for you,
You can till the fields and the gardens,
You all have your own duties of life,
Your village clans are prosperous and happy;
What is the use of your believing in false or heretical words?
You have, in consequence, been in trouble up to the present time.
Proclamations have been repeatedly issued;
You should have been aroused to the error of your ways a long time ago.
If you still wander in the error of your ways,
You will rush into the net of the law.
It is to be feared that your necks will not be saved,
And that your family and property will be utterly ruined.
Your aged father and mother will weep until the tears are dry;
Your brothers will weep until they are unable to utter a sound.
The evil you will have brought upon yourselves,
And your entire families will have suffered hardship.
Lay your hand on your heart, and in the night time, when all is quiet, ponder and reflect;
When you dream of the departed spirits, are you frightened or not?
From this time forth, you must repent of your misdeeds;
You will not then fall into the fiery pit and be in a state of misery.
If you are able to seize and arrest the leaders of the brigands,
And bring them before the court,
A reward will be given you.
You should take advantage of the opportunity and render meritorious service.
The Court will reward and punish:
Imperial favor or Imperial wrath.
The Governor entertains feelings of compassion for the suffering people;

He has thoroughly admonished them by proclamations.
This has been done repeatedly;
You people should reverently listen.
You are all good persons,[3]
You should therefore know that your duty is to obey the Sovereign.

NOTE. The above translation, labeled "Proclamation, in verses of five characters, issued by Yuan Shih-kai," was communicated to the State Department by Mr. Conger in his dispatch no. 356, of April 12, 1900. It is to be found in the manuscript documents of the Department of State, Dispatches from China, vol. 108.

B

Collective Note of December 22, 1900.

DURING the months of May, June, July, and August of the present year serious disorders broke out in the northern provinces of China, and crimes unprecedented in human history, crimes against the law of nations, against the laws of humanity, and against civilization were committed under peculiarly odious circumstances. Of these crimes the principal ones were the following:

1. On 20th June, his Excellency Baron Ketteler, German Minister, proceeding to the Tsungli Yamen, was murdered while in the exercise of his duties by soldiers of the regular army, acting under the orders of their chiefs.

2. On the same day the foreign Legations were attacked and besieged. These attacks continued without intermission until 14th August, on which date the arrival of foreign troops put an end to them. The attacks were made by regular troops, who joined the Boxers, who obeyed orders of the Court emanating from the Imperial Palace. At the same time, the Chinese Government officially declared by its Representatives abroad that it guaranteed the safety of the Legations.

[3] *I.e.*, born good; the opening couplet of the "San Tze Ching" says, "Man at his birth is good."

On 11th June, Mr. Sugiyama, Chancellor of the Japanese Legation, in the discharge of an official mission, was killed by regulars at the gate of the city. At Peking and in several provinces foreigners were murdered, tortured, or attacked by Boxers and regular troops, and only owed their safety to their determined resistance. Their establishments were pillaged and destroyed.

4. Foreign cemeteries, notably at Peking, were desecrated, the graves opened, and the remains scattered abroad.

These events led the foreign Powers to send their troops to China in order to protect the lives of their Representatives and of their nationals, and to restore order. During their march to Peking the allied forces met with the resistance of the Chinese armies and had to overcome it by force. China, having recognized her responsibility, expressed her regrets, and manifested the desire to see an end put to the situation created by the disturbances referred to, the Powers have decided to accede to her request on the irrevocable conditions enumerated below, which they deem indispensable to expiate the crimes committed and prevent their recurrence:

Article 1. (a) Dispatch to Berlin of an Extraordinary Mission, headed by an Imperial Prince, to express the regrets of His Majesty the Emperor of China and the Chinese Government for the murder of his Excellency the late Baron Ketteler, German Minister.

(b) Erection on the place where the murder was committed of a commemorative monument suitable to the rank of the deceased, bearing an inscription in the Latin, German, and Chinese languages expressing the regret of the Emperor of China for the murder.

Art. 2. (a) The severest punishment in proportion to their crimes for the persons named in the Imperial Decree of the 25th September, 1900, and for those whom the Representatives of the Powers shall subsequently designate.

(b) Suspension of all official examinations for five years in all the towns where foreigners have been massacred or have been subjected to cruel treatment.

Art. 3. An honorable reparation shall be accorded by the Chinese Government to that of Japan for the murder of Mr. Sugiyama, Chancellor of the Japanese Legation.

Art. 4. An expiatory monument shall be erected by the Chinese government in each of the foreign or international cemeteries which have been desecrated, and in which the graves have been destroyed.

Art. 5. Maintenance, under conditions to be settled between the Powers, of the prohibition of the importation of arms, as well as material serving exclusively for the manufacture of arms and ammunition.

Art. 6. (a) An equitable indemnity to Governments, Societies, private individuals, as well as for Chinese who have suffered during the recent occurrences in their persons or property, in consequence of their being in the service of foreigners.

(b) China shall adopt financial measures acceptable to the Powers, for the purpose of guaranteeing the payment of the said indemnities and the service of the loans.

Art. 7. The right of maintaining, by each Power, a permanent guard for its Legation, and of placing the Legation quarter in a condition of defence. Chinese not to have the right of residing in that quarter.

Art. 8. The Taku and other forts, which might impede free communication between Peking and the coast, are to be razed.

Art. 9. Right of military occupation of certain points to be determined by agreement between the Powers in order to maintain communication between the capital and the sea.

Art. 10. (a) The Chinese Government shall cause to be posted up for two years in all the Sub-Prefectures an Imperial Decree embodying:

Perpetual prohibition under pain of death of being a member of an anti-foreign Society.

Enumeration of the penalties which shall have been inflicted on the guilty persons, including the suspension of all official examinations in the towns where foreigners were massacred or subjected to cruel treatment.

(b) An Imperial Edict shall be issued and published everywhere in the Empire, making all Viceroys, Governors, and provincial and local officials responsible for order within their jurisdictions; and whenever anti-foreign disturbances or any other Treaty infractions occur therein which are not forthwith suppressed and in regard to which the guilty persons are not punished, these officials shall be immediately recalled, without the possibility of being given new posts or of receiving fresh honors.

Art. 11. The Chinese Government will undertake to negotiate regarding amendments to the Treaties of Commerce and Navigation considered useful by the Powers, and also other subjects connected with commercial relations with the object of facilitating them.

Art. 12. The Chinese Government shall undertake to reform the office of foreign relations, and modify the Court ceremonial relative to the reception of foreign Representatives in the manner which the Powers shall indicate.

Until the Chinese Government have complied with the above conditions to the satisfaction of the Powers, the Undersigned can hold out no expectation that the occupation of Peking and the Province of Pechili by the allied forces can be brought to a conclusion.

For Germany
(Signed) A. von Mumm.
For Austria-Hungary
(Signed) M. Czikann.
For Belgium
(Signed) Joostens.
For Spain
(Signed) B. J. de Cologan.
For the United States of America
(Signed) E. H. Conger.
For France
(Signed) S. Pichon.
For Great Britain
(Signed) Ernest Satow.
For Italy
(Signed) Salvago Raggi.

For Japan
(Signed) T. Nissi.
For the Netherlands
(Signed) F. M. Knobel.
For Russia
(Signed) Michel de Giers.

Peking, *December* 22, 1900.

Note. This translation from the official—French—form of the note is taken from *British Blue Books, China No. 6 (1901)*, document no. 91, inclosure.

C

Chinese Acceptance of the Collective Note.

Prince Ching and Li Hung-chang to the Doyen.

(English Translation.)

Peking, December 30, 1900.

Your Excellency,

On the 24th December, the foreign Ministers Plenipotentiary personally handed to us the Treaty in twelve Articles which, after joint consultation, they have adopted. We, the Prince and Minister, submitted by telegraph to the Throne the complete text of the Chinese translation, and on the 28th December we received the following telegraphic Decree dated the 27th December:

"We have duly perused the telegram of Prince Ching and Li Hung-chang. It behooves us accordingly to accept in their entirety the principles laid down in the twelve Articles."

As in duty bound we—the Prince and Minister—send this communication to your Excellency and beg that you will in turn transmit it to your colleagues. We have also to request that a time and place be fixed for an interview to discuss all questions. We beg that you will favor us with a reply.

The above Articles, having been agreed to by the Chinese Government, we would also further request that, until evacuation by the troops takes place, no further expeditions be undertaken by the troops of the Powers in the Departments and districts, to the end that the minds of the people may be pacified and relations of friendship strengthened.

(SEAL OF THE CHINESE PLENIPOTENTIARIES.)

NOTE. Taken from *British Blue Books, China No. 6 (1901)*, document no. 96, and inclosure.

Extract from the *Peking Gazette* of January 19, 1901.

ON the 27th December the following Imperial Decree was issued:

We have made ourselves acquainted with the contents of the telegraphic Memorial submitted by the Prince of Ching and Li Hung-chang, and also with the text of the accompanying Articles. How can we convey an idea of the extent to which these weigh upon our heart?

Considering, however, the dangers and difficulties of the present situation, we have no alternative but, in an indirect manner, to seek some satisfactory means of saving the same. We must therefore accord our sanction to the whole of the general principles laid down in the twelve Articles. As regards the detailed points which yet remain, the utmost endeavours to secure attenuation and reduction must continue to be made.

It is of essential importance that the Prince and others concerned put forth their best efforts and strain every nerve to wrestle with their hard task, in the hope that the interests at stake may be conserved.

NOTE. Taken from *British Blue Books, China No. 6 (1901)*, document no. 180, inclosure. Sir Ernest Satow reports that it was generally understood that this "masterpiece" was drafted by Wang Wen-shao.

D

Russo-Chinese Agreement Concerning Manchuria.

1. THE Emperor of Russia, being anxious to give evidence of his friendly feeling towards China, is willing to forget the hostile acts committed in Manchuria, and to hand back the whole of that country to China—its administration to be carried on as heretofore.

2. Under Article 6 of the Manchurian Railway Agreement, the Administration is authorized to maintain troops for the protection of the line. The country, however, being at present in an unsettled condition, and such troops few in number, a body of soldiers must be retained until order is restored, and until China shall have carried out the provisions of the last four Articles of the present Convention.

3. In the event of grave disturbances the Russian garrisons will afford China every assistance in suppressing the same that lies in their power.

4. In the recent attacks against Russia, Chinese troops having taken a prominent part, China agrees, pending the completion of the line and its opening to traffic, not to establish an army (in those provinces). She will consult with Russia as to the number of troops she may subsequently wish to establish there. The importation of munitions of war into Manchuria is prohibited.

5. With a view to safeguarding the interests of the territory in question, China will, on representations being made by Russia, at once deprive of office any Military Governor or other high official, whose conduct of affairs may prove antagonistic to the maintenance of friendly relations.

A police force, consisting of mounted and unmounted units, may be organized in the interior of Manchuria. Its numbers shall be determined after consultation with Russia, and from its armament artillery shall be excluded. The services of the subjects of any other Power shall not be employed in connection therewith.

6. In conformity with the undertaking given by China at an

earlier date, she will not employ the subjects of any other Power in training Chinese soldiers or sailors in North China.

7. The neighboring local authorities will, in the interests of peace and order, draw up new special Regulations with reference to the neutral zone (see Agreement of the 27th March 1898) treated of in Article 5 of the Agreement relating to the lease (of part of the Liaotung Peninsula).

China's autonomous rights in the City of Chinchou, secured to her by Art. 4 of the Special Agreement (of the 7th May, 1898) are hereby abrogated.

8. China shall not, without the consent of Russia, grant to any other Power, or the subjects thereof, privileges with regard to mines, railroads, or other matters in conterminous (*i.e.*, with Russia) regions, such as Manchuria, Mongolia, and the sections of the new Dominion known as Tarbagati, Ili, Kashgar, Yarkand, and Khoten. Nor shall China, without Russia's consent, construct railroads there herself.

9. China being under obligation to pay Russia's war expenses and the claims of other Powers, arising out of the recent troubles, the amount of the indemnity presented in the name of Russia, the period within which it will have to be paid, and the security therefore will all be arranged in concert with the other Powers.

10. The compensation to be paid for the destruction of the railway lines, for the robbery of property belonging to the Railway Administration and its employés, as well as claims for delay in carrying on the construction of the line, will form subject of arrangement between China and the Administration.

11. The above mentioned claims may, by agreement with the Administration, either in whole or in part, be commuted for other privileges. The grant of such privileges would involve a complete revision of the previous agreement.

In conformity with the undertaking previously given by China, it is agreed that a line may be constructed from either the trunk line or the branch line (of the Manchurian Railway) in the direction of Peking up to the Great Wall, its administration to be governed by the Regulations at present in force.

NOTE. This version, which was a translation of the Chinese text of the Agreement, was telegraphed to London by Satow on March 6; on March 19, he telegraphed the following amendments which had been made to the draft Agreement.

Article 4. The number of troops and military posts in Manchuria is to be determined with Russia. In accordance with common agreement to be made with the Powers, prohibition of importation of arms and ammunition. Meantime, prohibition to be made by China.

Article 5. Any Governor-General, or other high official, complained of by Russia as having acted in an improper manner in matters which affect foreign policy is to be transferred at once. China may maintain a police force of cavalry and infantry, determining its strength in consultation with Russia. This body is, however, not to have cannon until the pacification of the country, and only Chinese are to be enrolled.

Article 6. (Omitted.)

Article 7. The local authorities in the neighborhood of the neutral zone, provided for by Article V of the Convention relating to the lease of the Peninsula of Liaotung, are to frame a set of special Regulations suitable to the circumstances.

Article 8. Without previous consultation with Russia, China shall not grant to any other Power, or its subjects, railway and mining concessions and commercial advantages throughout Manchuria.

Article 10. The principles agreed upon by the Representatives of the foreign Powers and approved by their Governments shall be used to adjust the indemnities for the destruction of railways, of the Railway Company employés' property, and for losses due to delay of work.

Article 12. It is stated that China has contravened a previous Russo-Chinese Agreement by constructing a railway line direct into Manchuria, from Shanhaikwan to Newchwang and Sinminting, with money borrowed from a private Company, on the 28th September, 1898. China is to give compensation for this by conceding the right to the East China Railway Company to build an extension line of its main railway to the Great Wall, on the Chihli-Manchurian boundary.

NOTE. The other powers, especially Great Britain, continued to express their disapproval of Russia's procedure, and, on April 5, the Russian minister to Great Britain, M. Lessar, left the following note at the British Foreign Office.

Some time ago the Imperial Government entered into negotiations with China on the subject of an arrangement with the object of being able to proceed, as soon as circumstances admitted of it, to the gradual accomplishment of the intention expressed by Russia of restoring Manchuria to China. It is evident that, with this object in view, it was indispensable to know by a certain date if it was possible to establish, in accord with the Chinese Government, the conditions on which the evacuation of that province should take place.

It appears from information which has been received that, under the present circumstances, an arrangement of this nature, instead of serving as manifest proof of the amicable sentiments of Russia towards China, might occasion grave difficulties for the latter. Therefore the Imperial Ministry not only do not insist with the Chinese Government on the conclusion of the arrangement, but even refuse to enter upon further negotiations on the subject, and, with unswerving adherence to the programme which they have pursued from the beginning, will await with calm the development of events.

NOTE. These documents are all quoted from *British Blue Books, China No. 6 (1901)*, documents nos. 158, 192, and 237, inclosure.

Appendices

E

Transformation of the Tsungli Yamen.

Prince Ching and Li Hung-chang to the Doyen.

PEKING, *July* 27, 1901.

UPON the receipt of your dispatch, dated April 22nd, 1901, relative to the reform of the Office of Foreign Affairs as provided in Article XII of the Collective Note, we, the Prince and Minister, immediately requested the publication of an Imperial Decree in accordance with the different points enumerated in that dispatch.

We have now received the following telegram from Hsi-an-fu:

"On the 9th day of the 6th moon, the Grand Chancellary received the following Decree:

"The creation of officials and the determination of their duties have always been regulated by the necessities of the times. At this moment, when a new treaty of peace is being concluded, international relations occupy the first place in important affairs, and it is more than ever necessary to have recourse to men of ability who shall occupy themselves with all that relates to the establishment of friendly relations and mutual trust.

"The Office of Foreign Affairs, formerly created to treat with international questions, has existed for years, but, since the Princes and Ministers who composed it have generally exercised these functions only as accessory to others, they were not able to devote themselves exclusively to it. It now behooves us to create special functions, in order that each may have his special duties.

"We therefore command that the Office of Foreign Affairs (Tsungli Ko Kuo tze-wu Yamen) be changed into the "Ministry of Foreign Affairs" (Wai-wu-pu), and take rank before the six ministers. And we designate I-Kuang, Prince of the 1st rank Ching, as President of the Ministry of Foreign Affairs; Wang Wen-chao, Grand Secretary of State of the "Ti Jen Ko" is appointed Vice-President of the Ministry of Foreign Affairs; King Hong-ki, President of the Ministry of Public Works, is transferred with the same title to the Ministry of Foreign Affairs, of which he is appointed Vice-President. Sin Chou-peng, Director of the Imperial Stud, and Sin Lien-fang, expectant metropolitan sub-director of the 3rd or 4th rank, are appointed first and second under-secretaries.

"In all that concerns the determination of personnel, the regulations which should govern their choice, and the salaries of the Ministers, directors, and other agents, we order the councillors of the Government to consult with the Ministry of Civil Appointments, and to report to us promptly in regard to their conclusions."—By Imperial order.

In conformity with the orders of His Majesty, we, the Prince and Minister, consider it our duty to bring to the knowledge of Your Excellency, by this dispatch, the facts relative to the creation of the Ministry of Foreign Affairs sanctioned by Imperial Decree, and we beg you to communicate this dispatch to your colleagues.

NOTE. Taken from *Négociations de Pékin*, Annex No. 178.

F

Revision of Court Ceremonial.

Memorandum as to the Ceremonial to be observed at Audiences.

1. THE solemn audiences given by His Majesty the Emperor of China to the Diplomatic Body or to the separate Representatives of the Powers shall be held in the hall of the palace called "Kien-tsing-Kong."

2. In going to these solemn audiences or in returning therefrom, the Representatives of the Powers shall be carried in their chairs to the entrance of the King-yun gate. At the King-yun gate

they will descend from the chairs in which they have come, and be carried in a small chair (i-chiao) to the foot of the stairs of the Kien-tsing gate.

On arriving at the Kien-tsing gate, the Representatives of the Powers shall descend from their chairs and proceed on foot into the presence of His Majesty in the Hall—Kien-tsing-Kong.

On leaving, the Representatives of the Powers shall return to their places of residence in the same manner as they have come.

3. When the Representative of a Power has to present to His Majesty the Emperor his letters of Credence, or a communication from the Chief of the State by which he is accredited, the Emperor shall send to the residence of said Representative—to convey him to the Palace—a chair with trimmings and yellow tassels, such as are used by the Princes of the Imperial family. The said Representative shall be returned to his residence in the same manner. An escort of troops shall also be sent to the residence of the said Representative to accompany him in going and on his return.

4. In presenting his letters of credence or a communication from the Chief of the State by which he is accredited, the Diplomatic Agent, while he is bearing the said letters or communication, shall pass through the central openings of the gates of the Palace until he comes into the presence of His Majesty. In returning from these audiences, he shall conform, in regard to the doors through which he has to pass, to the usages already established at the Court of Peking for audiences given to Foreign Representatives.

5. The Emperor shall receive directly into his hands the letters and communications above mentioned which the Foreign Representatives may have to present to him.

6. If His Majesty decides to invite the Representatives of the Powers to a banquet, it is clearly understood that this banquet should take place in one of the halls of the Imperial Palace and that His Majesty shall be present in person.

7. In short, the ceremonial adopted by China with regard to the Representatives of the Foreign Powers shall not, in any case, be different than that which results from a perfect equality be-

tween the countries concerned and China, without any loss of prestige on the one hand or the other.

NOTE. Taken from *Négociations de Pékin*, Annex No. 198.

G

The Final Protocol.

THE Plenipotentiaries:

Of Germany: His Exc. A. MUMM VON SCHWARZENSTEIN;

Of Austria-Hungary: His Exc. Baron M. CZIKANN VON WAHLBORN;

Of Belgium: His Exc. M. JOOSTENS;

Of Spain: His Exc. B. J. DE COLOGAN;

Of the United States of America: His Exc. W. W. ROCKHILL;

Of France: His Exc. PAUL BEAU;

Of Great Britain: His Exc. SIR ERNEST SATOW;

Of Italy: His Exc. MARQUIS SALVAGO-RAGGI;

Of Japan: His Exc. JUTARO KOMURA;

Of the Netherlands: His Exc. F. M. KNOBEL;

Of Russia: His Exc. M. DE GIERS;

and Of China: His Highness I-KUANG, Prince of the first rank Ching, President of the Ministry of Foreign Affairs; and

His Exc. LI HUNG-CHANG, Count of the first rank Sou Yi, Tutor of the Heir Presumptive, Grand Secretary of the Wen-Hua-Tien, Minister of Commerce, Superintendent of the Northern Ports, Governor-General of Chihli;

have met in order to establish the fact that China has, to the satisfaction of the Powers, conformed with the conditions which were set forth in the Note of December 22nd, 1900, and which were accepted in their entirety by His Majesty the Emperor of China, by a Decree dated December 27th, 1900. [Appendix C.]

Art. I. (a). By an Imperial Edict of June 9th, last, Tsai Feng, Prince of the first rank Chun, has been appointed Ambassador of

His Majesty the Emperor of China and has been charged, in this capacity, to convey to His Majesty the German Emperor the expression of the regrets of His Majesty the Emperor of China and of the Chinese Government concerning the assassination of His Excellency Baron von Ketteler, the German Minister.

Prince Chun left Peking on July 12th, last, to carry out the orders which have been given him.

Art. I. (b). The Chinese Government has declared that it will erect, on the spot of the assassination of His Excellency Baron von Ketteler, a Memorial Monument suitable to the rank of the deceased, and bearing an inscription in the Latin, German, and Chinese languages, which shall express the regrets of His Majesty the Emperor of China for the murder committed.

Their Excellencies the Chinese Plenipotentiaries have informed His Excellency the German Plenipotentiary, by a letter of July 22nd, last, that an arch the entire width of the street is being erected, and that the work was commenced on June 25th, last.

Art. II. (a). Imperial Edicts of the 13th and 21st of February, 1901, have inflicted the following punishments upon the chief authors of the crimes and attempted crimes committed against the Foreign Governments and their nationals.

Tsai Yi, Prince Tuan; and Tsai Lan, Duke Fu Koo; have been sentenced to be executed at the Autumn Assizes and it has been stipulated that, if the Emperor thinks he should spare their lives, they shall be exiled to Turkestan and there imprisoned for life, without the possibility that this punishment shall ever be commuted.

Tsai Hsun, Prince Chuang; Ying Nien, President of the Court of Censors; and Chao Shu-chiao, President of the Board of Punishments; have been condemned to commit suicide.

Yu Hsien, Governor of Shansi; Chi Hsiu, President of the Board of Rites; Hsu Cheng-yu, formerly Director in the Board of Punishments; have been condemned to death.

Posthumous degradation has been pronounced against Kang Yi, Assistant Grand Secretary of State, President of the Board of Civil Appointments; Hsu Tung, Grand Secretary of State; and Li Ping-heng, formerly Governor General of Szechuan.

An Imperial Edict of February 13th, 1901, has rehabilitated the memory of Hsu Yung-yi, President of the Board of War; Li Shan, President of the Board of Revenue; Hsu Ching-cheng, Director of the Board of Civil Appointments; Lien Yuan, Vice-Chancellor of the Grand Secretariat; and Yuan Chang, Director of the Court of Sacrifices; who had been put to death for having protested against the abominable violations of international law committed in the course of the last year.

Prince Chuang has committed suicide on February 21st, 1901; Ying Nien and Chao Shu-chiao on the 24th; Yu Hsien has been executed on the 22nd; and Chi Hsiu and Hsu Cheng-yu on the 26th.

Tung Fu-hsiang, General of Kansu, has been deprived of his duties by an Imperial Edict of February 13th, 1901, until it shall be decided what definite punishment shall be inflicted upon him.

Imperial Edicts of April 29th and August 19th, 1901, have imposed suitable punishments upon the Provincial officials recognized as guilty of crimes and attempted crimes committed in the course of last summer.

Art. II. (b). An Imperial Edict, promulgated August 19th, 1901, has ordered the suspension of official examinations, during five years, in all towns where foreigners have been murdered or subjected to cruel treatment.

Art. III. In order to make honorable reparation for the assassination of Mr. Sugiyama, Chancellor of the Japanese Legation, His Majesty the Emperor of China has, by an Imperial Edict of June 18th, 1901, appointed the Vice-President of the Board of Revenue, Na Tung, as Envoy Extraordinary, and has charged specially to convey to His Majesty the Emperor of Japan the expression of the regrets of His Majesty the Emperor of China and of his Government for the assassination of Mr. Sugiyama.

Art. IV. The Chinese Government has undertaken to erect an expiatory monument in each of the foreign or international cemeteries which have been desecrated and in which the tombs have been destroyed. In agreement with the Representatives of the Powers, it has been arranged that the interested Legations shall give instructions for the erection of these monuments, and the costs have been charged against China; these costs amount to ten thousand taels for each of the cemeteries in Peking and the vicinity and five thousand taels for those in the provinces. This sum has been paid and the list of the Cemeteries is annexed.

Art. V. China has agreed to prohibit the importation of arms and munitions, as well as that of materials employed exclusively in the manufacture of arms and munitions.

An Imperial Edict has been issued on August 25th, 1901, prohibiting such importation for a period of two years.

Further Edicts may subsequently be issued, to extend this term by periods of two years, in case the Powers shall deem it necessary.

Art. VI. By an Imperial Edict dated May 22nd, 1901, His Majesty the Emperor of China has undertaken to pay to the Powers an indemnity of four hundred fifty million Haikuan taels. This sum represents the total of the indemnities for States, societies, individuals, and the Chinese mentioned in Article VI of the Note of December 22nd, 1900.

(a). These four hundred fifty millions constitute a debt in gold, and the value of the Haikuan tael, in the gold currency of each of the countries, is to be calculated as follows:

1 Haikuan tael	=	Marks	3.055
	=	Austro-Hungarian Kroners . .	3.595
	=	Gold Dollar	0.742
	=	Francs	3.750
	=	Pound Sterling	0.3s od
	=	Yen	1.407
	=	Dutch Gulden	1.796
	=	Gold Roubles (at the rate of Dolias 17.424)	1.412

This sum in gold shall bear interest at the rate of 4 per cent a year, and the principal is to be reimbursed by China in thirty-nine years on the conditions indicated in the plan of amortisation hereto annexed.

The capital and interest will be payable in gold, or at the rate of exchange corresponding to the different dates of maturity. The operation of the amortisation will commence on January 1st,

1902, and end at the expiration of the year 1940. The amortisations will be payable annually, the first date of maturity being fixed as January 1st, 1903. Interest will be reckoned from July 1st, 1901, but the Chinese Government will have the privilege of discharging, within three years beginning with January 1st, 1902, any arrears of the first half year ending December 31st, 1901, upon the condition of paying interest compounded at 4 per cent per year upon the sums of which the payment has thus been deferred.

Interest will be payable semi-annually, the first date of maturity being fixed at July 1st, 1902.

(b). The service of the debt will be arranged at Shanghai, and in the following manner:

Each Power will be represented by a delegate in a Commission of bankers, which will be authorized to bank the amounts of interest and amortisation which will be deposited with it by the Chinese authorities appointed to this duty, to apportion these sums among the interested parties, and to give a receipt.

(c). The Chinese Government will deliver to the Doyen of the Diplomatic Body at Peking a bond for the total sum, which will later be transformed into smaller bonds bearing the signatures of delegates of the Chinese Government appointed for this purpose. This operation, and all those relating to the establishment of claims will be carried out by the above-mentioned Commission in conformity to instructions which the Powers will give to their delegates.

(d). The revenue from the sources pledged for the payment of the bonds will be deposited monthly with the Commission.

(e). The sources pledged for guaranteeing the bonds are as follows:

1. The remainder of the revenue of the Imperial Maritime Customs after paying the interest and amortisation of the loans already guaranteed by these revenues, augmented by the result of increasing the present tariff to an effective 5 per cent on maritime imports, which shall include articles hitherto entering free of duty, with the exception of rice, cereals and flour for foreign consumption, as well as gold and silver currency and bullion.

2. The revenues of the "native" customs, administered in the treaty ports by the Imperial Maritime Customs.

3. The entire revenue of the "gabelle," except for the portion previously affected by other foreign loans.

(f). The increase of the present tariff to an effective 5 per cent is agreed to on the following conditions.

The increase will go into effect two months after the signature of the present protocol, and no exceptions will be made except for merchandise shipped within ten days of that date.

1. All the duties on imports collected "ad valorem" shall be converted into "specific" duties, so far as it is possible to do so, and with the shortest possible delay.

This conversion shall be accomplished in the following manner;

As the base of evaluation there will be taken the mean value of the merchandise, at the moment of debarkation, during the three years 1897, 1898, and 1899; that is to say the sales price after deductions have been made for the import duties and incidental expenses.

Until this conversion has been made, the duties will be collected "ad valorem."

2. The course of the Peiho and that of the Whangpu will be improved with the financial participation of China.

Art. VII. The Chinese Government has agreed that the quarter occupied by the Legations shall be considered as a quarter specially reserved to their use and placed under their exclusive police, where the Chinese shall not have the right to reside, and which may be put into a state of defence.

The limits of this quarter have been thus fixed in the annexed plan. . . .

By the protocol annexed to the letter of January 16th, 1901, China has recognised the right of each Power to maintain a permanent guard in the said quarter for the defence of its Legation.

Art. VIII. The Chinese Government has consented to raze the Taku forts and those which could prevent free communication between Peking and the sea.

Dispositions have been taken to this effect.

Art. IX. The Chinese Government has recognised, by the protocol annexed to the letter of January 16th, 1901, the right of the Powers to occupy certain points, to be determined by an agreement between them, in order to maintain free communication between the capital and the sea.

The points occupied by the Powers are: Huangtsun, Langfang, Yangtsun, Tientsin, Chenliangcheng, Tangku, Lutai, Tangshan, Lanchow, Changli, Chinwangtao, Shanhaikwan.

Art. X. The Chinese Government has engaged to post and publish during two years in all the district towns the following Imperial Edicts:

(a) Edict of February 1st, 1901, perpetually forbidding, under pain of death, membership in an anti-foreign society.

(b) Edicts of February 13th and 21st, April 21st, and August 19th, 1901, containing the enumeration of the punishments which have been inflicted upon the guilty.

(c) Edict of August 19th, 1901, suppressing the examinations in all the towns where foreigners have been massacred or subjected to cruel treatment.

(d) Edict of February 1st, 1901, declaring that all the Governors-General, Governors, and other officials, provincial or local, are responsible for order in their districts and that, in case of a renewal of anti-foreign troubles or of any other treaty infractions which are not immediately repressed and of which those guilty have not been punished, these officials will be immediately dismissed and shall not be appointed to new posts nor receive new honors.

The posting of these Edicts is being progressively carried out in the Empire.

Art. XI. The Chinese Government has undertaken to negotiate amendments, judged useful by the Foreign Governments, to the treaties of commerce and navigation, and other subjects affecting commercial relations, with the view of facilitating these.

For the present, and in consequence of the stipulations inscribed in Article VI on the subject of the indemnity, the Chinese

Government has undertaken to coöperate in the amelioration of the course of the rivers Peiho and Whangpu, as described below:

(a) The work of improving the navigability of the Peiho, commenced in 1898 with the coöperation of the Chinese Government, has been resumed under the direction of an international Commission.

As soon as the administration of Tientsin shall have been restored to the Chinese Government, the latter will be authorised to be represented in this Commission, and will pay annually a sum of sixty thousand Haikuan taels for carrying on the work.

(b) A River Council has been created charged with the direction and control of the work of rectifying the Whangpu and improving the course of this river.

This Council is composed of members representing the interests of the Chinese Government and those of the foreigners in the maritime commerce of Shanghai.

The necessary expenses for the work and the general administration of the enterprise are estimated at four hundred sixty thousand Haikuan taels annually during the first twenty years.

This sum will be furnished in equal parts by the Chinese Government and the foreign interests.

The detailed stipulations relating to the composition, the functions, and the revenues of this River Council are made the subject of an annex.

Art. XII. An Imperial Edict of July 24th, 1901 [see Appendix E], has reformed the Office of Foreign Affairs (Tsungli Yamen) in the sense indicated by the Powers, that is to say, has transformed it into a Ministry of Foreign Affairs (Wai-wu-pu) which takes rank before the other six Ministries of State.

The same Edict has named the principal members of this Ministry.

An understanding has also been reached on the subject of the modification of the Court ceremonial relative to the reception of Foreign Representatives, and has been the object of several notes from the Chinese Plenipotentiaries which are summed up in a memorandum hereto attached [see Appendix F].

Finally, it is expressly understood that, for the above-mentioned declarations and for the annexed documents emanating from the Foreign Plenipotentiaries, the French text is alone authentic.

The Chinese Government having thus conformed, to the satisfaction of the Powers, to the conditions enumerated in the aforesaid Note of December 22nd, 1900, the Powers have acceded to the desire of China to see the situation created by the disorders of the summer of 1900 come to an end.

In consequence the Foreign Plenipotentiaries are authorised to declare in the name of their Governments that, with the exception of the Legation guards mentioned in Article VII, the international troops will completely evacuate the town of Peking on September 17th, 1901, and, with the exception of the places mentioned in Article IX, will retire from the province of Chihli on September 22nd, 1901.

The present final Protocol has been drawn up in twelve identic copies and signed by all the Plenipotentiaries of the Contracting Countries. A copy will be delivered to each of the Foreign Plenipotentiaries and a copy will be delivered to the Chinese Plenipotentiaries.

Peking, September 7th, 1901.

SIGNED: A. VON MUMM.
M. CZIKANN.
JOOSTENS.
B. J. DE COLOGAN.
W. W. ROCKHILL.
BEAU.
ERNEST SATOW.
SALVAGO RAGGI.
JUTARO KOMURA.
F. M. KNOBEL.
M. DE GIERS.
I. KUANG.
LI HUNG-CHANG.

NOTE. Taken from *Négociations de Pékin*, Annex No. 200.

Appendices

H

Apportionment of the Indemnity.

	Haikuan Taels	*Per Cent of Whole*
Russia	130,371,120	28.97136
Germany	90,070,515	20.01567
France	70,878,240	15.75072
Great Britain . . .	50,620,545	11.24901
Japan	34,793,100	7.73180
United States . . .	32,939,055	7.31979
Italy	26,617,005	5.91489
Belgium	8,484,345	1.88541
Austria-Hungary .	4,003,920	.88976
Netherlands . . .	782,100	.17380
Spain	135,315	.03007
Portugal	92,250	.02050
Norway and Sweden .	62,820	.01396
International . .	149,670	.03326
Grand Total . . .	450,000,000	100.

Note. This division of the indemnity was agreed to by the representatives of the eleven signatories on June 14, 1902. The figures are taken from the official minutes of that meeting, as given in *Négociations de Pékin*, p. lvii; the writer has, however, taken the liberty of rearranging the names of the countries in order of the amount of their claims.

China and the Occident

I

Cities Involved in the Boxer Movement.

AN imperial edict of August 19, 1901 (see Art. II (b) of the Final Protocol) suspended, for a period of five years, all official examinations in the following cities where foreigners had been killed or cruelly treated:

In Manchuria:

Mukden[1]	Shu-lan-sien[?]	Kia-tze-chang[1]
Lien-chang[1]	Yu-king-sien[1]	Pei-ling-tze[?]

In Chihli:

Peking[1]	Hwai-lu[2]	Lwan-ping[1]
Tientsin[1]	Tung-chow[3]	Sin-gan[2]
Cheng-ting-fu[1]	Pao-ting-fu[1]	Cheng-te-fu[2]
King-chow[1]	Yung-ching[1]	
Wang-tu[2]	Wu-yi[1]	

In Shansi:

Tai-yuan-fu[1]	Pu-sien[2]	Yo-yang[1]
Kwei-hwa[1]	Chang-tze[2]	Ku-wu[1]
Ta-tung-fu[1]	Tse-chow-fu[2]	Si-chow[2]
Fen-chow[1]	Sui-yuan[1]	Ping-yang-fu[2]
Wen-shui[1]	So-ping[1]	Kao-ping[2]
Ta-ning[1]	Sin-chow[1]	Kiang-chow[3]
Ho-tsin[1]	Tai-ku[1]	
Shao-tang[2]	Shao-yi[1]	

In Honan:

Nan-yang-fu[2]	Kwang-chow[2]

In Shensi:	*In Hunan:*	*In Chekiang:*
Ning-yang[3]	Heng-chow-fu[1]	Chu-chow[1]

[1] Indicates cities where foreigners had been killed.

[2] Indicates cities where foreigners had been cruelly treated.

[3] Indicates cities where foreigners had been plundered and driven out.

[?] Indicates cities where no specifications were given in the foreign demands for punishment.

Bibliographical Note.

AN exhaustive bibliography of works relating to China—or even of works dealing with the relations between China and the West—would be out of the question in a book intended for general reading. The student who desires such a guide for his studies is referred to Professor Henri Cordier's *Bibliotheca Sinica* (2d edition revised, Paris, E. Guilmoto, 1904-1908; supplement and index, Paris, P. Geuthner, 1923). This is the best existing bibliography on China, and should be found in every library which attempts to maintain a section on the Far East. Instead of an imposing catalogue of publications on China, the author desires here to put before his readers a few of the books which he has utilized, and to give some indication as to their respective merits.

The study of China's relations with the non-Chinese world should begin with some study of the cultural and institutional bases of Chinese society. An invaluable work for such preliminary study is *The Chinese Classics*, translated by James Legge (8 vols., Hongkong, 1861-1872). In addition to the Chinese text and translation, Professor Legge has included in his work a tremendous amount of historical and critical material, which makes his work a veritable compendium of Chinese antiquity. *The Analects of Confucius*, translated by W. E. Soothill (Yokohama, 1910), gives the best-known of the Confucian classics in a more available form, with much useful comment and explanation. The Book of Mencius is included in Legge's translation of the classics.

The *Tao Teh King* of Lao Tze has been translated by Paul Carus, Remusat, von Strauss, Wilhelm, and others; while Professor H. A. Giles has translated the *Writings of Chuang Tzu* (London, 1889). Some reading of these two non-Confucian philosophers should be added to the study of the "orthodox" classics.

H. C. Chen's *Economic Principles of Confucius and His School* (New York, 1911) is a most useful interpretation of this aspect of Confucian philosophy, and goes far toward explaining some of the fundamental differences between the political development in China and the West. *The Three Religions of China*, by W. E. Soothill (London, 1913), is an excellent treatment of the position of Confucianism, Taoism, and Buddhism in China. E. Biot's *Essai sur l'histoire de l'instruction publique en Chine* (Paris, 1847) is the first of two works by this brilliant French scholar which must be included here. M. Biot has treated in great detail the history of the Confucian "literati" as a factor in the administrative system of the country.

On the institutional side, E. Biot's *Tcheou-li, ou rites des Tcheou* (published posthumously, Paris, 1851) must be mentioned, although few will be able to make use of it. This translation of the ancient work attributed to a brother of the first Emperor of the Chou Dynasty (about the end of the twelfth century B.C.) is remarkable for the light which it throws upon the extent of China's institutional development more than 3000 years ago. The work is very rare, and the present writer rejoices in the possession of a copy. Professor F. Hirth's *Ancient History of China to the End of the Chou Dynasty* (New York, 1908) is, perhaps, the most satisfactory available treatment of China's early history and development. Another modern work of very considerable value is *The Origin of the Chinese People*, by Dr. John Ross (London, 1916). *The Middle Kingdom*, by S. Wells Williams (New York, 1883), is a classic which is well known to all who have felt an interest in China, and, despite the fact that it was published more than forty years ago, has not been superseded by later publications.

The reader who desires some acquaintance with the legal system of the Chinese Empire is referred to two works: Sir George T. Staunton's *Ta Tsing Leu Lee*—Fundamental Laws and Supplementary Statutes of the Tsing Dynasty (London, 1810), and Alabaster's *Notes and Commentaries on Chinese Criminal Law and Cognate Topics* (London, 1899). The second of these works is a valuable supplement to the first. Staunton devoted himself chiefly to the fundamental laws—the "Leu,"—while Alabaster has paid particular attention to the statutes—the "Lee"—and to the study of cases which illustrate the actual practice of Chinese courts. Since the Tsing Dynasty took over, with few changes, the code of laws which was existing in China at the time they conquered the country, a study of these works will give a fair understanding of the legal system of China between 1400 A.D. and 1900 A.D.

The Chinese Government, by Wm. F. Mayers (Shanghai, 1896), is a very complete manual of China's political organization and deserves careful study. A more interpretative study of the government is to be found in H. A. Giles' *China and the Chinese* (New York, 1902), which contains an admirable discussion of the essential democracy of the Chinese state.

The literature of China is particularly rich in historical works, and some of the most valuable of these have been made available in translation by the labors of French scholars. Édouard Chavannes's translation of *Les Mémoires Historiques de Se-ma Ts'ien* (6 vols., Paris, 1895-1906) is a work of the first importance and supplements the historical portions of the Confucian classics. Of a different nature, but hardly less important, is de Mailla's *Histoire Général de la Chine* (Paris, 1777-1785), a translation from the Chinese. De Mailla's work is brought down almost to the date of publication, and covers more than a century of Jesuit missionary work at Peking; it is thus a most valuable source for the early contact between China and the West. The *Histoire des Relations de la Chine avec l'Annam-Vietnam*, translated from Chinese documents by G. Déveria (Paris, 1880), and *Tu-li-shin's Narrative of the Chinese Embassy to the Khan of the Tougourth Tartars*, translated by Sir George T. Staunton (London, 1821), throw considerable light upon China's attitude toward her neighbors and her relations with them. Additional information upon this point is contained in J. P. G. Pauthier's *Histoire des relations politiques de la Chine avec les puissances occidentales, depuis les temps les plus anciens jusqu'à nos jours* (Paris, 1859), which contains a translation of the court ceremonial at Peking for the reception of ambassadors, and also a list of the tributary states with the periods at which each was expected to send its tribute-bearing missions.

China and the Occident

The Coming of the West.

MARCO POLO is familiar, by name at least, to all readers, and the story of his travels is available in many editions. The earliest commercial activities of the English in the Far East are detailed by John Bruce in his *Annals of the Honourable East India Company* (London, 1810), and by John Anderson in *English Intercourse with Siam during the 17th Century* (London, 1890). This latter work covers much more ground than is indicated by its title, and deals with the early English, Dutch, French, and Portuguese rivalries throughout the Orient; it is especially useful for the bibliographical material which is to be found in its footnotes. Dr. H. B. Morse's *The East India Company* (4 vols., Harvard University Press, 1926) is an authoritative and exhaustive study of this important organization. *The Dutch in Java*, by Professor Clive Day (New York, 1904), is extremely valuable both for its text and for its bibliographical references. *The Journals of Major Samuel Shaw*, edited by Josiah Quincy (Boston, 1847), is source material for early American intercourse with China, and also for the general condition of the Canton trade at the close of the eighteenth century. *The "Fan Kwei" at Canton before Treaty Days, 1825-44*, by W. C. Hunter (London, 1882), is a fascinating description of the period immediately preceding the Opium War.

The early efforts of the Europeans to establish diplomatic relations with China may be studied in the records of the various embassies which were sent to Peking. Among these records are Nieuhoff's account of *An Embassy from the (Dutch) East India Company . . .* (English translation by John Ogilby, London, 1671-1673), E. Ysbrandts Ides' *Three Years Travels from Moscow Over-land to China* (English translation, London, 1706), Sir George Staunton's *Authentic Account* of the Macartney Embassy (London, 1798), Henry Ellis's *Journal* of the Amherst Embassy (London, 1817), and Dr. Robert Morrison's *Embassy to China* (London, 1820) which, like the book by Ellis, dealt with the fruitless Amherst Mission.

Bibliographical Note

The Conflict.

FOR the complicated story of China's relations with the West during the nineteenth century, a few general works can be recommended as most useful. First among these stands Professor Henri Cordier's *Histoire des relations de la Chine avec les puissances occidentales* (3 vols., Paris, 1901-1902). Closely following this comes Dr. H. B. Morse's *International Relations of the Chinese Empire* (London, New York, etc., 1910-1918), the first and second volumes of this work being especially valuable. Alexander Michie, in *The Englishman in China* (2 vols., Edinburg, 1900), has written the history of the period from the point of view of English relations, and around the outstanding figure of Sir Rutherford Alcock. Tyler Dennett's *Americans in Eastern Asia* (New York, 1922) treats America's share in the events with much detail and furnishes an excellent bibliography. Édouard Driault, in *La question de l'Extrême Orient* (Paris, 1908), discusses the relations between Europe and the Far East with sympathetic appreciation of the Oriental's view of the problems involved. *The Foreign Relations of China*, by M. J. Bau (New York and Chicago, 1921), is chiefly valuable for its references to the sources, for which it serves as a useful index.

The treaties between China and the Western Powers have been collected by:

L. de Reinach, *Receuil des Traites en Extrême Orient* (Paris, 1902),

G. E. P. Hertslet, *China Treaties* (2 vols., London, 1908),

J. V. A. MacMurray, *Treaties and Agreements with and concerning China, 1894-1919* (2 vols., New York, 1921),

W. F. Mayers, *Treaties between the Empire of China and Foreign Powers* (Shanghai, 1902), and

W. W. Rockhill, *Treaties and Conventions with or concerning China and Korea* (Washington, 1904).

Professor F. Wells Williams, in his *Anson Burlingame and the First Chinese Mission to Foreign Powers* (New York, 1912), recounts the effect which was made by China at the end of the '60's —with the aid of the former American minister at Peking—to modify the pressure of foreign aggression. Admiral Lord Charles Beresford's *The Break-up of China* (New York and London, 1899) is a protest, three decades later, against the contemplated partition of China; yet his own proposals with regard to the future of the country would have been hardly more acceptable to the people of China than the partition. Dr. Frank E. Hinckley, in *American Consular Jurisdiction in the Orient* discusses the development of Extraterritoriality in the Orient, and especially in China. These three books will supplement the treatment which is given to the several subjects by the more general works.

Of the many books which appeared during the nineteenth century describing the Chinese and their institutions, perhaps the most readable and, at the same time, the most sympathetic are those by Abbé Huc. His *Travels in Tartary, Thibet, and China* (English edition, London, 1852) and *The Chinese Empire* (English edition, London, 1855) have yet to be surpassed for the intimate view which they give of Chinese life. *Chinese Characteristics* by Dr. Arthur H. Smith (Chicago, 1894) and *Village Life in China* by the same author (New York, 1899) are second only to the writings of the genial French Abbé. T. T. Meadows, one of the missionaries who accepted the Taiping Rebellion as a Christian movement, has written interestingly—if not too wisely—on *The Chinese and Their Rebellions* (London, 1856). Not long after the publication of this book, the Protestant missionaries in China learned more about the Taipings, and repudiated their earlier sympathetic attitude toward the rebels.

The five books just cited contain much material upon the work of Christian missions in China, and much more will be found on this subject in the general works which have been mentioned. A less sympathetic treatment of missionary enterprise will be found in *China and Christianity*, by Alexander Michie (Boston, 1900), where most of the friction between China and the outside world is attributed to the aggressiveness of the missionaries and their dependence upon the political support of their home governments. A very able discussion of the problems arising out of the "treaty status" of Christian missions is to be found in Paul Boell's *La protectorat des missions catholiques en Chine et la politique de la*

Bibliographical Note

France en extrême Orient (Paris, 1899). In this monograph, which was occasioned by the decree of March 15, 1899,—granting official rank to Catholic missionaries in China,—M. Boell argues that the abolition of the protectorate would be equally beneficial to the missions, to China, and to France. A very different treatment of the religious question is found in *Sectarianism and Religious Persecution in China*, by Professor J. J. M. de Groot (Amsterdam, 1903). Professor de Groot reverses his own earlier opinion and runs counter to the opinions of most orientalists in his assertion that the Chinese government is essentially intolerant and addicted to religious persecution. While the critical reader will hardly accept this conclusion as justified by the material upon which it is based, much of this material will be found valuable.

La Chine qui s'ouvre, by René Pinon (Paris, 1900), was written and published just before the Boxer outbreak, at a moment when China seemed to be completely opened to the outside world. It is chiefly valuable as a presentation of French and Russian aspirations and a criticism of the policies of Great Britain and the United States. Alexander Ular's *Un Empire Russo-Chinois* (Paris, 1903), which is also available in an English translation, is highly sensational and should be taken with decided reservations; it can, however, be read with profit, as it is at least indicative of what many people at the time believed. The *Memoirs of Count Witte*, translated by Abraham Yarmolinsky (New York, 1921), is extremely valuable for the light which it throws upon Russo-Chinese relations between 1895 and 1900; the present writer has been informed, however, that the work has lost considerable in the process of translation. Max von Brandt, in his *Dreiunddreissig Jahre in Ost-Asien* (Leipzig, 1901) and his *Ostasiatische Fragen. China. Japan. Korea.* (Berlin, 1897), has given the fruits of long official residence in the Far East and an intimate connection with international diplomacy at Peking. Herr von Brandt's views with regard to the Orient derive especial value from the fact that his period of diplomatic service in that part of the world preceded the date of Germany's policy of aggression; he was thus in the position of a more or less neutral observer of the conflict between China and the West.

China and the Occident

The Boxer Movement.

FOR the official records of the Boxer movement, and of the "Battle of Concessions" which preceded, the reader is referred to the published diplomatic papers of the various countries:

AMERICAN: *Foreign Relations of the United States,* published yearly.

BRITISH: *British and Foreign State Papers,* which have been cited as *British Blue Books,* published as occasion demands.

FRENCH: *Ministère des affaires étrangères, Documents Diplomatiques,* published irregularly.

Negociations de Pékin (published by the Ministère des affaires étrangères, Paris ? 1902 ?).

Commision chargée d'etudier la question du payement des indemnités (a supplement of the above, no date, no place).

ITALIAN: *Ministero degli affari esteri, documenti diplomatici.*

The British and American documents are particularly full for this period, but it must be remembered that they have been carefully edited before publication and that much valuable material has—for diplomatic reasons—been withheld. Through the courtesy of the Department of State, the author was allowed access to the unpublished documents, for 1894-1900, and was thus able to fill several important gaps in the published material.

GERMAN: *Die Grosse Politik der Europäischen Kabinette, 1871-1914: Sammlung der Diplomatischen Akten des Auswärtigen Amts;* herausgegeben von Johannes Lepsius, Albrecht Mendelssohn Bartholdy, und Friedrich Thimme. (Berlin: Deutsche Verlagsgesellschaft für Politik und Geschichte. 1922-1925.)

This monumental publication, undertaken immediately after the close of the World War, contains a wealth of material for the student of foreign diplomacy in the Far East. Most of the documents relating to China before and during the Boxer period are assembled in three volumes. Volume IX deals with the Three-Power Intervention at the end of China's war with Japan; volume XIV relates to the lease of Kiaochow and to the "Battle of Concessions"; volume XVI contains the Foreign Office documents for the Boxer period, beginning in May, 1900, and continuing down to the evacuation of Shanghai in the autumn of 1902. Although considerable "editing" has been necessary, in order to reduce the work to the limits of possible publication, the editors have nowhere attempted to suppress material which might be regarded as damaging to their country. Much material which would be of interest and value to specialists in Far Eastern history has undoubtedly been omitted because of its insignificance in connection with great international problems; but *Die Grosse Politik,* where it does refer to Far Eastern questions, is more frank and more reliable than the official publications of the American, British, French, and Italian governments.

RUSSIAN: *Krasny Arkhiv,* published periodically.

Since the establishment of the present régime in Russia, the Soviet authorities have published, in the *Krasny Arkhiv* ("Red Archives"), a considerable number of imperial diplomatic documents. Those bearing on the subject of this work are found in volumes II and XIV.

In the absence of available Chinese government publications, the most valuable source for Chinese material is the *North China Herald,* the weekly edition of the *North China Daily News,* Shanghai. The greatest source value of this paper lies in the translations from the *Peking Gazette,* which constituted a regular feature in its pages. In addition to this feature, the *North China* enjoyed an unexcelled news service for "things Chinese"; its "Outport Correspondence" was kept up by a number of exceptionally well-informed foreign residents all over the Empire, and as the reports from these correspondents are accurately dated, the news items are an unusually reliable source for the historian. Editorially, the paper represented the ultra-aggressive element among the foreigners resident at the Treaty Ports, and consistently advocated the most vigorous policies in dealing with China.

Through the courtesy of the officers of the American Board of Commissioners for Foreign Missions, the author was allowed free access to the files of the Board's archives in Boston. The value of this privilege can hardly be overestimated. The North China

Mission of the American Board was located in the three provinces most vitally affected by the Boxer movement: Chihli, Shantung, and Shansi. Several of the Board's missionaries in these provinces were veterans who had resided in China for fifteen or twenty years, and their correspondence contains a wealth of material which cannot be duplicated from any other source.

A good deal of material regarding the Boxer movement, not elsewhere available, is to be found in two Catholic missionary publications. The first of these, *Les Missions Catholiques* (Lyon), is a weekly illustrated missionary paper, and contains telegraphic reports, correspondence, and numerous special articles. It is particularly valuable for its reports from China during the years immediately preceding the outbreak and during the early months of the movement. *Chine et Ceylan, Lettres des missionnaires de la Compagnie de Jésus* is a little magazine which was published, irregularly, at Abbeville. The portion relating to China was entirely devoted to the Jesuit diocese in southeastern Chihli, the district in which the Boxer movement made its earliest appearance—either simultaneously with, or before, its first appearance in the adjacent portions of Shantung. Many extremely valuable pieces of information have been gleaned from the pages of this little-known publication, and it has been cited on several points in the text of this book.

A number of diaries, narratives, etc., have appeared dealing with various phases of the Boxer year, and a few may be mentioned here as having especial value—either literary or historical. *La Chine contre l'étranger*, by Baron d'Anthouard (Paris, 1902), has, because of its author's position as first secretary of the French Legation, a semi-official character. Baron d'Anthouard was chargé d'affaires at Peking during part of February and March, 1900; returning from a vacation in Japan, he arrived at Taku on June 15, and was at Tientsin when the outbreak occurred. *The Siege of the Peking Legations*, the diary of the Rev. Roland Allen (London, 1901), is especially valuable for its details concerning events during the three weeks from May 28 to June 19. The picture which this writer gives—verified from official reports—of the calm that pervaded Peking for the greater part of this period does not comport with the violent measures which were being taken by the diplomatic body. Clive Bigham's *A Year in China* (London, 1901) is the work of a traveler and a shrewd observer who arrived at Tientsin, after an extended journey through the interior of China, in time to accompany the Seymour expedition. The writer gives evidence of his sympathy for the Chinese in their attempts to resist foreign invasion. *The Siege in Peking; China against the World*, by W. A. P. Martin (London and Edinburgh, 1900), is very different in tone. Dr. Martin, long a resident in China, attributed the entire movement to the machinations of the Empress Dowager, and considered that the Manchus should be driven from power and that the Western nations should set up a satisfactory government in China. *Martyred Missionaries of the China Inland Mission*, Marshall Broomhall, editor (London, 1901), contains much valuable material drawn from the diaries of missionaries in the province of Shansi, and is useful for the purpose of studying the movement in that province.

Alfred von Müller, in *Die Wirren in China und die Kämpfe der verbundeten Truppen* (Berlin, 1902), gives the most methodical account of the Seymour expedition and of the fighting around Tientsin. B. Lenox Simpson—B. L. Putnam Weale—in *Indiscreet Letters from Peking* (London, 1907) has given the world a masterpiece in the way of historical fiction, with the Boxer movement as his subject. The book is very readable, and has some value for the local color which it furnishes. *China and the Powers*, by H. C. Thomson (London, etc., 1902), is a collection of articles which first appeared in the *Monthly Review*, London. The author, a newspaper correspondent sent out to 'cover' the outbreak, considered that China had good reason to fear and resent foreign intrusion; he is also very severe on the foreigners for the atrocities of which they were guilty. Theodor von Winterhalder, the author of *Kämpfe in China* (Vienna, 1902), was an officer on the Austro-Hungarian cruiser *Zenta*. He accompanied the Austrian marine detachment to Peking on June 3, and was caught there by the destruction of the railway. As a stranger to China and the Chinese, his observations regarding conditions at

Taku, when the detachment landed, and at Peking, during the first two weeks of his stay there, are very instructive.

The third volume of Count von Waldersee's *Denkwürdigkeiten* (Stuttgart, 1923) is largely devoted to his experiences as commander-in-chief of the international forces in North China. This contains many of the field-marshal's reports to the Kaiser, a number of the Kaiser's dispatches, and a great deal of matter drawn from von Waldersee's diary; all of which serves to illuminate the international jealousies and rivalries during the period of the peace settlement. Some corroboration of the intrigues which are suggested by Count von Waldersee is to be found in the *Lebenserinnerungen und politische Denkwürdigkeiten* of Baron von Eckardstein (Leipzig, 1919-1920—also available in an English translation) and in W. R. Thayer's *The Life and Letters of John Hay* (Boston and New York, 1916), but the whole truth on this point will not be known until the archives of the several Western countries have been thrown open to investigation.

These from the Land of Sinim, by Sir Robert Hart (London, 1901), constitutes a plea in extenuation of China before the bar of public opinion. The several chapters of this book first appeared in the *Fortnightly Review*, beginning in November, 1900, and—with the books by Bigham and Thomson—helped to produce a reaction from the general condemnation of China. P. H. Clements, in *The Boxer Rebellion* (New York, 1915), has treated the movement as an international episode; he has accepted the traditional explanations regarding the outbreak, and concerned himself chiefly with the resultant diplomatic activities of the Western powers. An excellent bibliography is given in the appendix of this work. *The Real Chinese Question*, by Chester Holcombe (New York, 1900), like the book by Sir Robert Hart, was written by a friend of China who hoped to be able to counteract some of the wild extravagances of China's critics.

China in Convulsion, by Dr. Arthur H. Smith (New York, 1901), is, in many ways, the best treatment of the Boxer movement that has appeared, but is open to criticism on several points. Although Dr. Smith points out clearly the connection between the "I-ho Chuan" and the old "Tuan" or militia organizations and shows that the Boxers were not a secret society, and although he recognizes China's legitimate need for defensive reorganization in 1898 and 1899, he concludes by regarding the attack upon foreigners as the result of a deliberate conspiracy. While denying that Protestant missionary activities had any part in causing the anti-foreign outbreak, he appears to exaggerate the importance of Catholic missions as a cause for anti-foreignism. (Of the two forms of Christian propaganda, the Catholic—by reason of its freedom from nationalistic ties—would appear the less disruptive for the Chinese state.) The most serious criticism of Dr. Smith's work is, however, in connection with his treatment of the disturbances in Shantung during the winter of 1899-1900. The annual report from his own mission station—Pang-chuang—for the year ending March 31, 1900, states that there had been little personal violence, yet Dr. Smith cites the alarming telegram which he had sent to Mr. Conger on December 2 as proof that bloodshed and murder were rife at Pang-chuang throughout the winter. Ku Hung-ming, in *The Story of a Chinese Oxford Movement* (Shanghai, 1912), gives an able presentation of the essential conflict between the civilizations of China and of the West. This author maintains that the Empress Dowager had general popular support in her reversal of the reform policy of the Emperor and Kang Yu-wei, and that the growing antipathy to foreigners was cultural rather than economic.

The outstanding figure in the history of China, from the death of Hsien Feng in 1861 until her own death in 1908, was the Empress Dowager Tzu Hsi. This remarkable woman has been compared—not inaptly—with the great Catherine of Russia and with Elizabeth of England. *China under the Empress Dowager*, by J. O. P. Bland and E. Backhouse (Philadelphia and London, 1910), is a romantic study of this most interesting figure. The account which is given by Bland and Backhouse of the Boxer movement is chiefly remarkable for the diary of His Excellency Ching Shan. The portion of the book dealing with the "Hundred Days" and the *coup d'état* may be criticized for its undue emphasis of party struggles and its utter disregard of the critical state of China's foreign relations during this period. P. W. Sergeant, in *The Great Empress Dowager of China* (London, 1910), has told a much less dramatic story than that told by Bland and Backhouse, but gives a much more satisfactory discussion of the international problems which Tzu Hsi was compelled to face. Sergeant is one of the few writers to call attention to the fact that the "Battle of Concessions" increased in intensity throughout the period of the Hundred Days, and was terminated by the *coup d'état.*

Ching Shan's *Diary*, already referred to in connection with *China under the Empress Dowager*, has been retranslated and published separately by J. J. L. Duyvendak, *The Diary of His Excellency Ching-shan* (E. J. Brill, Leiden, 1924). Duyvendak's work consists of a brief critical preface, a more careful translation than that given by Bland and Backhouse, and a reproduction of the Chinese text of such portions of the diary as were available for his inspection. (The parts of the diary already published by Bland and Backhouse had been deposited in the British Museum, where Duyvendak secured photographic reproductions to serve as the basis of his work. Some portions, however, still remain in the possession of Sir E. Backhouse, who intends to publish them at some future date.) In the Chinese text, the editor indicates the places where the damaged condition of the original manuscript has necessitated "reconstructions," while valuable explanatory footnotes accompany the translation. Thus, fourteen years after the originally published translation by Bland and Backhouse, this interesting Chinese document—with the exception of those portions still in the possession of Sir E. Backhouse—has been made available for critical examination. A careful study of Duyvendak's text, translation, and notes—which I did not secure until my work was practically completed—leaves me still somewhat sceptical as to the historical value of the diary. In various passages of the work there are demonstrable errors of fact and date. As Duyvendak points out, the old gentleman frequently recorded rumors as facts; on one or two occasions, indeed, there is direct contradiction between entries. While these errors, being natural in a period of excitement and confusion, favor the authenticity of the document, they necessitate extreme care in using the diary as a source.

I have cited it, therefore, only as supporting evidence upon points which could be established by other sources.

Recent Events.

VOLUMES have been written on the Revolution, the Republic, and the foreign relations of China during the decade which has followed the outbreak of the World War. *Recent Events and Present Policies in China*, by J. O. P. Bland (Philadelphia, 1912), attributes most of China's disorders to the "procreative recklessness" of the race. The writer devotes considerable space to a valuable discussion of the deeply rooted Chinese objections to a highly centralized form of government, and expresses his utter disbelief in the stability of the newly established Republic—a disbelief which subsequent events seem to have justified. B. Lenox Simpson—B. L. Putnam Weale—in *The Fight for the Republic in China* (New York, 1917), takes a position diametrically opposed to that of Mr. Bland; his sympathies are all with the Republic, and he regards Yuan Shih-kai as the betrayer of the Republic and the chief cause of the difficulties which beset the experiment during its first five years. A much more reliable study of the revolution and the early years of the Republic is to be found in *Contemporary Politics in the Far East*, by Stanley K. Hornbeck (New York, 1918); while Professor K. S. Latourette's *The Development of China* (New York, 1917) is a good brief work which covers both ancient and modern history. These last two books are thoroughly unbiased and scholarly, and are free from any suspicion of propaganda—which cannot be said of the two mentioned immediately before them.

T. F. Millard's *Democracy and the Far Eastern Question* (New York, 1919), like the other works of the same author, takes a bitterly anti-Japanese stand with regard to recent events in the Far East; with this fact in mind, it can profitably be read for the very damaging material which is cited from Japanese sources. A similar attitude characterizes Dr. Gilbert Reid's *China, Captive or Free* (New York, 1921), although Dr. Reid includes the other outside nations in his condemnation. A pro-Japanese view of recent Far Eastern affairs is given by J. O. P. Bland in *China, Japan, and Korea* (New York, 1921).

A number of works dealing with China's political and international problems have been produced by Chinese scholars educated in Western countries. Four of these may be mentioned as being extremely useful. *A Survey of Constitutional Development in China,* by Hawkling L. Yen (New York, 1911), covers the period before the outbreak of the revolution. Cheng Sih-gung, in *Modern China, a Political Study* (Oxford, 1919), has devoted his attention almost exclusively to the post-revolutionary period. M. J. Bau, in *The Open Door Doctrine* (New York, 1923), and E. T. Yen, in *The Open Door Policy* (Boston, 1923) have contributed interesting studies on this important aspect of international diplomacy in the Far East. Of the two studies, Dr. Bau's is, perhaps, the more useful for the student by reason of its careful bibliographical footnotes; Dr. Yen has, however, approached the question with somewhat more originality and vigor.

Professor W. W. Willoughby, in *Foreign Rights and Interests in China* (Baltimore, 1920), and in *China at the Conference* (Baltimore, 1922), has added two valuable works to the literature on China; the latter of these, which deals with the Washington Conference, is of particular importance. Professor Bertrand Russell, after studying China and the Chinese student at close range, has attempted, in *The Problem of China* (New York, 1922), to forecast the solution of the conflict between the Chinese and Occidental civilizations—with what success, time alone will tell. Professor E. T. Williams, in *China Yesterday and Today* (New York, 1923), has written ably and interestingly upon the transition that has been taking place during the last generation. Long residence in the country, and familiarity with Chinese literature and language have enabled Professor Williams to treat his subject with sympathetic understanding. The reader who is interested in China often finds himself unable to obtain access to any very wide selection of books on the subject. For the use of such readers, *Modern Chinese History: Selected Readings,* by Professor H. F. MacNair (Shanghai, 1923), will be of great value. The selections cover the period which began with the Macartney embassy to Peking, and come down to the Washington Conference. In addition to the actual value of the selections which are included, the volume serves to indicate the location of further useful material.

INDEX

For Index to Bibliography see pages 347-349.

Index

Index

Index

Index

Index

Index

Index

INDEX TO BIBLIOGRAPHY

Index

Index